High School Ministry

High School Ministry

Mike Yaconelli
Jim Burns

ZONDERVAN PUBLISHING HOUSE
Grand Rapids, Michigan

HIGH SCHOOL MINISTRY

Youth Specialties Books are published
by the Zondervan Publishing House
1415 Lake Drive, S.E.
Grand Rapids, Michigan 49506

Copyright © 1986 by Youth Specialties, Inc.

Library of Congress Cataloging in Publication Data

Yaconelli, Mike.
    High school ministry.

    "Youth specialties."
    Bibliography: p.
    Includes index
    1. Church work with youth. 2. High school students—religious life.
I. Burns, Jim, 1953–   . II. Title.
BV4447.Y33   1986   259'.23   86-11183

ISBN 0-310-34920-6

Edited by David Lambert
Designed by Ann Cherryman

Printed in the United States of America

86 87 88 89 90 91 / DH / 10 9 8 7 6 5 4 3 2 1

Contents

High-school Ministry—An Overview   7

Part I. Defining the High-school Student
1. The High-school Student in the Real World: *The Cultural Dimension of High-school Ministry*   15
2. Is There Life After Puberty? *The Physiological Dimension of High-school Ministry*   39
3. Is There Life After Nerdness? *The Social Dimension of High-school Ministry*   53
4. Can a High-school Student Be Religious? *The Spiritual Dimension of High-school Ministry*   63
5. The Parents of High-school Kids   71

Part II. Defining the High-school Youth Worker
6. Characteristics of a High-school Youth Worker   93
7. A Strategy for High-school Ministry   103
8. The Problems of Programing   119
9. Ministering to High-school Kids in Crisis   129

Part III. Tools for High-school Ministry
10. Creative Learning Strategies   153
11. Family-oriented Activities   273

Appendix: Resources for High-school Ministry
     A Youth Ministries Bibliography   288
     Books on the Family   296

Notes   298

2/

75840

High-school Ministry—
An Overview

Bill became a Christian in Young Life. His girl friend Karyn had become a Christian at junior-high church camp. During the first three years of high school, both Bill and Karyn were active in their church.

But something happened their senior year. Bill started working; Karyn's parents were divorced—both Bill and Karyn found themselves no longer interested in church, Young Life, or anything religious. They both went on to college. Karyn started living with a guy, began partying, and eventually dropped out. Bill went on to law school, graduated at the top of his class, and no longer has any contact with Christianity.

What happened? What caused two young people who were active in their faith in high school to completely drop out of their youth group and the church?

Bennett grew up in a poor section of town. His father, an alcoholic, no longer lived at home. His home was windowless and located in a high-crime area. Bennett's mother worked six days a week and was too tired on Sunday to worry about whether Bennett should go to church. Bennett was invited to a church youth group by a friend at school. The church youth group was all white; Bennett was a Mexican-American low-rider. To attend, Bennett had to ride the subway forty-five minutes each way—by himself. Still, he came faithfully, began a serious relationship with Christ, and four years later is still active in the church.

Why did Bennett, when all the forces seemed against him, decide to stick with his faith and his youth group? Why did Bill and Karyn drop out? The answers aren't easy. High-school ministry isn't easy, either.

THE HIGH-SCHOOL YEARS

Years ago Ralph Keyes wrote a book entitled *Is There Life After High School?*[1] The implication of the title is clear: What we do in high school alters and shapes everything that is to come. Without a doubt, the high-school years are the most pivotal in the life of the adolescent. The American high-school experience, unique in Western culture, is for most of us the beginning of the rest of our adult lives. All the forces that have shaped our personalities and all of the developmental consequences of adolescence converge on us in high school and begin to push us from childhood into adulthood. Although it is widely accepted that early childhood is where we are *formed,* the choices we make during our high-school experience in response to those *formative years* is what determines the kinds of people we will be the rest of our lives.

In *Being Adolescent,* Csikszentmihalyi and Larson describe adolescence as the Age of Choice.[2] Originally the authors wanted to call their book *Catching Teenagers' Attention* because it is during the high-school years that students, faced with a barrage of competing options, are preoccupied with the life choices they must make—choices that will have lifetime consequences.

High school is the setting for the transformation of a child into an adult. Somewhere in those four years, a mature human being is supposed to emerge from the cocoon of childhood.[3] The high-school years have been called the pathway to adulthood—a pathway filled with dangerous obstacles and confusing turns. It is easy for a high-school student to be overwhelmed, to feel lost, alone, and afraid. Helping high-school students overcome these obstacles and negotiate the turns is one of the reasons we wrote *High School Ministry.*

8

Growing into healthy adulthood requires an environment of family, friends, significant adults, and a vital faith that counters and combats the negative forces at work in the high-school student's environment. The inclusion of the words *vital faith* distinguishes this book from others that deal with adolescence. Most people are concerned that high-school students *socialize* properly—that they move smoothly from a self-centered, nonproductive member of society to a socially conscious, other-oriented, productive member of society. As a result, many books about adolescence try to determine how we can ease young people into adulthood without incident. *High School Ministry* is not so much concerned with the socialization as the Christianization of high-school students.

Today's high-school student is surrounded by enormous pressures to conform, to mature, to adjust, and to fit into the framework of an increasingly cold and impersonal society. In truth, the American high-school student may be the most significant casualty of this technological age. More and more high-school students seem unable to cope with the pressures of modern living, so they are dropping out with drugs, alcohol, sex, and—tragically—suicide.

Today, high-school students live in a world so different from any previous generation's that comparisons are almost impossible. Alvin Toffler wrote many years ago about the exponential changes that were occurring in this society.[4] He suggested that the changes that all of us are facing are so radical that we are all falling victims to the disease of "future shock." The implications of *Future Shock* are obvious: It is not just that the world has changed—*change* has changed.[5] Although the external structure of the high-school years appears to be the same, the world of today's high-school student is radically different from that of other generations. It is not just that the high-school environment has changed; it has become a totally different experience. In his early eighties best seller *Megatrends,* John Naisbitt's suggestion that

9

we are seeing a restructuring of America is true not only of today's high-school experience but even truer in the overall life of the American teenager.[6] "Saturday Night Live," a satirical late-night comedy hour, illustrated this perfectly in a skit entitled *The Pearl Harbor Method*, comparing two methods of birthing. Using the Leboyer Method, every effort is made to bring the newborn into the world without undue shock or trauma. The lights are turned down low, and the delivery room personnel smile and speak in soft melodious voices. After delivery, the baby is not spanked but tenderly placed on the mother's stomach and gently caressed by the doctor and mother. Before the umbilical cord is severed, the baby is bathed in warm water to approximate the environment of amniotic fluid within the womb. Thus, the child is given an encouraging start in life.

Using the Pearl Harbor Method, the doctor snatches the baby as it emerges into the world. While the assistants shout and scream and set off firecrackers, the baby is tossed in the air, spanked, and used as a ball in an improvised football game in the delivery room.[7]

The Pearl Harbor Method, although done tongue-in-cheek, reflects more accurately than we'd like to admit the hostile, pressure-filled world where young people will be forced to grow up too fast and will be met with an overwhelming amount of hostility and stress from every possible direction, including places where, in the past, they could count on protection—the family and the church. In the magazine *Rolling Stone*, David Breskin, writing specifically about the exceptionally high suicide rate among today's adolescents, wrote a sobering profile of the modern adolescent that accurately describes the brave new world of high school:

> First off, chances are an adolescent's parents are divorced. Suicides come disproportionately from broken homes, and the increase in young suicides parallels the giddy divorce rate, now over 50 percent and the highest

in the world. Married or divorced, the adolescent's mother works outside the home. She prides herself on how quickly she goes back to work after he/she is born. (That the father is absent or away at work is a given.) His parents subcontract responsibility for raising him/her to day-care surrogates, nurses and sitters, and to Johnny himself. . . . There's no extended family around for him, not with the geographic mobility for which Americans are famous. The moving is hard on him. He must keep readapting to new environments.

American parents spend less time with Johnny than any other parents in the world. While he's a teenager, they spend an average of 14 minutes a week communicating with him. By the time Johnny graduates from high school, he'll have spent more time with his blue, flickering electronic parent than doing anything else but sleeping; he'll have seen 20,000 hours of TV, 350,000 commercials, about 18,000 killings. The family doesn't talk—they watch. On TV, problems resolve themselves in 30-minute spans. It's his only problem-solving role model, and it's unrealistic.

That his life is not as exciting as the life on TV may come as a disappointment. His pain comes as a nasty shock, and he'll learn to escape rather than cope. He has far more access to booze, dope, pills, coke, than any previous generation of kids, and at an earlier age. He also has easy access to the genitals of the opposite sex, and the sooner he scores, the more difficulty he'll have with intimacy later on. Chances are increasing that he will be sexually or physically abused by an adult at an early age.

Competition is tremendous. If he is middle or upper-middle class, his parents have already told him he had better start running, and fast, because the pie is shrinking. The number of his peers has doubled in 20 years, but the opportunities haven't. There are only so many spots on the basketball team or in the law firm. He feels pressure to be perfect. This "cohort effect" means he lives in a downwardly mobile, increasingly Darwinian world. It's called, trendily, the end of childhood. Johnny quickly learns that good grades and other tangible achievements are the currency in which he trades for his parents' approval and concomitant per-missiveness. The parents see the equation differently: They provide material well-being; he delivers good grades in return. His parents are permissive because it's easier to say yes than no. Besides, they don't know what rules are valid anymore. Everything in this world is negotiable now: Everything is shades of gray, and all that matters is green. They treat the kid like a little adult because they want him to be a little adult. They seek his friendship and fear his disapproval. When they give him too much freedom, he secretly desires rules; but they don't want to tell him about sex, about values, pain, problem solving, living with limitations. All is uncertain, nothing is shocking, everything is tolerated.

All told, Johnny lives in a bizarre warp of freedom and pressure at a stage of his life when neither is appropriate: when pressure makes him brittle and freedom's just another word for everything to lose.[8]

What is this brave new world high-school students live in? How is today's high-school experience different from past years'? How do you reach high-school students? How do you help them? Can the church make a difference to them? Is it possible for *you,* or any adult, to have a truly significant effect on this generation?

We have written *High School Ministry* to help you deal with these questions. *High School Ministry* is about *today's* high-school adolescent—about the personal, cultural, social, emotional, intellectual, and spiritual dimensions of adolescence that directly affect anyone who wants to understand and influence high-school students. Most of all, *High School Ministry* is a *practical* book—not an intellectual treatise, not a sociological masterpiece—but a *how-to* book, based on thousands of hours of ministry experience, that tries to put handles on ministry. We want to prepare you to go out and *do* youth ministry—not just theorize about it.

PART I

DEFINING THE HIGH-SCHOOL STUDENT

1 The High-school Student in the Real World:
The Cultural Dimension of High-school Ministry

It was Easter Sunday afternoon, 1985. A little cool in downtown Philadelphia—the thousands of young people milling around the arcades and theaters in the pedestrians-only inner-city mall wore jackets and sweaters. Twin theaters were showing *Friday the 13th Part V* and *The Last Dragon*, a kung-fu movie starring Taimak. At four p.m. *Dragon* ended, and hundreds of adolescents who'd been watching exited onto Chestnut street—right into a large crowd of disappointed young people who'd been turned away from *Friday* because the theater was full. It began as a minor shoving match, but soon escalated into a full-scale riot as the thousands of adolescents on hand joined in, breaking windows, looting stores, and causing tens of thousands of dollars worth of damage. Police in riot gear had to be called in to control the violence. Several people were treated for injuries.

What caused an ordinary group of adolescents to turn into a violent, uncontrollable mob? There were *many* causes, of course, but certainly the most immediate cause was the movies themselves. Is it any wonder that, after watching two hours of glamorized violence, these young people decided to try a little violence themselves?

Even though we believe that the violence in Philadelphia was largely culturally induced violence, we aren't suggesting that American culture is a sin—even though modern society has, on occasion, been likened to Sodom and Gomorrah,

15

cities that had become so evil, so corrupt, that the word "sodomy" comes from one of their names. What should frighten us about two cities like Sodom and Gomorrah is not the sin of sodomy; what should frighten us is the realization that the people in those cities *no longer thought that what they were doing was sin*. The blurred distinctions between right and wrong were so pervasive that you could not live in Sodom and *not* be affected by the environment.

America is not Sodom and Gomorrah. But neither is it neutral. It is a *new* environment, and because of the accelerating rate of social change, many of the aspects of modern American culture are untested. No one knows how our culture will affect the adolescents growing up in it. Some of those effects will undoubtedly be positive; but the kung-fu-movie incident in Philadelphia is a frightening reminder that there will be other effects—powerful, destructive, and universal.

One thing is sure: Our cultural environment is influencing every adolescent every moment of every day. The question, of course, is: What kind of effect? What is this society doing to its children?

THE CULTURAL THREAT TO ADOLESCENCE

Adolescence is a phenomenon unique to Western culture. Adolescence exists in our society because there are certain structures, or underpinnings, here that support it. In past generations, those underpinnings protected the adolescent from forces in society that could harm or permanently retard his development. But now, something is happening to those safeguards of adolescence, and the world of the adolescent has begun to collapse under the weight of change. The underpinnings are crumbling—and our young people are becoming increasingly exposed to the harsh and destructive forces of a brave new environment.

Some of those destructive forces are the disintegration of the traditional family, the disappearance of morality, the worship of technology, the rise of consumerism, the worship of self, and the loss of meaning. Let's examine how those forces have affected the modern adolescent.

THE DISINTEGRATION OF THE TRADITIONAL FAMILY

Traditionally, adolescents have been able to count on one stable reality—the family. Children could grow into their teenage years trusting that Mom and Dad would be there to guide them; adolescents would discover that part of their journey through adolescence to adulthood would involve the inevitable battle for independence from those parents. That was a long time ago. Now one divorce occurs every twenty-seven seconds. In 1986, a general sampling of youth workers by Youth Specialties indicated that 35 percent to 75 percent of the adolescents in any group are not living with both of their natural parents. The stable underpinning of the family is not just buckling—it has collapsed. Even those young people whose parents are not divorced are not free from anxiety. Every time their parents have an argument, they wonder: *Is my family next?* The adolescent of today has been deeply affected by this family permutation. In the past, the family was stress *re*ducing, now the family is stress *pro*ducing.

THE DISAPPEARANCE OF MORALITY

John Naisbitt, in his book *Megatrends,* explains that in the past we lived in an "either-or" society[1]; all of our choices (including our moral choices) were simple. Either you were married or you weren't; most were. You drove either a Chevy or a Ford. You were either male or female, and either you had sex when you were married or you didn't have sex at all. Because there was a clear cultural consensus on most moral choices, even the structures of society supported the "right" choice. But now, we live in the "multiple-option" era; now, there are so many choices that the issue of right and wrong

17

has become irrelevant. There are no longer any *moral* choices—now, there are only *personal* choices. What makes something right today is the fact that you *choose* to do it. Adolescents, who in the past could cruise through the teenage years making only a few moral decisions, are now immersed in a bewildering sea of choices, forced to make decisions daily, and left alone to suffer the consequences.

THE WORSHIP OF TECHNOLOGY

Not only is technology out of control, it is beginning to control us. In this age of Alvin Toffler's "third wave,"[2] adolescents are growing up with an awe of technology. Although there is a growing concern among young people regarding nuclear and military technology, there is still the well-entrenched belief that technology is making our world a better place to live. Technology is the response of science to the question, "What *can* we do?" But the Christian feels it necessary to ask as well, "What *should* I do?"[3] The trouble, as Jacques Ellul points out, is that modern man has transferred his worship of God to a worship of technology.[4] As a result, the young people of this society tend to accept new technology uncritically, never questioning what the consequences of that technology might be. Consider, as a minor example, the proliferation of the Walkman among young people. The consequences of the popularity of the Walkman are much more than damaged eardrums: increased exposure to popular music, decreased communication among peers and families, decreased reading, privatism, and much more. Again, the Walkman is not evil—but neither is it neutral.

Howard Snyder, in his classic evaluation of the effects of technology on our society, says that technology is robbing us of five important qualities:[5]

1. Spontaneity. In simple terms, in a highly technological society "the worst sin of a machine, computer or human being is to be unpredictable."[6] A highly technological society values homogeneity. It runs better when everyone "cooperates" and does the predictable. Creativity, imagination, and uniqueness are discouraged in favor of compliance. And yet, it is the quality of unpredictability that we associate so closely with Jesus Himself. He was always doing the *unexpected*, which, we now know, was a characteristic of His deity.

2. Individuality. Snyder says, "Technological society, of course, is not ultimately interested in what is unique in each individual but rather in what is identical—what can be counted, standardized, computerized."[7] How many high-school students live under the tyranny of their SAT scores or their IQ? How many high-school students has the church lost because we communicate to them that the Christian faith can only be expressed in a particular, preprogramed way? The truth is that the Bible is a collection of unique characters—true individuals who were about as alike as night is to day. That is the *Good News*—that when Christ appears in our lives, our uniqueness suddenly matters and can be expressed so beautifully in the Body of Christ.

3. Moral sense. What happens to morality in a technological society? Jacques Ellul says that we develop a "technological morality"[8]—in other words, a morality that accepts as right whatever is technologically possible. Take the issue of abortion, for example. If abortions are technologically possible and if the techniques for abortion are scientifically and medically sound, then, technological society reasons, why not? Human, emotional, and spiritual values have no place in a technological society—nor does the Gospel, since it works to *deepen* our moral capacity. The presence of the Holy Spirit "convicts us of our sin," says the Bible.[9] The closer we are to Christ, the more our moral sense is quickened so that we *know* what is right and what is wrong.

4. Self-consciousness. "Orthodoxy is unconsciousness"[10] says George Orwell in his classic *1984*. The more you can reduce a person's self-awareness, the more you can keep him from *thinking*, the easier it is to control him. Neil

Postman's recent book *Amusing Ourselves to Death* gives a powerful description of how today's society is numbing our minds. He contrasts the vision of George Orwell's *1984* with Aldous Huxley's *Brave New World* and comes to a startling conclusion:

> Huxley and Orwell did not prophesy the same thing. Orwell warns that we will be overcome by an externally opposed oppression. But in Huxley's vision, no Big Brother is required to deprive people of their autonomy, maturity and history. As he saw it, people will come to love their oppression, to adore the technologies that undo their capacities to think. What Orwell feared were those who would ban books. What Huxley feared was that there would be no reason to ban a book, for there would be no one who wanted to read one. . . . Orwell feared that the truth would be concealed from us. Huxley feared the truth would be drowned in a sea of irrelevance. Orwell feared we would become a captive culture. Huxley feared we would become a trivial culture. . . . In *Brave New World*, they are controlled by inflicting pleasure.[11]

We believe, along with Postman, that Huxley was right. Too many young people are being sucked into a vortex of mindlessness.

5. Volition. We are living in an age of manipulation. We all—but adolescents in particular—are the targets of highly effective advertising, propaganda, and other persuasive techniques. Adolescents are motivated so effectively by these techniques that many young people are limited in their ability to make *significant* choices on their own. They have, to some extent, lost their volition—and become the puppets of the manipulators in our society. The ability to make meaningful choices is an expression of spiritual growth and maturity and is vital to healthy adolescent spiritual development.

THE RISE OF CONSUMERISM

The sixties and the seventies were the decades of materialism—the obsession with things. But the onset of the eighties brought us into a new age—the age of consumerism. Consumerism goes a step further than materialism. Consumerism not only worships things—it causes people to begin treating *each other* as things. Father John Kavanaugh defines it as the process of being "thingified."[12] David described it perfectly in Psalm 115:2–8:

> But their idols are silver and gold,
>   made by the hands of men.
> They have mouths, but cannot speak,
>   eyes, but they cannot see;
> they have ears, but cannot hear,
>   noses, but they cannot smell;
> they have hands, but cannot feel,
>   feet, but they cannot walk;
>   nor can they utter a sound with their throats.
> Those who make them will be like them,
>   and so will all who trust in them.

Father Pat Brennan puts it this way: "The dominant spirituality of this generation is the spirituality of consumerism."[13] Today's young people not only believe that they can find happiness by buying it, driving it, or chewing it—they also believe that they themselves are *its* that can be defined in some quantifiable way.

These observations are not universally true, of course—in most parts of the world, poverty and hunger are real, and affluence is restricted to an elite minority. But it is demonstrably and overwhelmingly true of the American middle class. And in that middle class, consumerism has left two significant legacies for today's adolescent—premature affluence and downward mobility. Premature affluence means that adolescents today have already attained a level of affluence that most adults did not attain until they were adults. These days, it isn't unusual to see an adolescent driving a $10,000–$25,000 automobile. Young people today have experienced only one lifestyle—affluence—and they expect that lifestyle to continue. There's the problem: These young people are also victims of downward mobility. This is the first generation of young people who can expect *less* than their parents. There is a good chance that the adolescents of today will not be able to afford the same kind of house and car that their parents have. If that is true, we can look forward to future generations of young people becoming extremely frustrated with not being able to have what they want (see "An Ominous Sign," on page 37).

THE WORSHIP OF SELF

The bottom line in today's society is simple and pervasive: "What's in it for me?" And today's high-school adolescent has grown up with that phrase ringing in his ears. Narcissism has permeated every aspect of our culture; selfishness has been institutionalized and is looked upon as a positive value. All of life is evaluated using one criterion: benefit to self. "To live for the moment is the prevailing passion—to live for yourself, not for your predecessors or posterity."[14]

One of the developmental characteristics of adolescence is a concern for self to the exclusion of others. But narcissism is more than the inability to acknowledge that there are concerns other than your own; it is the subtle attempt to make your "self" the center of the universe. This self-worship has four very worrisome characteristics: an obsession with self-fulfillment, a loss of perspective, an inability to empathize, and a loss of the ability to *know*.

1. Obsession with self-fulfillment. Many adolescents evaluate heir relationships, their activities, and their values according to how much pleasure they receive—in other words, the desire to *feel* fulfilled and satisfied overrides any other concern. That's why so many youth workers plan for their young people only activities that are pleasurable, entertaining, and interesting. The question is not, "Was the activity good for me?" Rather, it is: "Did it feel good? Did it give me lots of pleasure?"

2. Loss of perspective. Bishop William Temple once told a story about some thieves who broke into a jewelry store but didn't steal anything. Instead, they just rearranged the price tags, so that the expensive items had inexpensive price tags and vice versa.

That is exactly what has happened in modern culture. The price tags have been rearranged. Things that should matter don't, and things that shouldn't matter do. Having grown up in a value vertigo, our young people find it increasingly difficult to know what *does* matter. As a result, they spend much of their energy, time, and money seeking what this culture says are the expensive items—self-satisfaction, pride, money, and power—and very little of their time seeking what Jesus said were the items of real value—humility, self-denial, service, sacrifice, and loving. For example, a generation ago virginity was an expensive value. It was important to maintain one's sexual purity until marriage. Although it appears that the pendulum is beginning to swing back toward the attitudes of the previous generation,[15] today virginity is looked upon as a negative value. Virginity connotes inexperience, ineptitude, and inadequacy. Although many high-school students are still virgins, even those who are often go out of their way to give the impression they are *not* virgins. Why? Because society values sexual experience and does not value sexual inexperience.

3. Loss of empathy. Because one of the developmental characteristics of adolescence is selfishness, high-school students already have a built-in self-centeredness. It eventually goes away as they get older—unless society *affirms* that quality by encouraging young people to "look out for number one." The result of that encouragment is a monster who is unable to empathize, sympathize, or understand someone else. These narcissistic products of our society learn to

23

interpret experience only in terms of its effect on themselves. Too many of today's adolescents are neither taught nor encouraged *how* to understand others. A high priority of high-school ministry should be the development of caring adolescents who are able to empathize with those who are in need.

4. Loss of ability to know. In our narcissistic society, knowledge is viewed as a commodity, something outside yourself. It has become a thing you *use* for your own personal gain. There is no accountability, no responsibility for what you know.

The biblical view of knowledge is radically different.[16] From the very beginnings of the Old Testament, God made it clear that once you knew something, you were responsible for that knowledge. In the New Testament, Paul implies in Romans 12:2 that knowledge *transforms* a person. It is that concept we must communicate to a generation that views knowledge as a ticket to a better job. Knowing God is not just a way to get God on our side—knowing God is a relationship that transforms us daily.

THE LOSS OF MEANING
It sounds vague and philosophical to talk about "the loss of meaning," especially in reference to high-school students. But our technological society has created a generation of high-school students who are more and more alienated *from* meaning instead of set free *through* meaning.[17] As our society speeds toward a high-tech environment where work requires an "absence rather than a presence," and as the technological environment generates increased standardization, commodification, and technique, high-school students begin to believe that performance is all that matters.[18]

Where do they get their first job? McDonald's—where they quickly discover that speed and productivity are what matter, that their personalities only get in the way, and that what is important is selling hamburgers and French fries.

Even high-school students find it difficult to see ultimate meaning in a hamburger and fries.

Sports are not exempt. Surprising as it may seem, many high-school students are already experiencing burnout in athletics because they have been taught that the only thing that matters is winning. There's meaning in being a winner—but the pressure to win robs the sport of any *other* meaning. It doesn't take a high-school student long to see that there must be more to life than winning.

As a result, too many adolescents today are desperately trying to make sense out of life in general and *their* lives specifically. Why is the teenage suicide rate at an all-time high? Because when a girl friend says good-by, or Mom and Dad lose their jobs and the money dries up, or the grades get bad, young people don't feel worthwhile anymore. They found meaning in the immediate experience of a relationship—but when the relationship was over, their basis for meaning was also over. Many young people feel insignificant. And, to be honest, the reason they *feel* insignificant is because they are. They have never been allowed to do anything significant. Never have they been in a position where their life and their gifts really made a difference. For the high-school youth worker, that means that today's high-school students are more than ready to hear the Good News, which tells all of us how significant and worthwhile we really are.

HOW SOCIETY AFFECTS ADOLESCENTS

The culture we have just described has a profound effect on young people; it is a large part of the reason high-school students are the way they are. Let's look at those effects in some detail, and discuss how we should deal with them.

ANXIETY AND STRESS

Young people are living under a load of stress and anxiety that would traumatize most adults. When you combine the stress caused by instability of the family with the academic pressure to get good grades and the social pressure to grow up fast and to perform, it is not surprising to see adolescents escape to drugs, alcohol, and even death. Then to those pressures, add the pressure to perform for God and the church—and the coping powers of the high-school student are pushed to or beyond the limit. Strange, isn't it? The Good News of the Gospel is that Jesus promised to carry our yoke and give us rest, but too often the church youth group demands a level of spirituality that very few adults, if any, could attain—creating in the adolescent a load of guilt that, in turn, creates more stress and more anxiety.

How can we help adolescents deal with this stress and anxiety?

1. Create an atmosphere of openness in which adolescents are free to discuss all of the areas of their lives without fear of immediate criticism or rejection. High-school youth group should be a place where students *want* to be because it is a place to *unload* stress—not to add on more. You create an atmosphere of openness when you communicate unconditional love and when you are willing to listen.

2. Emphasize the grace of God. Almost all adolescents suffer from guilt. One of the characteristics of adolescents is an extreme case of self-consciousness. They are aware of every flaw in their appearance as well as every flaw in their character. No one has to tell them when they fail. They want to know whether God loves them even *with* the flaws. The essential task of high-school ministry is *to convince high-school young people that God loves them and is present in their lives even though they are not perfect.* That message should permeate every part of your youth program.

3. Have fun. That's right—have fun. Many high-school ministry programs are too serious, too somber, and too religious. The young people in those groups begin to equate religious commitment with the absence of fun. But fun is a normal part of being a kid. Play is a healthy part of the growing process. You should not apologize for doing the Egg and Armpit Relay with a group of kids.

INCREASED ACTIVITY

In a performance-oriented society, kids have a lot to do. It isn't unusual for a youth worker to try to make an appointment with one of the girls in her youth group and get this response: "Well, uh, Monday I have a tennis lesson. Tuesday I have a dance lesson. Wednesday I have volleyball practice. Thursday I have singing lessons plus my geometry tutor comes over. Friday our school has an away football game and I'm a cheerleader."

Most high-school students start working their junior year. Twenty years ago, you could plan a weekend retreat for high-school students and have the bus leave on Friday at 5 P.M. and return Sunday at 2 P.M. Not anymore. Now the *first* van leaves at 5:00 Friday. The second van leaves at 11:00 Friday night with all the kids that were in the football game or had to work. The first van returns Saturday night because some kids have to work on Sunday.

You won't be able to return your high-school kids to the "thrilling days of yesteryear" when kids weren't so active, but there are some things you can do:

1. Accept the fact that high-school students are more active today. Don't try to compete with the activities they're involved with, and don't try to add more activities to their already overactive lives. Instead, recognize that high-school students today have to be selective in their activities. Offer as many activities as you want—but understand that most high-school kids are so busy they have to pick and choose their activities carefully. Few kids, if any, will come to everything you plan.

2. The older the high-school student gets, the more individualized your ministry must become. If you want to maintain contact with juniors and seniors, you will probably have to meet with them one-on-one after work, early in the morning, and on weekends.

This approach requires a whole new way of thinking about high-school ministry. In the past, we used to evaluate an adolescent's spirituality by how many meetings he attended. The more meetings he attended, the more spiritual he was. That isn't true any longer (if it ever was). Most high-school students will not be able to attend all your activities. They will select only the ones they feel are important. A high-school senior may have a deep commitment to Christ, yet attend only your Tuesday night Bible study—because that's the only night he has off work.

3. If your weekly activities conflict with a heavy schedule of mandatory activity at the high school, cancel your activities and do what you can to support the activities at school. (For more on this, see pages 59 and 60.)

4. Of course, you can challenge high-schoolers to make a choice about the activities they do attend. Make sure that you do not assume that every choice should be made in favor of a church-related activity. It may be that God does not want the most important leader in your youth group to become a student body president. On the other hand, God may want that leader to be involved in student government as an influential witness for Jesus Christ. You have no way of knowing. Your role is to help this student make intelligent, God-directed decisions about the use of his time and energy—not to make those decisions for him or to insist that he do what *you* think is important.

THE IMPORTANCE OF PEER RELATIONSHIPS

Peer relationships are becoming more important to high-school students than adult relationships. As this techno-logical society becomes more impersonal, as the family structure continues to disintegrate, adolescents are turning to their friends to find the security and warmth they seem unable to find in their families, with other adults, or anywhere else. High-school students are more interested in *who* is at your meeting than in *what* you are doing at the meeting. Many high-school students find it easier to trust their friends than to trust any adult. There are a number of significant implications:

1. Peer ministry can be a very effective part of your youth program. Because friendships are so important to adolescents, friends ministering to friends is a much more effective way to evangelize than adults ministering to kids.

2. High-school students are becoming more suspicious and wary of adults. They are beginning to distrust all adults, in general. This doesn't mean high-school students *won't* trust an adult or don't *want* to trust you. Quite the contrary. Adolescents want to have significant adults in their lives— they are just more cautious.

3. Ministry to high-school students needs to be person-centered rather than program-centered. Adolescents respond to relationship more than they respond to program. We're well aware of the resurgence of program-oriented ministries. Rally-oriented programs will get high-school students to attend—as long as the program continues to be entertaining. As soon as the program falters, so do the kids. Their loyalty will not be to the organization sponsoring the event—their loyalty will be to *you*. But you have to earn that loyalty.

4. Think in terms of "friendship clusters"[19] rather than individuals. Take a good look at any group of high-school students. You will notice that high-school students, even though they have many acquaintances, tend to have one or two close friends with whom they spend nearly all of their time—a friendship cluster. Rather than focusing your efforts on the individual student, it would be much more effective to spend time with that student's friendship cluster. Spend the day with Bob and his two friends, Gil and Larry, rather than just spending time with Bob. One advantage of this approach to ministry is that you'll reach three kids instead of just one. And another advantage, just as important, is that the kids will feel more at ease and be more likely to enjoy the day.

ADDICTION TO EXPERIENCES

In a technologically sophisticated culture like the United States, technology becomes an ever more subversive

29

force. Technology begins to replace the unpredictability of human behavior with the reliability of computerized behavior. Soon machines will not only replace humans, they will replace human experience. Jacques Ellul suggests that when humans experience a loss of meaning, they are susceptible to "distractions."[20] These "distractions" cause people to become addicted to experience. High-school students are becoming more and more addicted to experience. They constantly need to have some activity to look forward to. Looking forward to the weekend, for instance, becomes the reason for putting up with school and parents during the week. But the weekend has to contain *activities*—parties, for example.

Another aspect of this "experience-orientation" is the increased interest among adolescents in *spiritual* experience. More adolescents every day are becoming interested in spiritually-oriented experiences: Dungeons and Dragons, for instance, and Satanism. Not all of the effects have been so negative; for example, the upsurge of interest in charismatic Christianity in the past several years can be partially attributed to this fascination with experience. The reason for all this is simple: Kids would rather feel than think. They want to experience spirituality with their senses. The positive implication is that young people are more likely to be open to worship and liturgy. The negative implication is that young people are often open to *any* mystical experience, regardless of the source of that experience. High-school ministry involves adolescents' minds and emotions. We should be giving kids opportunities to experience God *and* understand God.

The third and most serious side effect of "experience-orientation" is that high-school students are easy prey to the *illusion of intimacy*. In other words, they easily mistake a relationship of *experience* for a relationship of *quality*. This most often occurs in a relationship with someone of the opposite sex. Because high-school students are so susceptible to the sexual, it is easy for them to become involved with someone from the opposite sex and (as a result of the lack of sexual mores) suddenly experience intimacy so powerful and overwhelming that everything else in life seems dull and insignificant. The *experience* of intimacy is addictive to the adolescent. It isn't unusual for high-school students to lose interest in everything except their relationships with boy-friends or girl friends.

What does this illusion of intimacy mean to those of us who are involved in high-school ministry? It results in one of our most difficult tasks: to convince adolescents that real intimacy is not always easy and is always accompanied by a lot of hard work. Our role is to capture the hearts of high-school students and to help them begin to experience *real* relationships.

Depressed? Discouraged? Ready to throw in the towel after reading about all the sinister forces at work in our culture? We hope not. We hope you feel as we do that the opportunities for ministry are better than they have ever been. The good news is that, although this culture is constantly changing, the Gospel is *not* changing. It is the "same yesterday, today and forever." Let us spend some time discussing just how that Gospel intersects with high-school students in this culture.

BRINGING THE UNCHANGING GOSPEL TO ADOLESCENTS

There are three principles that should shape your presentation of the Gospel to adolescents; fail to grasp these three ideas, and your work with high-school students will suffer.

1. Realize that many of these problems are not conscious problems. Preaching a sermon or teaching a series of lessons on narcissism, for example, is not the total answer. There is a famous story told about a young girl who went to a psychiatrist because she was drinking too much, partying too much, and fooling around sexually too much. The psychiatrist suggested that she stop doing some of these things for a while. The girl looked up with surprise and said, "You mean I don't have to do what I *want* to do?" Surprising as it may seem, it does not occur to most young people that they have the option of choosing to say no to their feelings.

2. Give high-school students room to move realistically *to higher levels of responsibility and commitment.* Young people may be able to go from sinner to saint after a weekend retreat, but within a few days, they begin the *real* process of rebirth, which takes time.

3. Accept the fact that you must start with high-school students where they are, not where you want them to be. You'd probably like all your students to be dedicated disciples—but chances are not all of them are ready for that yet. They should not be made to feel like there is something wrong with them because they are not ready to be where you want them. Our role in ministry is to give high-school students the *opportunity* to grow.

Now—with those three principles in mind, what are the elements of the Gospel we hold out to kids? What is it that we're really offering them?

1. The Adventure of Following Christ. It is tempting, faced with the hostile forces in this culture, to circle the wagons—to try to *protect* the students we minister to from a threatening environment by insulating them from it. In other words, we tend to try, as much as possible, to hold the world at bay and keep things from changing. We become so cautious that we are afraid to allow our students to experience the consequences of following the living Christ. That's a mistake. Our role is to help adolescents insulate themselves from the Evil One. *Change is the way God does His work—not an obstacle to it.* "The symbol of our religion is a hoisted sail, not an anchor."[21] The practical application of this is simple: We need to *challenge* high-schoolers, to put them into situations where they are forced to do the heroic.

Too many youth are unchallenged and unthreatened. It was the liberating power of Jesus Christ that called some simple fishermen to leave the "security" of their nets and stumble into the "insecurity" of following Christ. High-school young people need to be nudged into situations where they can learn responsibility, accountability, and trust.

2. The Grace of God. As we have pointed out, high-school students live in a performance-oriented society. It is easy for adolescents in the church to get the impression that the sincerity of their faith is evaluated on the basis of performance. Young people in the church are under a lot of pressure to perform for Jesus. As a result, many adolescents in the church suffer from constant guilt. In the words of Robert Capon, young people are "like ill taught piano students; they play their songs, but they never really hear them because their main concern is not to make music but to avoid some flub that will get them in dutch."[22]

As a result, the word that describes the relationship of most high-school students with God is not *grace*—but *guilt*. They act more like citizens of a police state than like children of the King. Of course, there is such a thing as true guilt; but more often than not, high-school students are made to feel guilty rather than loved. Young people need to be told they are loved more than they need to be told how badly they are doing. Going back to Father Capon's analogy of the piano student, we need to give adolescents a chance to hear the music.

3. The Love of God. It is important to emphasize to young people in this society that God is a lover. When we sin, it is not just that we break the *law* of God—we break the *heart* of God. Most young people don't really believe God loves them. Paul tells us that it is the "love of Christ that constrains us."[23] It is not our love for Christ, but Christ's love for us that is the motivating force compelling us to live a godly life. Too many youth ministers try to pressure kids into living godly lives instead of helping them to fall in love with a God who has already fallen in love with them—forever.

33

God is not a stern taskmaster sneaking around to catch young people in sin so He can punish them. He is a loving, caring Father who understands young people better than they understand themselves and appreciates everything they do for Him.

Chap Clark tells the story of a friend of his who had a three-year-old son. Every day the father would come home after work and go through the same routine: walk into the kitchen, pour a glass of milk, grab a couple of cookies, and walk back into the living room to unwind while watching the evening news. One night the father came home a little late, and as he walked in the door he noticed his three-year-old son hurrying toward the kitchen. The father, sensing something was up, hesitated. The little boy rushed over to the kitchen counter, climbed up, reached into the cupboard, and grabbed a glass—knocking down two others in the process and breaking one of them. Then he climbed down from the counter, went over to the cookie jar, grabbed two cookies (one fell on the floor), and ran to the refrigerator. The carton of milk slipped out of his hands as he pulled it out; it fell, spilling some. Undaunted, the boy poured some of the remaining milk into the empty glass and set the carton back down on the floor.

By now, the kitchen looked like a tornado had struck. The cupboard was open, a glass was broken, cookie crumbs and milk were all over the floor. Behind the open carton of milk sitting on the floor, the refrigerator door was open. Any other night, the boy might have been punished for all the rules he had broken. But as the father watched his son run down the hall with the glass of milk and cookie, he realized what love was in the boy's heart—and threw his arms around his son and said, "Thank you, son, for that wonderful gift."

Too many young people view God as a stern father standing at the end of the hallway yelling, "You broke that glass! You spilled the milk! Get that refrigerator door closed!" But God isn't like that. He stands at the end of the hallway, throws His arms around us, and says, "Thank you for the wonderful gift you have given me." That's the God we want high-school students to see.

4. The Peace of God. The peace of God is not some mystical complicated truth. Young people don't have to become monks to understand it. The peace of God can be understood with just one word—quiet. High-school students today need to be quiet. They need time alone with God with no noise, no distractions, no activity whatsoever. High-school ministry must provide ample opportunities for students to be quiet. The fruit of the spirit is not a meeting—it is peace.

5. The Call of God. The reality of the call of God is a truth that every high-school student needs to understand. It is knowing we are in the right place that gives meaning to all that we do. When Jesus spent the day with Zaccheus, He said He had come "to seek and to save what was lost" (Luke 19:10). The word "lost" means "in the wrong place." Jesus came to save those who are in the wrong place and put them in the right place. So many young people today, as well as adults, have no idea what they want to do with their lives. They haven't any sense of place—of being where they belong. The expression of a high-school student's identity (Erik Erickson suggests that identity formation is the primary task of adolescence[24]) and the exercise of his gifts is *not* done for himself, for his family, for the company where he will eventually work, or even for the good of humankind. It is done as a response to a summons for service from the Lord Himself.[25] The call of God transcends all else and gives meaning to all that we do.

6. The Church of God. Too many high-school ministry programs exist outside, or apart from, the church—even those that are closely identified with a church. Youth programs often become "youth ghettos" where the young people's program is isolated from the life of the church. It is a tragic mistake to keep high-school students outside the church. God did not just *say* we were different; He created a place where those differences matter—the church. The church must not be just a parent corporation that provides the money and resources for youth ministry. The church must include, involve, and depend upon young people. High-school students are *not* the church of tomorrow—they *are* the church. Now.

7. The Hope of God. Depression and loneliness are two of the biggest problems facing adolescents today. High-school students often wonder if life makes sense. It is vitally important that we hold up before our young people the hope of the Christian faith. God is at work, and adolescents especially need to understand that no matter how bad things may seem, or how many times they fail, God's love is constant, and He will see us through to the end—which is really only the beginning.

AN OMINOUS SIGN

There may be a very disturbing trend emerging that will affect future generations of adolescents. So far, it's only a hunch. And we hope we're wrong. But the signs all point to an emerging generation of adolescents who could erupt in anger.

The late sixties produced an angry generation of young people who had specific complaints and a clear agenda about what needed to be corrected in our culture. Our fear is that the emerging generation of young people will be angry but have *no* specific targets, no agenda; it will simply be anger directed at anything and everything. It will be anarchy.

This is, we realize, a sobering and negative view. But the signs are beginning to emerge, both in the society around us and in the research being done into the adolescent mind. One sign, for instance, is the rapidly increasing distance between the have's and the have-not's. A second sign is the tendency of our institutions to overpromise the future to each new generation; we are creating a generation of young people whose expectations will far exceed our society's ability to fulfill them.

We would be wise to continue to watch for signs of this new age of anger and to do what we can to create a new generation who will look to Christ, rather than society, for the fulfillment of their longings.

2 Is There Life After Puberty?
The Physiological Dimension
of High-school Ministry

Because most high-school students have already passed through puberty, most adults assume that high schoolers are prepared for the emotional and physical *consequences* of puberty. Not so—*helping high-school students deal with the emotional and psychological consequences of puberty and their emerging sexuality is one of the major goals of an effective ministry to high-school students.* The most significant developmental struggles of adolescents are associated with the radical changes happening in their bodies. High-school students spend a great deal of time worrying about their bodies and their sexuality. The process of physical change brought about by puberty (menstruation, breast development, body hair) and the adjustment to sexual development (sexual experimentation, sexual desire) can overwhelm the average high-school student. The *process* of puberty can become the *peril* of puberty for even the most normal of teenagers, causing overwhelming stress.[1]

—Darrell refused to go to school because he had a serious case of acne.

—After growing over six inches in the last six months, Glenn has no energy, his grades are falling, and he is not getting along with his parents.

—Carol is frightened and depressed. One breast is growing faster than the other one.

—Heather is worried about her Christian faith. Lately it seems that all she can think about is her boyfriend. He is pressuring her to have sex, and she is surprised at herself because, although she knows it is wrong, she wants to say yes.

—Don was the all-time great jock in junior high. He was bigger and stronger than any other guy in his class. But just two years later, all of his friends are bigger than he is. What's wrong with him, anyway? Now all his buddies are playing football, and he's too small even to get on the team.

Spiritual problems? Not primarily. Each of these is, first of all, a physiological problem. Physiological problems can and do affect every area of a high-school student's life, but far too many youth workers ignore them.

Let's take a look at the most common physiological concerns of high-school students.

APPEARANCE

High-school students worry that they are too tall (girls worry if they are over five foot, seven inches). They worry that they are too fat (at least 30 percent of today's teenagers are overweight) or too skinny (eating disorders, such as anorexia and bulimia, have become serious problems with adolescents). Basically, adolescents worry about every conceivable part of their body—ears (too long, too stuck-out), lips (too fat, too thin), mouth (too big), neck (too thick, too long), head (too big, too pointy, too little), nose (too big, too pointy, too long, too flat), eyes (too close together, wrong color, too squinty, too wrinkled), eyebrows (too thick, too close together, too thin, funny-shaped), chest (too flat), breasts (too big, too small, too pointy), legs (too long, too fat, too skinny), thighs (too fat), hips (no shape, too big), feet (too big, too small), hands (fingers too long, fingers too short).[2]

A recent survey of adolescents revealed that 56 percent of high-school girls were not satisfied with their bodies.[3] High-school boys can just as easily be obsessed with their height (they don't want to be smaller than their girl friend or date) and their body proportions (they don't want to be called a "wimp").

As a result, adolescents are apt to judge a person's worth by how that person looks. It is still an axiom of adolescence that how you look means more than who you are, so adolescents are continually concerned about what people see.

Because adolescents are so obsessed with the physical, the sensitive youth worker will exercise some precautions:

1. Be extra sensitive about what you say regarding high-school students' appearances. Youth workers often make jokes about kids in their youth groups. Too many times, the jokes focus on someone's appearance, such as "Hey, Bob, what happened to your hair?" or "Linda—just learn how to walk? Way to go." Making fun of Bob's hair or Linda's momentary clumsiness may not seem very significant, but sometimes those comments can be upsetting. We are not suggesting that you never have fun with high-school students; sometimes jokes, for example about someone's tripping, can relieve the pressure and make things better. But generally, we believe that the more you as a youth worker refrain from joking about kids' bodies, the less chance you have of deeply hurting and offending someone.

2. Try not to relate to high-school students on the basis of how they look. To be blunt, many (if not most) youth workers are attracted to the good-looking kids and find it harder to relate to the unattractive kids. The more time you can spend with *each* high-school student, regardless of appearance, the more effective your ministry will be, and the more powerfully you will be able to communicate that external appearance really doesn't matter.

3. Take high-school students' physical problems seriously. Many adults who work with adolescents, when they encounter an adolescent with a physical problem, assume that it would be best for them not to get involved in the treatment of that problem because the parents are aware of their children's physical problems and are doing whatever needs to be done to remedy them. In reality, many parents are either used to the problem (and therefore don't see it as a problem) or they are unaware of the seriousness of the emotional trauma the problem causes.

Ed Connor was a senior in high school, eighteen years old and heavy-set. His voice, which had never changed, had become a constant source of embarrassment and ridicule, resulting in serious emotional problems. Because Ed's voice problem caused him so much emotional pain, his youth worker found it hard to talk with him about the problem. It wasn't until after years of building a relationship with Ed that the youth worker mustered up enough nerve to ask Ed the source of his voice problem. To the youth worker's astonishment, Ed didn't have any idea. Because Ed's parents were poor, he had never been to a doctor about his voice. (His parents were too embarrassed to admit they didn't have the money.) Within a few weeks, the youth worker raised enough money for Ed to see a specialist in voice disorders. The prognosis: There was nothing wrong with Ed's voice that one or two speech therapy sessions couldn't fix. In two short weeks, Ed Connor's voice was normal, and the youth worker had built a bond between Ed and him that would never be broken.

EMOTIONS

If there is a given in adolescent development, it is the onset of sudden mood shifts. Adolescents can be elated one minute and superdepressed the next; they can be withdrawn and uncommunicative and a few minutes later be the life of the party.

Mood swings and emotional change are a normal part of the adolescent landscape, but they can signal serious problems as well. And that emotional roller coaster and the potential problems associated with it are unfortunately too often ignored by youth workers. Here are some thoughts that may help.

1. Adolescents have different temperaments. Some kids are shy and withdrawn; others are loud and outgoing. We can't change a kid's temperament, nor should we. Our role is to help all members of the group, regardless of their temperament, to feel accepted. It's easy to gravitate toward the outgoing kids, the extroverts, and to all but ignore the shy ones, the socially awkward kids who keep to themselves. But often it's those withdrawn kids who are developing, during those years of being ignored by their peers, the quiet strengths and skills that will make them leaders as adults— or artists, musicians, engineers, pastors, poets, or writers. Let's be careful not to squelch anyone just because his temperament is different.

2. More often than not, there are physical reasons for moodiness. Accelerated physical changes or menstruation can both cause shifts in mood. Remember that the young people you work with are bewildered and possibly frightened by their runaway emotions. It is important to assure them that moodiness caused by physical change is normal and expected.

3. Solitude can cause moodiness. Some adolescents try never to be alone because they find solitude intolerable; others are alone a large percentage of the time. Loneliness and solitude can lead to depression, aimlessness, boredom, anxiety, and sadness. Solitude can also lead to a deep appreciation of others, along with other positive results; still, it's important when you are involved with an adolescent who is moody or depressed to check out his solitude. Is the adolescent alone a lot? Are his parents working? Does he have any friends or outside interests? The solution may be as simple as cutting back on his periods of solitude.

4. Entropy vs. negentropy. Entropy is a psychic disorder that expresses itself in bad moods, tiredness, loss of motivation, and an inability to focus or use attention constructively. Entropic experiences are normal for adolescents and motivate them to overcome adversity and set

43

higher goals. However, a consistent pattern of entropy may signal difficulty in adjusting to being an adult. If a teenager is bored all the time, it could mean trouble, and you should look for outside help. The opposite of entropy is negentropy, characterized by positive feelings toward self and others, psychological activation (the adolescent experiences a sense of energy when performing an activity), intrinsic motivation, and effective concentration.[4] How does the youth worker strengthen the negentropic characteristics and lessen the entropic characteristics? *Enjoyment.* The job of the youth worker is to help adolescents have experiences that combine pain and pleasure—to help teenagers find "pleasure and pain in the right objects."[5] There is nothing wrong with the high-school youth group taking a break from their work in a Mexican orphanage for a wild fireworks show one evening or having great evening campfires with skits and singing. The kids spend all day experiencing the pain of hard work, then enjoy the evenings with each other.

SEX[6]

Even in this sophisticated age, two common myths still exist regarding teenagers and sex.

The first is that secular sex education has made this generation of teenagers much more knowledgeable about sex than previous generations. Most adults assume that high-school students have been exposed to extensive sex education courses. The truth is that, although most high-school students have taken sex education in school, they have only been exposed to the technical aspects of sex. Most high-school students know little about the moral and emotional consequences of sex. Interestingly, the most common complaints adolescents have about sex education in the schools are the same complaints they have always had about sex education with their parents: The teachers don't talk about the things we want to know and are embarrassed to talk about difficult areas.

Actually, today's high-school students are often as frustrated and as ignorant about sexual matters as previous generations.

The second myth is that most parents who have a strong relationship with the church talk to their adolescents about their sexual values. Not true, unfortunately. Most parents *assume* their kids know what their sexual values are. But they don't. Most adolescents know that their parents don't want them to practice sexual intercourse or get pregnant but *don't have a clue about any other sexual values their parents may have.* Even in the eighties, few parents actually sit down with their high-school children and talk frankly about sex.

Compounding the problem is the sad fact that much of what high-school students have learned about sex occurs in a supposedly *neutral values* environment. Not only do kids not know their parents' values, *the only sexual values they have been taught have been the prevailing cultural values,* which, in many cases, are directly opposed to biblical sexual values. Here are some of the most dangerous of those cultural values:

1. Sex is only a physical act. When the Bible says that during sexual intercourse two people become one, sex is not just a physical act but a mystical experience in which the two people involved give up something of themselves that can never be reclaimed. Part of a person's inmost being is transferred to someone else during intercourse, whether the participants believe it or not. Help your high schoolers understand that sex is much more than a physical act. Sex was created by God to be the vehicle through which two committed people become one.

2. Sexual technique is the most important part of sex. Obviously, concern about sexual technique is not a conscious concern for most high-school students. Still, they're constantly hearing through television, movies, books, records, and other propaganda channels that *the better lover you are, the better sex you will have.* It is easy for them to become more concerned about sexual performance than they are

45

about moral performance. The slang phrase for sexual intercourse among teenagers is "do it." That is more than just a slang expression; it is an expression of how high-school students view sex—a performance. The appropriate questions afterward are "How was it?" and "Was I good?"

Our role as youth workers is to once again counter this cultural view of sex with the biblical view: Sex is not a performance; it is an expression of a committed relationship. The Creator of sex has come to set us free from worrying about our performance, so we can find real meaning and satisfaction in our sexual activity.

3. There are only two moral restrictions when it comes to sexual behavior: You should not be responsible for giving someone a social disease and you should not hurt other people. Those *are* important values. But consider this: If people adhered to the basic biblical sexual premise—that sexual intercourse should be reserved for a permanent relationship—those two rules would be unnecessary. They *are* necessary in a pluralistic society, when the fundamental value upon which sex was created is often completely ignored.

4. There are no consequences to our sexual behavior. The prevailing belief in our society is that if you take the proper precautions and don't hurt anyone, sexual activity has no consequences: It is merely an isolated experience. The truth is that sexual activity *always* has consequences. It changes us; we lose something. Prostitutes are not like they are portrayed in the movies. They are hardened, cold people because their sexual behavior has changed them. The implications are clear for high-school ministry: Adolescents need to understand that sexual activity has consequences, and that although God cannot stop the consequences, He can forgive us and begin to heal us of the results of sexual misuse.

How important is it to dispel this cultural misinformation? Vitally important. The youth worker should spend *whatever* time it takes to convince young people of the fallacies of our society's notion of sex. The Bible does, after all, have a better idea.

THE BIBLICAL ALTERNATIVE

1. Sex is good. High-school students need to hear that God created sex not only as part of the process of procreation but also to be enjoyed. The Christian response to the playboy ethic that encourages sex for pleasure only is not to deny that sex is pleasurable but to suggest that pleasure is not the primary function of sex. Sex was given by God to make two people one, so sex is not only good, it is a mystery.

2. Sex is a mystery. There is no adequate way to explain what happens to people during intercourse because sex is a mystery—a mystical experience that is unique for everyone. It is never the same and can never be reduced to a measurable process. High-school students must hear about the mystery of sex as well as the morality of sex.

3. Sex requires constant moral surveillance. Some who work with high-school students in the church believe that, according to the Bible, there should be no sexual activity of any kind until marriage. Hand holding maybe, but other than that, nothing sexual between couples until marriage. Well, that does make it easy to decide about sexual behavior. You hold hands and then you get married.

We respect those who come to that conclusion. We have concluded differently. We believe that some sexual activity among high-school students is not only inevitable, but with plenty of prayer and thought, within the limits of Christian behavior.

What do we mean by "some sexual activity"? We answer with another question: What does the Bible say about masturbation, oral sex, French kissing, and mutual masturbation? The answer is that the Bible doesn't say anything specific about any of those things. Even so, Christian high-school students have to make decisions about all of those activities. How? Another of the important functions of high-school ministry is to *help adolescents develop sexual standards based on biblical principles*. There may not be specific verses regarding French kissing, but there are a lot of verses about moderation (1 Peter 4:7, for instance), putting others' interests ahead of our own (Phil. 2:3–5), and putting ourselves in situations where we are tempted beyond our capacity (1 Cor. 10:13).

Sexual desire and sex-related decisions are as much a part of adolescence as homework and parents. We cannot keep our heads in the sand and refuse to talk about sex because we are afraid of the issues. High-school students are making decisions about abortion, homosexuality, living together before marriage, sexual abuse, incest, oral sex, and a host of other sex-related issues. Will they have the input from the church they need to help them make positive, solid, biblically-based decisions? Effective high-school ministry should provide that input.

HOW TO DISCUSS SEX WITH TEENS

Unfortunately, when it comes to discussing sexuality with teenagers, adults have a lot of problems to overcome. Here are some suggestions that will help:

1. Talk frankly about sex. It *is* hard to talk frankly about sex in church—but what better place? Still, we're not naive. We realize that there are some obstacles to frank discussions of sex in church youth groups. Not only is it hard for youth workers to talk about sex—it's also true that many church parents don't *want* you talking frankly about sex in church.

There are dangers in frank discussions of sex. An immature or unknowledgeable adult may end up raising more questions than he has answered, but the risks are worth it. The important thing is to do your homework: Know your subject well, anticipate responses, and make sure you have lots of biblical foundation for what you say. Let parents know ahead of time that you are going to talk with the high-school students about sex, so if they object, they can keep their children away. You may believe, as we do, that those students are the ones who need to be there the most, but you cannot violate the parents' right to make decisions they believe are in their children's best interests.

2. Create an open and safe environment. One of the most important ingredients of high-school ministry is a safe environment where high-school students feel free to say what they believe, even if we, as leaders, strongly disagree with them. They must sense that we love them unconditionally, even when they have opinions we disagree with. For some reason, many churches subtly or not so subtly give young people the impression that they are to say what the churches or the youth worker want to hear rather than say what they believe.

3. Avoid simplistic answers. Too many youth workers and churches look for an easy way to teach sex education with a nice list of black-and-white answers. Packaged answers don't work now or later. We cannot be afraid to admit to the complexity of sexual decision making.

4. Don't be afraid to talk about all the issues. The myth that knowledge leads to promiscuity is exactly that—a myth. Knowledge can't hurt kids, but withholding knowledge can. A word of caution: Sexuality is a sensitive area for everyone, so you must be wise and careful. We are not suggesting that it is okay to discuss oral sex with students in junior high. We are saying if *they* raise the question, then you must attempt a careful and biblical response, no matter what the issue.

5. Don't forget to talk about the grace of God. Most of our churches teach, explicitly or implicitly, that sexual sins are the worst kind of sins. That's why many high-school students believe that sexual sins are unpardonable. They also believe that because sexual sins tend to be repeated, there comes a point where God will no longer forgive.

There is a tension between calling kids to a discipleship

that demands responsible decision making and the grace of God that proclaims adolescents forgiven even when they continue to do the same sin over and over again. Recognizing that tension, we would still rather err on the side of Grace than Law. Most adolescents have no trouble at all visualizing a *policeman God*, holding them accountable for their decisions and actions. But it's hard for them to believe that God really does love them unconditionally. For that reason, we believe it is important to reaffirm continually God's love to them, especially when the question of sexual sin arises.

6. Don't be afraid to tell kids what they don't want to hear. Darla comes to you and says that she is dating a guy she really cares a lot about, but she is not happy with their sexual behavior. In fact, he is beginning to push her to have sexual intercourse. She doesn't want to have sex but she doesn't want to lose her boyfriend either. She asks, "How can we back off from our sexual activity and still keep the relationship going?"

This is a difficult question with an even more difficult answer. Unfortunately, in nearly every case, couples cannot go backward when it comes to sexual activity. The difficult answer is: "Well, Darla, I'm afraid it probably won't work to try and go back, and I doubt if your boyfriend will go for it anyway. I am afraid that the best advice I can give you is to break off your relationship." That is not what Darla *wants* to hear, but it is what she *needs* to hear.

Even though you have to tell kids what they don't want to hear, it's unwise to force them to respond the way you want them to respond. Let them hear the hard news and then make the decision on their own. Darla may decide she can't break up with Todd. You may be upset by that, knowing what it means for Darla, but *you must let her live with the consequences of her decision*. Does that mean that you must condone her decision or agree with it? No. But you must let it be *her* decision.

Tell kids the truth about sex. Don't be afraid to tell

them that sexual intercourse before marriage is wrong. Don't apologize for upholding the biblical sexual ethic. Let them respond to their options, then be willing to love them and help them even when they make the wrong decision.

DATING

Helping high-school students deal with their sexuality doesn't mean that we only tell them what they *shouldn't* do. We should also give them suggestions about what they *should* do. Strange as it may seem, American high-school students are very much interested in dating, but most high-school students don't often date. It's been estimated that half of high-school girls won't have had even *one* date before they graduate from high school.

Consequently, youth workers have a dual task. On the one hand, we need to make it clear that you do not have to date in high school to be normal. On the other hand, encouraging teenagers (boys especially) to look at dating as more than just going to a movie or dinner and parking is a very important function of high-school ministry. It is our conviction that if more high-school students rediscovered the old-fashioned date, there would be less sexual conflict and more healthy adolescent relationships. The church can help high-school students understand that dating can be great fun. Why do so many high-school students have a hard time integrating their dating lives with their spiritual lives? One reason is that dates have become just another occasion for sexual pressure. Too many adolescents are unaware (because they have never been taught) that a date can be much more than merely a romantic or sexual experience. When the church begins to encourage and educate high-school adolescents about dating, then the kids in our youth groups will recognize that healthy dating can be a very practical expression of their faith.

MARRIAGE

The church can no longer expect that marriage preparation is taking place at home. Whether it is because of the alarmingly high divorce rate, the growing acceptance of living together, or some other phenomenon, high-school students are simply not being prepared for marriage. In a society where living together is increasingly becoming an acceptable option, the church needs to do more than merely say that living together is wrong. The church needs to educate its young people about the biblical view of marriage. The strange fact is that although more and more students are choosing to live together without marriage, there is also emerging a new idealism about marriage. Most adolescents still believe in marriage and still believe that they will be the exception when it comes to divorce.

How do youth workers help adolescents learn to respond to their sexuality? Consider the comments of David Elkind in his book *All Grown Up and No Place To Go.*

> Puberty brings with it a host of worries and anxieties, some of which are serious, others less so. These worries are symptoms of a constructive form of growth and are therefore healthy in the long run, even though they may be painful in the short run. Even in times of social stability, the stresses associated with the perils of puberty are considerable. They are clear evidence of teenagers' need for a special place and a protected time in society to cope with the transformations of their bodies and the social consequences those transformations entail.[7]

The church can be—*must* be—that special place of protection where high-school students can learn to cope with their new sexuality.

3 Is There Life After Nerdness?
The Social Dimension of High-school Ministry

> The early adolescent wants many friends, for he needs peers to help him sculpt his beliefs, verify his new conclusions, test his new attitudes against an alien set to evaluate their hardiness, and obtain support for his new set of fragile assumptions.[1]

You cannot talk about high-school ministry without taking into account the *social realities* of adolescent life. The older the high-school student, the less he is influenced by the home and the more he is influenced by his social environment (peers, friends, school).

The question for those of us who minister to high-school students is not "*Are* adolescents affected by their peers and their school?" but "*How* are adolescents affected by their peers and school?" Will the effects be positive or negative? Is there anything we can do in ministry to help high-school students survive the social realities of high-school life? To answer that last question, we need first to understand what the social realities are.

PEER PRESSURE
Since we are beginning with the safe assumption that high-school students are influenced profoundly by their peers, it would be wise to take a look at the dynamics of peer pressure.

All adolescents are affected by their peers. All adolescents need relationships outside their family to begin to develop their own identity. They need others, especially peers, for support and acceptance at this critical period in their lives. *"It is important to remember . . . that peer pressure has no power in and of itself.* The peer group is powerful only because there are teenagers . . . who lack the inner strengths that would weigh against conforming."[2] *Peer pressure in itself is not the problem.* In many cases, it can be beneficial, depending on the individual adolescent. That's good news because it means peer pressure *can* be a very positive, productive force.

Adolescents are most susceptible to peer pressure. The reasons adolescents are susceptible to peer pressure are more developmental than sociological. First of all, adolescents are beginning to turn away from their parents and look more toward their friendships and their peers for support and growth. Secondly, they are beginning to think differently—as David Elkind calls it, "thinking in a new key."[3] The primary characteristic of this "new key" is that high-school students are very self-conscious. They begin to suffer from the imaginary audience syndrome—the feeling that they are always on stage and that everyone is watching them. They'll do anything to keep from drawing attention to themselves. For them, the *worst* thing that can happen is to be different or odd. This extreme concern for being noticed is a significant cause of an adolescent's susceptibility to peer pressure. (It's encouraging that this imaginary audience syndrome decreases as teenagers grow older.)

Peer banding vs. peer bonding. In her book *Children Without Childhood*, Marie Winn points out that many adolescents band together out of a sense of shared *weakness*—not out of a sense of shared *strength*.[4] It is in these groups—the ones who band together out of weakness—that the high incidence of drug and alcohol abuse and sexual experimentation occur most frequently. The bonding that takes place is a forging together of weak people who depend on the group's escape activities to give them strength. In contrast, *the church youth group should be a place where adolescents band together to build each other up*—where the adolescents find security. In a church youth group, peer bonding should not be the result of shared weakness, but rather of shared strength.

Positive peer influence vs. negative peer influence. Too often when the term "peer pressure" is used, it is used in a negative context, synonymous with "bad influence." We assume whenever adolescents are influenced by their peers, it is almost always negative. Not true. Peer pressure can be a positive force; adolescents can influence each other in positive ways.

Peer Ministry. Adolescents need to realize they have gifts and abilities that are necessary, and important, to the life of the church. There is much young people can do and need to do:

1. Run vacation Bible school
2. Teach children's Sunday school
3. Plan youth meetings and youth retreats
4. Participate in the worship services
5. Plan and participate in work camps and mission trips
6. Get involved in service projects[5]

Peer Counseling. Almost everything a teenager does in this culture is based on competition and performance. Peer counseling is one of the few things a teenager can do that actually helps someone. *Every* adolescent is a potential resource of caring. They all have the right credentials—age and similar experiences and problems.[6]

Adolescents can help other adolescents in ways that adults cannot. More and more youth groups are beginning to realize that *high-school students themselves are sometimes the best resource for helping another high-school student.*[7] Peer counseling does require some learned skills, but the skills required are easily learned. Brian Reynolds lists six qualities that peers can use to help each other: affirmation, to need and be needed, trust, support, recognition of potential, and cohesiveness (unity).[8] Any counselor can tell you that what adolescents need most when they are in trouble is not advice but someone who cares enough to listen. Peers are the perfect resource to provide that caring and listening.

55

Teaching teens about peer pressure. As strange as it may seem, many high-school students are not aware that they are being pressured to conform. It should come as no surprise that most high-school students do not want to be influenced by their peers in a negative way but often they don't have the tools or the strength they need to refrain. Teaching about peer pressure can be preventive medicine. A good peer pressure education program can help adolescents know what peer pressure is, recognize that everyone faces it, and see that it can be a force for good as well as bad.

THE HIGH-SCHOOL CASTE SYSTEM

The basis of adolescent relationships in high school is homogeneity. The high-school subculture is a web of homogeneous groupings, each of which has its own criteria for acceptance and inclusion. In every high school, those groupings possess distinct characteristics and exist in a definite hierarchy. The groupings may have different names and characteristics from one high school to another, but a highly structured caste system is operating at every high school.

We are all familiar with the most obvious manifestation of the high-school caste system: class structure by grade—the "mighty" senior vs. the "lowly" freshman. The grade caste system is operative at every high school and affects every member of the class, regardless of the other social groupings that exist. The lowliest of seniors still has power over the most revered freshman. Tragically, in most church youth groups, *the higher the grade, the smaller the participation*. It should be a real cause for concern when the older an adolescent becomes, the more irrelevant his faith seems. Youth workers should be concerned when this happens in their youth group and should make every effort to address the causes of this problem.

Here are some of the possible causes:

Economics. Because of spiraling inflation and increasing unemployment, more and more middle-class adolescents are being forced into the work force just to survive economically in high school. To have spending money, to operate a car, and to buy clothes for school, high-school students are going to work at a much earlier age than in the past. "In America, at least a third of high-school students (18.6 million) hold part-time jobs in any given week."[9] The older the high-school student, the more likely he will be working and the more likely his working hours will conflict with your youth program. To minister to older high-school students, youth workers must find creative ways to minister individually, one-on-one, during nonworking, nonschool hours.

Maturity. When high-school students become seniors, they begin to perceive themselves as more mature. Parents and teachers are also beginning to expect more from the seniors and to push them to think about the future. For possibly the first time in their lives, they need to take life seriously. Your youth program should recognize this new-found maturity and offer a more distinctive program for older high-school students. For example: Offer classes and special seminars on "How to Choose and Finance Your College Education," "How to Know What You Want to Be When You Grow Up," "How to Survive Living Alone," "What to Expect Your First Year of College," "Who Wants to Go to College? What to Do if You Don't."

Service. When high-school students become seniors, they want to be accepted and recognized as older and more capable of giving as well as taking. The more you can involve seniors in leadership and in activities that require them to give as well as receive, the more they will feel motivated to stay. Getting seniors involved in service projects is great. Give them responsibility. Challenge and encourage them to stretch beyond themselves.

SOCIAL GROUPINGS

You remember all the terms: jocks, nerds, dopers, brains, cowboys. You could probably name more. But they all have one thing in common: They describe one of the many social groupings that exists in every high school. Every one of these social groupings centers around common interests—athletics, cheerleading, a particular fad (punkers, valley girls, mods, preppies), intellectual interests, and so on.

The social group provides the adolescent with instant security and identity. The group becomes a safe place where adolescents feel included, instead of excluded. There are many high-school students who would not consider themselves members of any of these obvious groupings, but even they are members of the "adolescent" grouping itself, which provides a sense of identity, of belonging.

One of the goals of high-school ministry is to create an adolescent community in which these social groupings no longer exist. In school, jocks have nothing to do with nerds. In the youth group, jocks and nerds should be able to be together and not be affected by their social grouping. If the youth group is really practicing the gospel, then if a member of the youth group happens to be considered a nerd in high school, his nerdness will not be noticed in the youth group because it simply won't make any difference.

A note of realism: Although it should be the goal of every youth group to have no caste distinctions, it is important to recognize that social groupings *do* exist. Not only does the youth worker try to minimize the groupings, he also tries to *use* the social groupings for ministry. Most commonly, it works like this: Adults of a particular social grouping tend to have more effect on adolescents of the same social grouping. For example, if an adult is very athletic, he will tend to have more influence on a high-school jock, or if an adult works with computers, he will have a greater effect on a high-school computer whiz.

It's important for those of us who work with adolescents to realize that social groupings have changed in nature in the past few years. Previously, there was a *hierarchy* of social groupings (see figure 1). Even though the social groupings were sharply defined, some groups were admittedly higher on the social scale than others and influenced the other groups. If, for example, the jocks endorsed something, other groups were influenced by that endorsement. Interestingly, many Christian organizations who worked with adolescents (Campus Life, Young Life, Campus Crusade) based their ministry strategy on that assumption.

Things have changed. Now there is no hierarchy. The punkers couldn't care less what the jocks endorse. Each group is a separate entity, and each has equal *noninfluence* on the others (see figure 2).

Figure 1

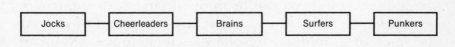

Figure 2

CLIQUES

A clique is an exclusive group of adolescents whose basis of exclusivity is related to location (the kids have all lived in the same neighborhood for years), status (each one of the kids lives in Emerald Bay Estates), talent (they all take ballet from Mrs. Dirkson), special information (they all buy drugs from the same person), or length of relationship (they have been friends since first grade). Cliques are the result of an arbitrary, conscious decision on the part of the members. A clique *wants* to limit its membership; the members *want* others to feel excluded. Although the members of a clique may be very close, it is just as possible that they are not close. The relationships within a clique are secondary—what matters is keeping others out.

Cliques are a serious problem. The biggest problem for the members is that they begin to define their identity by the parameters of the clique. In other words, they begin to believe that living in Emerald Bay actually *does* determine how much a person is worth. The second problem is that cliques stunt the growth of the members because they withdraw into themselves and become too comfortable to change. The third problem is that cliques that exist within a larger group harm the larger group because they usually put a damper on larger groups by forcing them to do what the clique wants to do. If the larger group ignores the clique, the clique often becomes uncooperative and refuses to participate.

What do you do about cliques? The answer depends on the clique. If the clique *is* the youth group and refuses to accept anyone new, then focus on the individual members of the clique you feel you can be most effective with and ignore those who are so exclusive they refuse to respond to you. At the same time, minister outside the clique to see if you can develop a new group that has no connection with the clique.

If the clique is part of a larger group, begin with the strategy above. If that doesn't work, your choices are to (1) ask the clique to cooperate or leave, or (2) ignore them and work with the larger group.

SCHOOL

> My entire life is really school. I don't mean the work,
> but my friends. My family life is falling apart, so I look
> forward to seeing my friends and talking to them. Also,
> it's the only place I can meet boys.[10]

There is no other nonfamily setting that consumes so
much of an adolescent's time. High-school students are not
only *in* school from 8 A.M. to 3 P.M. every weekday, they are
also involved in school-related activities (sports, cheerleading, school politics, homework) for another one to four hours
a day. Because school takes up a significant portion of the
high-school student's week, youth workers need to recognize
the opportunities for ministry that school provides rather
than complain about how school keeps adolescents from
doing important things, such as attending youth group
meetings. Want to take advantage of school-related opportunities and not compete with them? Here are some suggestions:

Don't deliberately compete with school. For instance, don't force high-school students to choose between a
school activity and a church activity. Accept the fact that
school is an important and necessary part of adolescent
development and try to work your youth group's schedule
around school activities, such as Fifth Quarter programs that
start *after* the Friday night football games. Fifth Quarters are
not planned to compete with the aftergame dance (many
youth groups do not have a Fifth Quarter if there is a dance)
but rather to be another option for aftergame activity. A
number of high-school youth groups across the country also
sponsor Breakfast Club that meets once a week for an hour
before school starts, provides breakfast, skits, announcements, and a short program with a speaker. Breakfast Club is
usually held in a church close to the school and is very
popular. Whatever activities you plan, don't give the
impression that there is something wrong with the kids if
they choose the school's activity rather than yours.

Provide a ministry of academics. There are many ways to help kids with their schoolwork, such as group leaders' tutoring or the group's sponsoring a study hall once a week, where kids can come not only to study but also to get help from interested sponsors. During finals week, the church can provide a nightly study hall complete with typewriters and computers so the kids can study and finish term papers or reports. The youth worker who helps his high-school students with their schoolwork accomplishes a number of important goals: He helps the student through school, supports the parents, and spends time with the kids. Keeping tabs on your young people's grades (not by sneaking around and finding out their grades but by asking) and watching for problems that might affect a student's learning (family trouble, learning disabilities, sickness, and so on). All of these school-related activities result in deeper relationships.

Look for opportunities to help school officials. School officials are generally leery of religious people who want to help, but if you take the time to gain the trust of the administrators, there's no limit to the help you can provide and the inroads you can make onto the high-school campus. You can volunteer to help the coaches (if you have coaching experience); you can provide rides to activities; you can substitute teach; you can help with school projects, such as homecoming activities; you can chaperone dances, help organize and plan baccalaureates. Most schools *need* a lot of outside help.

Cooperate with parachurch organizations like Young Life and Campus Life. Although parachurch organizations are for *unchurched* young people, your support of them will encourage your youth group to see them as an opportunity for outreach. Then nonchurched kids who have recently found new faith through parachurch organizations will find it easier to come to your church and your youth group.

4 Can a High-school Student Be Religious?
The Spiritual Dimension of High-school Ministry

You don't have to be around high-school students very long before you begin to wonder whether the terms "spiritual" and "teenager" can coexist or whether, perhaps, "the spiritual adolescent" is a contradiction in terms. We don't think so. "Spirituality" describes a person's capacity for the spiritual more than it describes a person's external behavior. During the high-school years, adolescents actually seem far more open to the spiritual dimension of their lives than they will be later in life. They have reached the age where they are becoming mature enough to *understand* faith, but they aren't old enough to have developed the defense mechanisms against faith that adults often have. Obviously, spirituality means something different for adolescents than it does for adults. Adolescent spirituality has a shape all its own.

CHARACTERISTICS OF ADOLESCENT SPIRITUALITY
High-school students need a firsthand faith. Too many youth programs attempt to *program* high-school kids into a relationship with God, when what students really need is *time to build their own relationship with God*. The primary side effect of too much programing is the creation of a youth group that knows more about Amy Grant's faith than their own and more about your walk with God than theirs. Tragically, many high-school students graduate from their church youth group with a "secondhand faith in a second-

hand God." In his best-selling book, *The Road Less Traveled*, Scott Peck quotes Alan Jones:

> One of our problems is that very few of us have developed any distinctive personal life. Everything about us seems secondhand, even our emotions. In many cases we have to rely on secondhand information in order to function. I accept the word of a physician, a scientist, a farmer on trust. I do not like to do this. I have to because they possess vital knowledge of living of which I am ignorant. Secondhand information concerning the state of my kidneys, the effects of cholesterol, and the raising of chickens I can live with. But when it comes to questions of meaning, purpose, and death, secondhand information will not do. I cannot survive on a secondhand faith in a secondhand God. There has to be a personal word, a unique confrontation, if I am to come alive.[1]

Even if we agree with this statement, can we really set aside our programs and our activities and allow kids quiet, solitary, personal time with God? Can we actually *program* times of no program? Yes, but only by consciously planning into our activities moments of no activity, such as daylong trips to the mountains, moments of silence during retreats, or quiet times after meetings.

When we do give young people time to think about God, the results will be overwhelming. The reason is very simple. Kids are seldom quiet—when they are, God can really work.

High-school students need spiritual experiences as well as spiritual content. Some believe the only way to know God is to experience Him; others believe the only way to know God is through the intellect. The truth is high-school students need *both* spiritual experience *and* intellectual content. What happens when kids come back from camp? They're ready to live for God twenty-four hours a day—but in three short days, they forget all about it. Still, kids *need* those emotional highs. They need to experience God, not just hear about God. That is why one of the imperatives of high-school ministry is to provide kids with good experiences. Good camping programs, rallies, and conventions are essential because kids not only need to experience God individually, but they also need to experience God corporately. They need to see that they are not alone.

Caution: Experiences alone are not enough. They must always be balanced with a clear emphasis on what happens *after* the experience. Making a first commitment to Christ at camp is a wonderful experience, but then comes the work—living that commitment when we don't feel like it. We must always live with the tension of balancing experiential truth with propositional truth.

High-school students find it difficult to relate their spiritual life to other parts of their life, such as home and school. High-school students can practice community in their church youth group by being friends with kids they consider nerds—but what happens as soon as they are back at school? They tend to have nothing to do with those same kids.

This generation of high-school students has grown up in a society that has taught them that faith is a private matter and should not interfere with the public areas of our lives. Because of that, many young people believe that faith is only a *part* of life, not something that influences all of life. The result is that high-school students can come to church, be very vocal and involved in their faith, then walk out the door and ignore their faith all week long, *and see no contradiction in their behavior*. The implication for high-school ministry is obvious. We must help students relate their faith to every other area of their lives, not by making them feel guilty but by helping them realize that faith in Christ affects all of life. We must teach our young people that faith is not merely one of the things we do in life; rather, it is the basis of *all* that we do.

High-school students are becoming more aware of the ambiguity of life. Every generation of adolescents realizes, at some point, that life is more complex than they had previously understood it to be. That's a normal and healthy part of maturation. What is *not* normal or healthy about this generation of adolescents is that they have been exposed to the ambiguities of life *much earlier* than previous generations. And the question is: Can this generation and future generations of adolescents handle ambiguity so early in life? They may have been taught that homosexuality is wrong—but then they take a class with a homosexual high-school teacher, and suddenly the issue of homosexuality isn't quite so simple. Because the Christian faith is based on absolute truth, and because Christianity is often defined with very clear black-and-white parameters, young people are increasingly bewildered by it—after all, an absolute faith seems like an anomaly in a society that has no certainties. To be sure, the Christian faith *is* based on the premise that certain things are true and certain things are not true. We must continue to stress those truths. *But we cannot ignore ambiguity (that would be dishonest) and we must help kids develop a faith that is able to function in the midst of ambiguity.*

High-school students need to express their faith in concrete terms. It is important for high-school students to learn about their faith in all its aspects, such as the feel of worship, the emotional highs, but it is also important that high-school students learn to express their faith concretely. Knowing *about* God is not the same as knowing Him. Talking about God is not enough, longing for God is not enough— young people need to live their faith in the real world, not the artificial world of the Sunday school classroom or the sanctuary. Faith needs to be fleshed out in the real world.

There is a practical way to get the truth into kids' lives—service. The more kids are given the opportunity to serve others, the more real their faith becomes. The more kids can focus on others rather than on themselves, the more they will begin to understand the needs and hurts of others. The more kids can minister to those who suffer, the more they understand the ministry of the One who suffered for us all. If we want high-school students to have a personal faith that functions in the real world, then we need to teach them to serve.

CAUTIONS

Caution #1. *When it comes to the spiritual, high-school students can be easily manipulated.*

High-school students don't have many adult role models. When they find an adult they respect and admire, it is easy for them to be influenced by that adult, especially if he or she is a model of spiritual commitment. All of this adds up to a strong potential for manipulation.

Adults must take every precaution to ensure that adolescents over whom they have influence are not enticed into making spiritual life-decisions simply out of loyalty, respect, or admiration. Adults must be very careful not to create situations where kids are responding solely to them and not to God. There are some youth workers who see nothing wrong with using their personalities to seduce kids into the kingdom of God. But the end does not justify the means. What works for the short term may not last for the long term. Ministering with integrity to high-school students means that what is done today must be evaluated by what it will mean tomorrow.

Our role is not to see kids respond to us during high school; it is to confront high-school students with the truth about Jesus Christ and to help them give their lives to Him once and for all. We cannot and should not expect every high-school student we work with to make a commitment to Christ. Paul made it very clear in 1 Corinthians 3 that reaping the results is not the only thing that legitimizes our ministry. *Planting and watering* also are legitimate functions of our ministry with kids. When we become so myopic, so narrow, in understanding our function as youth ministers that our only justification is overt commitments to Christ, we

67

are dangerously susceptible to using manipulation to justify our existence.

Caution #2. *High-school students often have unrealistic expectations of their faith.*

How many times have you heard high-school students give their testimony at a concert or youth night? Their testimonies are often filled with glowing statements about how wonderful the Christian faith is. Those of us who are adults appreciate those testimonies, but we also recognize that faith is not always so simple and so wonderful. Kids, more often than not, really do expect their lives to be free of failure with total consistency and effortless faith. *The most common reason for spiritual problems among high-school students is disappointment over their inability to live up to what they think the Christian life should be.*

If guilt over failure is the number-one spiritual immobilizer of high-school kids, what should our response be? Not to deny true guilt nor to burst the bubble of kids' idealism. Our role is to balance high-school students' idealism with realism and give them experiences that put their faith into action.

Caution #3. *Recognize that each kid's spiritual pilgrimage is unique.*

One of the more common mistakes youth workers make with high-school students is to give them the impression that there are only one or two legitimate ways to express their faith, so many young people grow up believing that everyone's pilgrimage with God is the same. For example, we often give prominence to those who are very outgoing and find it easy to talk about their faith. Then kids who are shy or quiet begin to doubt whether their faith is real because they can't talk about it. We need to make it clear to high-school students that although the Christian faith is based on the absolute truth of God's grace through Christ's death, each person's response to that truth and to the presence of God in their lives will be unique. That is why we must continually talk to high-school students about the body of Christ and spiritual gifts.

Caution #4. *Learn to accept each student wherever he is spiritually.*

High-school students are under a great deal of stress. Often we compound that stress by communicating that only *serious* Christians are acceptable. Is it our role to make everyone in the high-school group a serious Christian? No, our role is to accept kids where they are, push them lovingly to where they are not, and love them no matter what. *We never know what God is doing in the lives of the kids we are working with.* We need to trust God and respond to each kid's faith individually.

Caution #5. *High-school students act like high-school students.*

We often give high-school students the impression that being spiritual means acting like an adult. We shouldn't be surprised, then, when we find high-school students rejecting spirituality because they think they have to start behaving like adults.

Nothing could be further from reality. High-school students are adolescents, and everything about them is changing. They have short attention spans, they like to have fun, they are inconsistent, moody, idealistic, simplistic, naive, and make lots of mistakes. Those who work with high-school students must always consciously concern themselves with spiritual issues, not developmental issues. When a high-school student disrupts a meeting, the disruption needs to be stopped, but the leader needs to recognize that the disruption was probably the result of a developmental problem, not a spiritual problem. Adolescent spirituality does not change high-school kids into adults; it changes high-school kids into spiritual high-school *kids*.

THE LAST FRONTIER

We cannot emphasize enough that the high-school years are the last frontier of opportunity. We believe that high-school students are more open to faith than at any other time

69

in their lives. It is becoming increasingly obvious that if you do not reach kids while they are in high school, the chances of reaching them in later life will be reduced significantly. More and more studies show that high-school students have already become aware that life is more than grades and jobs and money. They are already conscious of longings deep inside and are beginning to recognize that those kinds of longings need to be filled by God. Author and radio personality Garrison Keillor describes these longings in his own son:

> My son is fifteen years old. He has been crazy about the electric guitar for about a year and a half. He plays what I would call "heavy-metal blues." He has a small amplifier, but in our house the sound really gets around. I can be sitting downstairs at my typewriter and will hear him playing very clearly.
>
> And what I hear is miraculous. Here's a kid whom I have known since he was conceived—in fact, I have known him ever since he was theoretical. I hear him playing his guitar, and his music has such *soul* to it. It's so wrenchingly sad. There is such anguish in it. Now, where did he find that anguish? Where did he learn that? I give him enough money. I'm a nice dad. We get along well. I give him lots of things. He does well in school. He swims on the swim team. Where does he get this anguish? What does the anguish mean? Maybe it means that the gospel is true. Maybe it means that getting enough allowance and being reasonably accomplished at what you do and having a nice dad are not, in the end, enough. Maybe it means that there is another reality and it is not this one.[2]

The anguish that Garrison Keillor's son expressed is the same anguish that all of us experience in the spiritual part of our lives. It is in the high-school years when young people begin to recognize their need to find the "other reality" Garrison talked about. That is the challenge of high-school ministry—to help high-school students make the spiritual part of their lives an everyday reality and to help them see that Jesus Christ is that "other reality."

5 The Parents of High-school Kids

American parents today are worried and uncertain about how to bring up their children. They are unclear about the proper balance between permissiveness and firmness. They fear they are neglecting their children (and, indeed, many of them are). They resent the demands their children are making on them. Many parents worry that they are not doing a very good job raising their children, and yet they are unable to define just what a "good job" is. In droves they seek the experts, expecting them to solve their children's problems. And many parents frankly feel that their children are not just out of control, but *beyond* their control.

> As a result, the parent today is usually a coordinator without a voice or authority, a maestro trying to conduct an orchestra of players who have never met and who play from a multitude of different scores, each in a notation the conductor cannot read. If parents are frustrated, it is no wonder: for although they have the responsibility for their children's lives, they hardly ever have the voice, the authority, or the power to make others listen to them.[1]

Today's parents are glad to have their children in your youth group. They know they need help, and they are counting on the church and the youth worker to save their child from the ravages of a culture that has gone so wrong in so many places. Parents are frightened and often feel impotent, so they look to you, the youth worker. No youth worker should have to be in the position of saving someone

71

else's children—but since we are, we should be as concerned about the kids as the parents are. Even so, it is impossible to undo in one, two, or three years what has taken fifteen years to do. No one knows better than you that youth workers are not miracle workers; still, there's a lot you can do.

It is becoming increasingly more apparent that high-school youth workers do more than minister to youth; they also minister to parents. We are not suggesting that youth workers try to fix parents' marriages or substitute for parents. What we are suggesting is that *every youth worker understand that youth ministry exists for the purpose of supporting and strengthening the family (whether headed by a single parent, stepparents, or natural parents).*

GUIDELINES FOR WORKING WITH PARENTS

COMMUNICATE WITH PARENTS
Most youth workers assume that parents understand what the youth workers are doing and why, and that the members of the youth group can be trusted to pass on necessary information to parents. Wrong—on both counts.

First of all, most parents are, and should be, somewhat leery of *any* youth worker. Before they'll be completely comfortable in turning their kids over to any youth worker, they need to know him well enough to know what makes him tick.

Secondly, adolescents can never be trusted to pass on information to their parents. It is up to the youth worker to communicate to parents. Here are three of the most effective ways we have found for youth workers to keep the communication lines open:

Parents' information meeting. At least twice a year invite parents to attend a meeting that will provide information about scheduling for the coming year, the costs of activities, dates for camps, and a short explanation of your goals for the next few months. Pass out a sheet with a list of topics to be covered in the coming weeks. Don't be afraid to ask for help. Have some fun as well. Start the evening with a skit, game, or some singing, so the parents get the feel of how you run your youth group.

Parents' newsletter. A parents' newsletter does not have to be fancy. It can be mimeographed or xeroxed, folded or stapled together. The newsletter can include anything from a schedule of upcoming events to articles by the kids or research information on parenting. You may even want to include book reviews for books about family (see appendix).

Visits to parents. Most youth workers hate nothing more than visiting parents because it's so awkward. But it's a must. Parents need to know you, your values, and your philosophy of youth work as well as see the rapport you have with their child. If you can't visit, you can at least call—a few minutes on the phone to tell the parents about their child, about how much you appreciate them, and ask whether they have any questions for you. Phone calls make a real difference.

SUPPORT, DON'T COMPETE

If the parents of your high-school students are to trust you, they need to know that you are supporting them, not competing with them. That doesn't mean you'll be on their side every time, but it *does* mean that you won't always be on the teenager's side, opposing the parents.

Supporting parents means that you try to understand their position and that you don't always assume the interests of your youth program are more important than the parents' interests. For example, you may believe that Don needs to attend winter camp for important reasons, but his parents say no. Before you get upset, try to find out their reasons. You may discover that Don's parents have been feeling guilty because they haven't spent any time with him, so they have decided to go skiing as a family the weekend of your retreat. Obviously, a weekend as a family is more important. Of course, Don's parents could want him to stay home because they have decided to paint the inside of the house and they need his help. To be needed and to work with his family is important too. So be careful.

From the beginning, it is important to let parents know that all of your discussions with their children are confidential and only in a life-threatening situation might you be tempted to violate that confidence. Assure·them that your confidential discussions with their children don't mean that you'll always take the kid's side or that you won't encourage the kids, when necessary, to share information with their parents.

There are many other ways you can show parents that you are supportive. Here are some of the most effective.

PROVIDE RESOURCES

Most parents do not keep up on parenting resources; most youth workers do. The youth worker can be the catalyst that brings resources and parents together. Parents really do want resources—they just don't know where to find them.

Tape and book library. With little funding, you can collect enough books and tapes to start a family resource library. Be familiar with the material because often parents will want a summary of what the tape or book is about. Collect material on the following subjects: parenting, marriage, discipline, communication, family spiritual life, drugs, alcohol, and sex. You will be surprised how many parents will start using the library.

Parents' seminar. There are two ways to help parents with seminars: Watch for seminars in your area that are sponsored by other churches, clinics, colleges, hospitals, local school systems, and so on or sponsor your own seminar, such as the video and film series by family experts. One caution: If you are very young, unmarried, or married without children, be careful that you don't give advice in areas you are not sure about. For example, don't tell parents how easy it is to talk about sex. It may be easy for a youth worker to talk to kids in the youth group about sex but difficult for a parent to talk to his kids about sex. You can report what other parents have suggested about the subject as long as you make it clear you are only passing on information.

Support groups. Many churches provide weekly, bimonthly, or monthly support groups for parents. The youth minister, minister, or professional counselor can function as the facilitator, so the parents can give each other mutual support, share ideas, and develop friendships. You can organize the parents by geographical area, by topic (drugs, divorce, sex), or by situation (single parents, stepparents).

PROVIDE OPPORTUNITIES FOR INVOLVEMENT

Many parents *want* to be involved with their children but don't know how. You can provide nonthreatening activities that, by including the parents, bring the parents and their kids closer.

Parents' discussion sheet. This idea takes work, but the dividends are high. With each Sunday school lesson (Tuesday night Bible study or Sunday night youth group), provide a discussion sheet for the parents. The discussion guide provides a great opportunity for parents to discuss the same issues that have been discussed at church with their children.

Family nights. The youth group can sponsor a special night of family entertainment, consisting of games and activities designed for family participation. Most families don't play together anymore; the more opportunity you give them to play, the more they will begin to see each other in a new way.

Family camps. Plan an overnight or weekend retreat for families. Most family camps separate the kids from the parents—but not *your* camp. The idea is to bring families together, so kids can get to know their own families better and see how similar their families are to everyone else's. Give the families plenty of free time; structure the activities so each family member can participate.

Parent sponsors. Many parents are afraid to sponsor a youth group, especially the one their own kids belong to, because they don't feel spiritually qualified. But there are plenty of other needs that parents can meet, such as driving, chaperoning, cooking, and helping with service projects or work weeks. You will be surprised how many parents would love to help *if they knew they were not locking themselves into a permanent commitment.* Often we only want parents to participate in the youth group if they will give us a long-term commitment, but there are many legitimate ways parents can perform on a one-time basis, and many parents who would be willing to give their time *once.* Nine times out of ten, if the parent has a good experience once and if he likes what's happening in the group, he is much more willing to volunteer again or begin to consider a longer commitment. Just make sure *the parent* is the one to suggest being used again.

Parents' panel. Many parents are glad to participate in a panel where their points of view are presented to the kids, *except* most are hesitant to participate if their child is in the youth group. Try to find parents whose children just graduated or are in the junior-high group.

HEAR BOTH SIDES

When adolescents come to you with parental problems, make sure you hear both sides before coming to a decision. Too often adolescents come to a youth worker with a family problem, and the youth worker, trying to be a sympathetic listener, makes it obvious that he agrees with the adolescent. *Always hear both sides first.* In most cases, you'll find that the student has left out some important information.

Hearing the other side of the story isn't always easy because you cannot violate the confidence the student placed in you—he may not want his parents to know you have talked at all. In those cases, you simply have to withhold judgment and become a good listener.

UNDERSTANDING PARENTS

What are parents like today? What pressures and forces are at work in their lives that affect the high-school students you work with? We'll address those questions in this section—but first here are two principles that affect your ability to understand the parents of the kids in your group:

1. You'll never completely understand the parents of adolescents if you've never parented an adolescent. Until you've spent forty-five minutes arguing with your teenager about why it's important to hang up a wet towel, you'll find it hard to understand what really goes on in a home with adolescents. You may be able to understand the adolescent himself just fine, and even be able to help him in his relationship with his parents—but if you haven't parented one yourself, your advice to parents, though possibly helpful, will always be flawed.

2. Parenting is overrated. These days we tend—especially in the church—to lay *all* of the responsibility for how a child turns out on the parents. Certainly, parents have a primary effect on their children, but just what that means is not clear. We've all seen, for instance, abominable family situations that produced children who turned out to be absolute saints. And we've also seen the opposite—the saintly parents who turned out kids who were hellions. How much did the parents actually influence those results? To what extent could they actually be given the credit—or blame? No one can really be sure. It's important, therefore, that you don't punish parents whose children have problems and add more guilt to their lives.[2]

Let's look, now, at some of the pressures on parents today, and at their effect on our strategy of ministry to parents.

WORKING PARENTS

Depending on which statistics you read, in 50 percent to 75 percent of American families both parents work. In 1984, there were 5.2 million latchkey children in America, and that number is increasing rapidly.[3] Most of the kids in your youth group, then, have parents who are both working. Many of these parents see their high-school children very little, and when they do see them, they are too tired to do much more than acknowledge each other's presence. As a result, most parents experience the ambivalence of wanting to spend more time with their children and resenting their children for interrupting their limited leisure time. One of the most significant contributions a youth worker can make to a working family is to attend activities when the parents can't. By taking snapshots, videos, or tapes during the activity, you communicate how much you want to support the family.

NEGATIVE COMMUNICATION

Most of a parent's communication with his adolescent is negative. It isn't that parents *mean* to be negative; it is just that often the only conversations they have are about chores and responsibilities. Here is the summary of a typical parent's dialogue with his high-school student:

7:00 Wake up, Mark, it's seven o'clock. Hurry up and take a shower and don't use all the hot water! Oh, and don't get water on the floor; hang up your towel and clean up your room. Breakfast is at 7:30, don't go eating junk food, and I'm leaving at 7:45 whether you are ready or not.

7:45 Did you hang up your towel? Did you clean up your room? Did you brush your teeth? Did you eat a decent breakfast? Okay, so when you get home today, mow the lawn, stack the wood, and help your mother with dinner.

6:00 Did you mow the lawn? Did you stack the wood? Did you help your mother with dinner? Do you have homework? Okay, then after dinner and after you help stack the dishes, do your homework, don't watch TV, and be in bed by ten.

An exaggeration? Maybe, but not much. This parent isn't a bad person, nor does he dislike his child. It is just that parents are so busy, they don't realize that the only dialogue they are having with their children is negative. You can help parents recognize their negativeness and help them with ideas for giving positive input to their kids. You can encourage parents to write their teenagers a letter or sneak notes into their lunches, books, or cars. You can suggest that parents send a love message to school or fix the kids a special surprise meal. Parents are usually not aware of how long it has been since they have said anything positive to their children.

FEARFUL PARENTS

Most parents are afraid—afraid of a lot of things. Especially during their children's adolescent years. Some of those fears are normal, and some aren't. But a high-school student who understands his parents' fears can go a long way toward establishing empathy and understanding in his family. You can help parents, therefore, by helping their adolescents understand some of the fears parents have:[4]

Parents are frightened of their teenager's new-found independence. Parents still remember when their adolescent was totally dependent on them. Now that their child is an adolescent and becoming more independent, parents worry he will make a serious mistake in judgment, so they want to be included in all their adolescent's decisions. Their real basis of the fear is that the new independence of their teenager will result in a repudiation of their own values. That is a normal fear, but usually unjustified because adolescents are strongly influenced by their parents' value system. As a youth worker, you must be conscious of the parents' reluctance to let go of their child. You can help alleviate the family tension caused by this fear if you explain to your high-school students what their parents are afraid of.

Parents are afraid their child will not make up for

the parents' failures. We have all seen parents who are living out their frustrations through their children. A dad wants his son to be the football player he never was. A mother wants her daughter to be the dancer she couldn't be. Often parents project onto their children their own frustrated dreams. The youth worker can intercede by helping the parents see what they are doing and helping the child understand his parents' frustrations.

Parents are afraid that their child will make a life-changing mistake. It's true that some decisions we make live with us the rest of our lives. Choosing to drive drunk one night can result in disaster; having sex one time can create a nightmare of complications; taking drugs can permanently damage a child. The fear that their son or daughter will make some such mistake can cause some parents to restrict their child unreasonably. Can you help the parent take a more reasonable stance? Possibly, but not always. And if you do, you will assume, in some parents' eyes, an element of responsibility for that adolescent's future decisions. If nothing else, you can help the young person understand how concerned his parents are and why they are concerned.

Parents are afraid because they feel like they can't communicate with their child anymore. High-school students consistently rate lack of communication as *the* biggest problem between parents and adolescents. What is so amazing is that most parents are aware of the problem but aren't sure what to do about it. Here is one problem where the youth worker can be a help.

There are two main reasons parents have difficulty talking with their high schooler. First, *parents have a hard time listening to their child.* Here is the most common complaint from kids: "My parents won't listen to me. When I try to talk to them, they keep interrupting or they stop me and say what they wanted to say." As a result, adolescents decide not to talk to their parents. *Listening* should be the easiest of a parent's many roles. Youth workers need to help parents learn to listen, without interruption and without advice.

The second block to communication is that *parents cannot be neutral* because they are too close to their children and care too much to be neutral. There's nothing wrong with that—parents are *supposed* to care too much. But parent-child closeness and caring is also the reason adolescents need adult friends other than their parents. As a youth worker, you can help parents recognize that other adult friends can listen much more objectively and still give mature advice. Parents should *hope* their children have other adult friends because they can often be much more helpful to an adolescent during a crisis than the parents.

PROTECTION VS. PREPARATION

In the past, parents believed that they were to *protect* their child from the harsh realities of life as long as possible. They withheld unpleasant information until their child was ready psychologically and emotionally to handle it. Today, parents believe that the best way to help their children is to *prepare* them for life by exposing them to reality now.[5] They also believe that protecting children from the truth is potentially harmful because the shock of new knowledge on previously protected children may be more than they can handle. For example, if eight-year-old kids are told their parents are flawed, then they won't be shocked when they turn eighteen and see those flaws. But what is happening is that many adolescents are unequipped to handle this new knowledge. Rather than preparing kids for adulthood, this new philosophy is turning kids into little adults who are being robbed of their childhoods.

High-school youth ministry can help kids rediscover the childhood they never had. You can teach kids and parents to have fun again by sponsoring family game nights and special events that require both adults and kids to participate. You can try to slow the "hurried-child syndrome" by showing parents how to let their kids be kids.

81

LOSS OF PARENTAL RESPONSIBILITY

Many parents feel that the responsibility for raising their children has been taken over by the schools and other agencies. They feel impotent. As a result, they no longer know how to discipline their children—nor want to. These parents see no need to talk to their kids about sex (the schools do that) or talk to their kids about God (the church does that) or talk to them about their future (the school counselor does that) or counsel them about their problems (professional counselors do that). Many modern parents see their primary parenting role as that of the provider of material comforts.

Youth workers can help parents see that even though adolescents have many people other than their parents giving advice and education, *none of them can take the place of an adolescent's parents.* Parents are abdicating their responsibilities for no good reason. Although other agencies may appear to function in place of parents, they are not nearly as effective as parents themselves—and kids know it. The more a youth worker can give parents the motivation and the tools to parent their adolescent, the happier the kids will be.

PROBLEMS WITH PARENTS

High-school students have lots of problems with their parents. Characteristic of adolescent development is the battle for independence between parent and teenager. And when high-school kids are polled, they complain about their parents in the same ways:

My parents don't trust me. High-school students don't understand why their parents don't trust them. The most common reason parents give for not trusting their children is that, sometime in the past, their children violated their trust. And once trust is violated, it's hard to earn it back. Sure, there may be a *few* parents who don't trust their kids for reasons that aren't valid. But in most cases, high schoolers don't realize that trust is a fragile and sensitive commodity.

Because of that, they have violated their parents' trust at one time or another, making it difficult for their parents to trust them again. You'll make life easier for the adolescents if you'll help them see the connection between what they do and what their parents do in response.

How do high-school students win back their parents' trust after losing it? Just do what they say. If they say they'll be home at 11:00, then they need to be home at 11:00. If they promise to call when the concert's over, then they have to call. That's all. When it has been demonstrated to the parent that his child is trustworthy, he'll be willing to bestow trust gradually again.

My parents don't love me. Parents often find it hard to tell their high-school son or daughter they love them. The most common reason is embarrassment—their own. Also, they're afraid their son or daughter will get embarrassed. Most parents do love their teenagers; they've just developed bad habits when it comes to telling them.

Here are some suggestions for parents:

—Encourage them to verbally tell their high-school kids that they love them, even if it's embarrassing.

—Encourage them to find creative ways to show their love, such as writing notes, fixing surprise meals, or doing something special.

—Make sure the fathers understand how important it is for them to express love.

And for high-school students:

—Encourage them to express verbally their love to both their parents.

—Encourage them to find creative ways to show their love, such as writing notes, fixing breakfast, doing the laundry, cleaning the house.

My parents don't listen to me. Try your best to make parents aware of their lack of listening skills and encourage them to work on improving them.

My parents pick on me a lot. In almost every case, the

solution to this problem is simple—quit doing whatever it is that bugs your parents.

Parents don't normally pick on kids; instead, they pick on something their kids do that irritates them. For example, Wayne slouches in his chair at meals. Slouching drives Wayne's parents crazy, so they ask him to sit up straight. He half-sits up, and they ask him again to sit up straight. This goes on for a few minutes until the parents become exasperated and blow up at Wayne. From Wayne's perspective, his parents are picking on him—they're making an issue out of something that isn't an issue. Wayne is probably right; "slouching" is not an issue worth arguing over. Our advice to high-school kids whose parents are bugging them about slouching is to quit slouching. Wait until there is something worthwhile to fight over.

My parents are hypocrites. Many high-school students become disillusioned with their parents when they notice that their parents are one person in public and another in private. The truth is that almost *every* parent—every *person*—is different in public than in private. There is nothing wrong with that. Hypocrisy is when the difference is *deliberate*—when there is a definite attempt to deceive others about what kind of person you are. High-school students need to understand the true meaning of hypocrisy.

They also need to understand that all of us—especially high-school students—to some extent deliberately set out to deceive people about who we really are. We wear masks because we fear that people won't like us as much if they *really* know us. Parents are as guilty as anyone of wearing a facade, but it's a characteristic more deserving of understanding and sympathy than of contempt and anger. It's one of those common traits that should bind kids to their parents in mutual understanding rather than push them apart.

HELPING HIGH-SCHOOL STUDENTS SHARE RESPONSIBILITY FOR THEIR PARENTS

Part of the youth worker's job is to help high-school students see that they must assume some responsibility for resolving family conflicts. Getting along is not solely the responsibility of the parents. High-school students are old enough to make their own contribution to family harmony. Here are some of the ways it's done:

Encourage high-school students to take the initiative in communication with their family. It isn't easy and may even be awkward, but there's no reason why a high-school student can't initiate a conversation with his parents about a family problem.

Encourage high-school students to try to understand their parents. Often high-school students see things only from their own perspective. They need to try and understand the pressures and problems of their parents. It may be true that Carrie's father has been "on her case" all the time. It may also be true that her father is losing his job. Once Carrie understands what's happening to her father, she'll see why he's been so edgy. If Carrie were to go to her father, give him a hug and say, "Dad, I'm really sorry you're losing your job. Is there anything I can do to help?", the tension in the family would probably be reduced.

Encourage high-school students to spend time with their parents. The responsibility for families spending time together usually is given to the adults in the family. There's just one problem: It's usually the schedule of the high-school member of the family that prevents the family from getting together. High-school students need to arrange their schedules to spend quality time with their parents.

Encourage high-school students to "honor and obey" their parents. (See Exod. 20:12, Col. 3:20, Eph. 6:1.) Too often, youth workers forget to remind high-school students that honoring their parents is not an option—it is something all of us have been commanded to do. It is granted there are cases of sexual abuse, incest, or physical abuse that would make parental honor practically impossible. But in most families, there is no significant hindrance to honoring and respecting the parents.

WORKING WITH KIDS FROM A BROKEN HOME

We are all aware of the startling and sobering statistics regarding divorce. In most church youth groups, 50 percent of the kids are from broken homes and are living with either one parent or a stepparent. Broken homes have become so common that we sometimes forget this truth: *Even in families where the divorce seems justifiable, even in families where the parents seem much happier and better off after the divorce, all children are seriously damaged by divorce.* The conclusion is obvious. *High-school youth ministry must have a significant ministry to the children of divorce.*

CHARACTERISTICS OF ADOLESCENTS FROM BROKEN HOMES

Guilt over the divorce. Most children of divorce suffer some amount of guilt over the separation. Adolescents, especially, believe that they were the cause of the divorce or that they could have done something to stop it.

Our response: Give the student the opportunity, without being pushy, to verbalize his feelings of guilt. Point out that such feelings are normal and that children are never the cause of their parents' divorce. Encourage them to talk to their parents about their feelings of guilt.

Loneliness. When families are in crisis, it is common for the children in those families to withdraw from activities and friendships. The extent to which they withdraw will depend on how badly the adolescent is affected by the divorce.

Our response: As a youth worker, you will usually be aware of which families are in crisis. Watch the kids closely. If you notice them withdrawing, start spending time with them and provide nonthreatening opportunities for them to talk. Obviously, when someone is going through a great deal of pain and turmoil, it is not the time to suggest that he go party. But when you are with him, he won't be totally alone.

Depression. Depression and self-pity often go hand-in-hand in a broken home. Adolescents suffering from the hurt of family turmoil will often act out intense feelings of self-pity and self-hatred. As adolescents continue to withdraw, they often push themselves into a serious depression.

Our response: When you suspect that a child is depressed, watch him carefully, call him often, drop by and see him, and *inform the parents of your concern.* Divorcing parents are often so wrapped up in the divorce they forget about what's going on with their children. If the depression persists, have him seek professional help, with the parents' consent.

Divorced kids see themselves as different. In a sense divorced kids *are* different. Even though many of their friends' parents are also divorced, adolescents see themselves as victims of a tragedy that has forever scarred them, which is partly true.

Our response: The more you can understand how different they feel, the more effective you will be with kids from broken homes. Be very sensitive when you announce family activities that you include these kids and their single or broken family as well. You should also offer special, nonpublic, nonthreatening classes for kids from broken homes. They desperately need a place to discuss what has happened, but they will not seek out that place on their own.

Anger. Anger is common in children of broken homes. Some anger is normal, but extreme anger directed at specific family members may be a sign that professional counseling is necessary.

Our response: Try to become an outlet for the adolescent's anger. Let him know that you understand he's angry and you are willing to be a person he can share his anger with.

Inability to trust. Adolescents from broken homes often

feel betrayed. Many times their defense mechanisms move into overdrive and they quit trusting everyone, including God.

Our response: The important thing is not to panic. Don't try to force the teenager to trust someone else or lecture him about the need to trust God no matter what. By ignoring his unwillingness to trust and by spending time with him, you can become a person he can start trusting.

Lack of direction. Kids from broken homes can easily fall into the "who cares" syndrome. It is easy to decide that nothing matters anymore, because instead of making decisions with the help of their parents, now they have to decide *between* their parents. The stress can become too much, and sometimes they just don't care anymore.

Our response: Give the kids some room. Don't force them to make any more decisions, but just stick with them. Try to be a person to whom they can verbalize their "who cares" feelings and lovingly help them see that life does go on. Talk to the parents—tell them what you are seeing in their children and ask them to quit putting their children in the position of choosing between them.

Inability to love. When there is a crisis in anyone's life, especially in adolescents, it is easy to shut down the emotions. It is not uncommon for the child of a broken home to become hard and calloused, seemingly unable to give or receive love. Time usually eases the hurt and heals these emotions.

Our response: Kids can make silly mistakes when they have shut off their emotions. They can reject anyone who reaches out to them. They can pretend that everything is okay. They can decide to take drugs, drink too much, or have sex with someone without any thought of the consequences because they supposedly don't care. These kids are hard to reach. The best approach is to stick with them no matter what. Refuse to be put off by their callousness; continue to be a friend. It could be a long and painful process—but·it's the only one that works.

WHAT THE YOUTH WORKER CAN DO TO HELP KIDS FROM BROKEN HOMES

Don't ignore the divorce. Those of us who are part of the church must be sure that our theology doesn't get in the way of our ministry. We cannot pretend that only good marriages exist. Regardless of our views about the rightness or wrongness of divorce, the victims of divorce need help. Talking about divorce will not condone it nor will it cause more divorces to happen. The church should be a sanctuary of love and support where kids can admit they are from a divorced home and feel free to talk about divorce.

Let the kids see good marriages. We do not show kids good marriages to judge those whose marriages didn't work. High-school kids, especially high-school kids whose parents are divorced, need to see models of good marriages and know good marriages are possible. As part of the church, we dare not imply that all Christian marriages are perfect—but good marriages are still possible.

Encourage kids from broken homes to talk. The hard truth is that kids from broken homes often have no one to talk to because talking to one parent is considered betrayal by the other parent. Since people take sides in a divorce, the adolescent doesn't feel free to express his real feelings of frustration and anger, so he doesn't talk to anyone. Don't be afraid to ask kids how things are going at home, not forcing the conversation, but making it clear that you are more than willing to be there if they need to talk to someone.

Encourage the parents. We often assume that the parents who are going through the divorce can handle it. They must have friends and relatives they can lean on for help. But the sad truth is that many parents don't have anyone to go to, especially when it comes to understanding and advice about their children. If the youth worker is sensitive to divorced parents, he can often provide a good ear and refer them to someone who can really help.

Help kids see the long view. When a family crisis

89

occurs, it is normal for adolescents to feel overwhelmed and to lose hope. They begin to wonder if life will ever be normal again, if they will ever get used to the divorce, or if they will ever see their father or mother again. One of our most important roles is to help kids from broken homes see that life really does go on and that, besides being with us, Christ can heal us and make us well again.

Talk about forgiveness. Strange as it may seem, kids from divorced homes, more often than not, are angry at one or both of their parents and need to forgive them. It isn't easy but it is necessary. The youth worker must emphasize Christ's forgiveness of us that enables us to forgive others.

Teach high-school students about marriage. High-school students recognize that it will take years to train for their profession, yet when it comes to marriage, they receive no training. The best place for premarriage training is the church. Although many youth groups have kids *talk* about marriage, few youth groups ever spend time *teaching* kids about marriage. Your high-school group should have a series of lessons on marriage at least once a year.

Being a parent isn't easy, especially these days. The very fact that you are a youth worker who ministers to high-school students is a sign of encouragement to every parent. You really can minister to parents, and you really can help kids in those tough relationships with their parents. Youth workers are probably in the most strategic position of all to help both parents and adolescents. We hope this chapter has helped you become even more strategic. What an opportunity! What a privilege!

PART II

DEFINING THE
HIGH-SCHOOL
YOUTH
WORKER

6 Characteristics of a High-school Youth Worker

Which of the following youth workers would you expect to be most effective with high-school students?

Mr. Nerd. Mr. Nerd is an engineer with a large computer company. He is bright, quiet, and good at anything mechanical. He wears very thick glasses, dresses kind of nerdy, and is serious about his faith. Mr. Nerd is nonathletic, reads a lot, doesn't watch much television, and can't stand rock music. He hasn't a clue as to what the latest teenage fads are—he never has, even when he was a teenager. He has a high-school daughter and wants to help the youth group.

Mrs. Resthome. Mrs. Resthome is sixty-three years old. She wears the same two dresses all the time. She is very much overweight and lives by herself. She hasn't a clue regarding the latest teenage fads or current lingo. She does have kids over quite a bit and likes high-school students. She has taught high-school Sunday school for twenty-five years. Quite a few of the kids who attend her Sunday school class think it's sort of boring, but Mrs. Resthome is nice.

Mr. Jock. Mr. Jock is twenty-three. Not only is he good looking, but he excels in everything he does. He is an athlete, a successful manager in his company, drives a Porsche, is married, and has two little kids. He loves high-school kids and knows them very well. He always dresses in the latest styles and has a great tan. He really understands the kid's culture, their language, their music, and he is a great communicator.

Traditionally we have been led to believe that Mr. Jock would have the most success with a group of high-school students. Although it is true that *initially* young people often respond to a person's appearance or ability to communicate, it is *not* true that those externals have any real or lasting effect on a young person's life in the years ahead. Ask any of us who had the greatest influence on his life in high school. The response is always the same: Those we remember as significant adults in our lives are always the adults who genuinely cared. *Caring about high-school kids is the primary prerequisite for working with them.* It's that simple.

Volumes have been written about the importance of adult modeling. It is always suggested that what kids need today are role models—adults who live what they say, who evidence in their lives the kind of Christian faith they want their young people to live. We would never want to suggest that modeling is not significant; but, on the other hand, no adult can live a flawless life. Our flaws are bound to evidence themselves. Should our flaws keep us from working with kids? No—but if an adult is deliberately living in contradiction to the values of his faith, that's more than just a flaw. And if an adult is unwilling to admit the presence of flaws— if he is trying to maintain an image of perfection—then there should be serious doubts about his competency to work with kids.

With those reservations, our mistakes should not destroy our ministry to the young people who look up to us. The most effective model for high-school young people is not an adult who lives a perfect life but an adult who unconditionally cares for kids. No adult can do that unless he himself is experiencing the unconditional love of Jesus Christ.

There is another prerequisite for working with high-school kids. You cannot work with high-school kids very long if you do not understand this principle: *Whatever you do with a high-school kid will make a difference.* Often, adults become frustrated because they don't have much time or because there are others who can do so much more than they can. Our effectiveness with high-school kids cannot be quantified—doing something is better than doing nothing.

Some studies indicate that the average father has *seven minutes of significant conversation with his child per week*. If those studies are accurate, devoting even a half-hour a week to youth gives you twenty-three more minutes with a high-school student than the parents have. You may only have time to drive kids for a Polaroid Scavenger Hunt or pick up kids from camp, but the conversations you have with the kids while driving could be the most significant conversations of their lives.

SIX CHARACTERISTICS OF THE PERSON WHO MINISTERS TO HIGH-SCHOOL STUDENTS

There are six qualities that always seem to be present where there is effective high-school ministry: helplessness, truthfulness, ability to see the significance of the insignificant, listening, nurturing, and affirming. You may not have all of these qualities; you may not have any. The important thing is to recognize that these six characteristics are actually the basic ingredients of ministry. Programing, communication skills, management of time, and counseling skills are all helpful, but these six qualities describe what ministry to high-school students really is.

HELPLESSNESS

Anyone who decides to work with young people has to wonder what he could possibly offer to young people that could help them. Integral to the call to youth work is the recognition of the impossibility of the task, the inadequacy of the one called to do the task, and the adequacy of the One who has called you. You probably are reading this book because you feel inadequate. You are looking to this book for encouragement, for help in overcoming your feelings of helplessness. This book is not written to rid you of those feelings, but rather to help you understand that helplessness or humility is far preferable to arrogance. People who feel totally adequate for youth ministry don't belong there.

You're afraid of kids? Good. You are worried that they won't like you? That's encouraging. You look at your skills (or lack of them) and ask, "God, why me?" Terrific! You went to a parents' meeting and raised your hand to ask where the restrooms were and now you're chairman of the youth department? Great! You cannot have an effective, long-lasting ministry with kids unless you feel like you don't know enough, unless you are a little bit frightened, unless you recognize how desperate you are for God's power and direction.

In a few years from now, what a thrill you will experience when you bump into one of the kids who was in your youth group and she says to you, "I have never forgotten that talk you gave, Mr. Donaldson, at the high-school winter retreat. Thanks, it really helped." At first you can't remember giving that talk, and then when you do, you immediately want to apologize for the poor quality of the talk until you realize that somehow God used that talk and you, with all your flaws, to communicate the lasting truth of the gospel.

TRUTHFULNESS

It may sound hard to believe, but the most common mistake made by youth workers is *unintentionally not telling the truth to kids*. Not that youth workers attempt to deceive young people. But sometimes youth workers give simplistic answers or answers that merely *sound* true because they are afraid to admit they don't know the answer.

The problems high-school students face today are complex and difficult. Because the implications of the gospel in the real world are not easy to live, we are all attracted to the simplistic answer, the quick solution, the formula. But life is not that simple. We must resist the temptation to simplify and, instead, tell the kids the truth, even though the price may appear high at the moment. When a young high-school student comes to you and asks, "Why did God let my mother die of cancer?" we are all tempted to alleviate his grief with some simple answer instead of saying, "I don't know." The high price of the truth may be that the young person turns from his faith in God and becomes full of bitterness and resentment. But Paul says that when people come to us in grief, we are to grieve with them, not temporarily relieve their grief with a simple response (Rom. 12:15).

There are three answers that are appropriate when some kind of answer is needed in discussions with kids. (Remember that most of the time we're talking with kids, the kids need a sounding board more than an answer man.)

1. I believe the answer is . . .

2. I don't know what the answer is, but I will find out.

3. I don't know. Here's what some people have said; here's what the Bible says or doesn't say. Here's how I feel about it, but I honestly don't know.

We want high-school kids to know the truth—the truth may be that we don't know, can't know, and won't know until we are with God. There is nothing wrong with helping kids learn to live with the unknown.

ABILITY TO SEE THE SIGNIFICANCE OF THE INSIGNIFICANT

You don't have to work very long with kids to discover that *significant events* with kids happen at the most insignificant times. A youth worker we know invited the guys in his youth group to help him move. On each trip back and forth in the pickup, the youth worker took a different boy in the front cab. By the end of the day, this youth worker had had some of the most meaningful conversations he had ever had with the guys in his youth group.

Every moment you spend with a high-school student is

significant. You never know when a high-school student is ready to talk, deeply impressed by how you live at your house, or encouraged by something you said in passing. The important thing is to recognize that every moment is important, even when it doesn't seem to be.

If we do not see every moment as significant, then two problems can occur. One is burnout. Many of us evaluate the significance of our ministry by the significance of people's response and when we get no response, we give up. Often there are many significant things happening in kids' lives; we are just unaware of it. The second problem is manipulation. It is easy to ensure some kind of response by programing our kids to give artificial responses to our ministry. For example, we can be tempted to demand some kind of black-and-white response from our kids every few weeks. The tragedy is that when we investigate our motives, we discover that *we need the kids to respond more than they need to respond.* We manipulate them to make commitments, so we can prove to ourselves or to our church that we are doing a fine job.

Effective high-school ministry is not determined by programing, it is determined by presence. Being with kids is how ministry occurs. We can never plan *when* significant events occur, we can only plan to be with kids, so when significant events occur, we're there.

LISTENING
Have you ever had a young person come to you and say something like this:

Could I talk to you for a second? Uh . . . I need some help, I guess. See, my dad has been in a real bad mood for the past three weeks. He's been drinking a little too much and giving my mom and me a hard time. Well, this week is finals week, and I have a very big test, so I've been studying real hard. Well, last night, my dad came in and started yelling at me for a bunch of things. I finally got real mad and told my dad to shut up and I left. I stayed at a friend's house last night. I don't know what to do. I mean, I know my dad has been in a bad mood because he's being laid off and we're tight on money, but still, that doesn't mean he can treat Mom and me like that. Course, I have been under a lot of pressure with finals and everything, and I know my dad is really having a hard time. I don't know . . . maybe I should just call him at work and explain to him about my finals and stuff. Maybe I should tell him that I know he's been under a lot of pressure too. I think that's what I'll do—thanks a lot, you've been a great help!

You just sat there with your mouth closed. You didn't give one piece of advice, not one kernel of a suggestion. Obviously, no advice was needed. This young person just needed someone who would listen.

There is so much noise today, so much activity, so many advice-givers, but there are very few people who will listen anymore. Joe Bayly lost a son to cancer. While Joe was in the hospital with his boy, he was barraged with visits from well-meaning Christian people who offered prayers, advice, tapes, books, and conversation, and Joe said he could hardly wait for each of them to leave. Then a man came in who had lost his own teenage son in a tragic car accident. He slid a chair next to Joe's, reached out and grabbed his hand and never said a word. Joe said he never wanted that man to leave.[1]

There are high-school students everywhere who would give anything if someone cared enough to listen.

You may not be able to speak very well in front of kids. You may not be able to give great advice. But anyone can listen.

NURTURING
It is great to be a friend to a high-school student. It is important to listen to them and spend time with them. But, once we have done that, or as we are doing that, we must always be conscious that we can do more. We must help kids grow. And helping them grow requires that we take risks with them. We risk our relationship with them and we risk their relationship with God.

The process of nurturing is the process of confronting

kids with the claims of the gospel and giving kids responsibility. Kids need to be pushed onto new ground, they need to hear new things, they need to be nudged to the edge of their faith. Many of us would rather bask in the experience of being with kids without taking the risks required to help them grow. It is not fun to force one of our high-school kids to attend Easter work camp, but on Friday night of work week when we see her stand up misty-eyed and tell how wonderful her week was, then we know it was worth the risk. Nurturing is fraught with danger, but it is well worth the risks.

AFFIRMING

When does a high-school student get affirmation? Who tells high-school students that they are gifted people, that they are a joy to be around, that they are okay? The harsh truth is that high-school students get little affirmation, if any. Adolescent life is characterized by turmoil and tension at home. Even in the most loving of homes, genuine affirmation is hard to come by.

What does this mean for the youth worker? Giving genuine affirmation to a high-school student is one of the most effective and long lasting ways you can minister. Here are three different ways to accomplish the ministry of affirmation:

See what they can't see. Affirming kids is believing in kids. You can see their potential, even when they can't. You are a person of hope who finds the specialness in each high-school student you work with and you affirm it. Jesus saw Peter and called him Cephas (rock) (Matt. 16:18). Peter thought he was a weak betrayer of friendship, but Jesus saw the real strength of Peter. Likewise, we can encourage the shy, overweight girl who never says a word because we see she is a thinker, a person who is not easily swayed by externals. Then, we help her know what a valuable asset contemplativeness is.

100

Say what they can't say. Adolescents don't hear much praise. Our ministry is one filled with liberal praise. Praise kids when they do well, and even when they fail, praise them for trying hard, for taking risks that others wouldn't take. We heard of a father who wrote each of his kids an individual Thanksgiving letter listing all the positive characteristics that he as a parent was thankful for. The kids have never forgotten those letters. Kids will not forget the praise you give them. It means a lot.

Be there when others can't be. Because your schedule is different than a high-school student's parents, you can make a track meet or basketball game or an event after school when the parents can't. Your presence at an activity can make a deep impression on a kid and give you an opportunity for a continuing relationship. It is a good idea to take pictures and give them to the kid's parents to let them see you are working *with* them and not against them.

THE 15-15 PLAN

We have given you what we think is a model for effective ministry with high-school kids. Ministry takes time: The more time you have, the more opportunity for ministry you have. But ministry doesn't have to take *much* time. If you have just thirty minutes a week (even a month), we have a plan that we know works.

Anyone can take fifteen minutes a week or a month to talk with kids on the telephone. We'll be honest, it's not easy for an adult to talk to kids on the telephone (just getting through is a problem), but it can be rewarding. All that is necessary is a quick call to say that you are thinking about them as they take their finals the next day, or you heard they were sick and wanted to know if there was anything you could do, or you were thinking of them and wanted them to know how much you appreciate them. They may sound startled or awkward, but you can know they are impressed by your message. Just call as many kids as you can in fifteen minutes.

101

Anyone can also take fifteen minutes a week or month to write a quick note to some of them. Notes are very powerful in this technological age. Few people write letters anymore, and high-school kids very seldom get a personal letter or card, so receiving a note or card from you is special for them. If you travel a lot, take postcards with you and write them while you are on the plane. Kids will never forget your notes, and once the word gets out, they will look forward to them.

We sincerely hope that this model of ministry will not frustrate you. We meant it to encourage you, to let you know that as long as you love kids you can't really do anything wrong. Oh sure, you can make mistakes—and you will. But love covers a multitude of mistakes.

7 A Strategy for High-school Ministry

High-school ministries come in all shapes and sizes. Although there are hundreds of effective high-school ministries across the country, no two programs are exactly alike. That's good news for you because it means there is no perfect high-school program. There are many effective ways to program.

The kind of program *you* decide on will depend on a number of variables. A youth worker who is a very spiritual person will want to focus on discipleship, structuring a program best suited to that emphasis. A youth worker gifted with an outgoing, charismatic personality will probably be more effective structuring a program that is program-oriented.

PICKING A STRATEGY

Before you can decide on a strategy of ministry, you need to ask a number of fundamental questions:

Does our program have specific, measurable goals? Most youth programs are run by the seat of the pants. There are no well-defined goals for the high-school students other than to keep their interest. That is not enough. These questions should be asked of every program:

1. *What do these kids need to know before they graduate?*
2. *How can we measure what they know?*

A youth program should be more than a baby-sitting service. It should be a structured, functional process that has specific goals and looks for specific results.

Are we preparing high-school students for the future? Unfortunately, many youth programs do nothing more than wrap the kids in a protective cocoon during high school. These youth programs provide lots of neat friends, great activities, support, advice, fun, counseling, everything except good, solid, Christian education that will last. As soon as the high-school student graduates, he drops out of the church altogether because he no longer needs a cocoon. A good youth program continually challenges high-school students to see the implications of their faith in the real world beyond what they know now.

Are we giving high-school kids what they need, not just what they want? It is easy to give kids what they want. And high-school students often believe that what they want and what they need are synonymous. A good youth program manages to balance kids' wants (to keep interest) and needs (to foster growth), so kids are motivated to grow in their faith.

Many youth programs start with a program and then look at the need. That is the opposite of what should happen. The old statement "find a need and fill it" should be the philosophy of every good high-school ministry.

Part of the problem is that leaders tend to be need-oriented while students are want-oriented. One youth worker asked his high-school kids to list the needs of their group. Here's their list:

Disneyland Trip
Beach BBQ
Ultimate Frisbee Contest
Pizza Party
Car Rally
Water-ski Trip
Snow-ski Trip
Bible Study on the Book of Revelation

These, obviously, are not needs; they are wants. Of

course, this list would meet some of the social needs of the high-school group, but they would not even touch the spiritual needs. It is up to the youth workers to take a serious look at the needs of the kids in the group and the community in which they live. One group we know was located in an area where parents and schools put a lot of pressure on the kids to get good grades. The youth program structured a number of tutoring programs led by adults in the church. Other youth groups we know have started recreation leagues when school districts cut intramural athletics. Some groups started free employment agencies, baby-sitting services, or coffeehouses. The spiritual needs of the youth group as well as the needs of the community can all be addressed by any church that takes the time to mesh *need* with *program*.

FIVE INGREDIENTS OF AN EFFECTIVE HIGH-SCHOOL PROGRAM

PERSON-CENTERED MINISTRY

High-school students want to be heard, they want to be known, and they want to be understood—they want to feel significant. Program-centered youth ministry usually treats adolescents as spectators. Kids respond better to a *person-centered ministry* where the primary focus is on the high-school students and not the program.

In a person-centered ministry, youth workers spend one-on-one time with kids, so each person in the youth group gets individual attention. It is not difficult to have a one-on-one ministry with kids. Here are three effective methods for person-centered ministry:

Get-acquainted time. Each high-school student in your group should have a time during the year (the earlier in the year the better) when you spend time (half-hour to an hour) getting acquainted. Take them to the local McDonalds or some place that is comfortable for them. You wouldn't want to meet them at some intimidating place like your office, home, or church. This is not the time to preach or pontificate, this is a time to find out as much as you can about the person you're talking to. You may spend the entire time talking about soccer or cheerleading, but what is important is that you get acquainted with the high-school student and they leave knowing that you are really interested in them.

Shepherding time. You as a youth worker (whether a layworker or a paid employee) are a pastor to your group of high-school students. You and the other youth leaders are the spiritual shepherds for your flock, interested not only in building a relationship with kids but also in guiding and helping them in their spiritual lives. You must take the initiative in talking with kids about spiritual matters.

Counseling. Every high-school youth worker is a counselor. You may not be a professional counselor, but you will be called upon constantly to counsel the kids in your group. Statistics show that most people in crisis go to people who are peers or friends more often than to a professional counselor. Most counseling is listening, and any youth worker can listen.

Even though a little knowledge can be a dangerous thing, it is important for every youth worker to get as much basic counseling training as possible. The more relationships you have with kids, the more of your time will be spent listening and helping them through the crises of adolescence.

PEER-CENTERED MINISTRY

The most exciting single development in youth ministry over the past twenty years is the emergence of *peer ministry*. Peer ministry is more than just high-school students getting involved in the actual program—it is kids ministering to each other. Peer ministry doesn't mean that you give control of the youth group over to the kids. It does mean that you allow them to participate in every aspect of your youth program. Here are some suggestions:

1. Adolescents should not just *go* to youth group; they should be allowed to *do* the youth group. Kids should have the opportunity to use their gifts in your youth ministry program, not just occupy a seat and watch.

2. Provide lots of small group activities in which kids (without adults or with silent adults) discuss the lesson and come up with their own conclusions. Small group activities are the primary source of peer ministry opportunities. Too many youth groups either don't have small groups, or, when they do, use them to accomplish some activity rather than share with each other.

3. Keeping a journal and letter-writing provide great opportunities for peer ministry.

4. Service projects are another great environment for peer ministry.

Today's youth worker has no excuse for not using his best programing resource—the kids in the youth group. Kids can participate in almost any aspect of the program, often more effectively than an adult. *They aren't always* more effective. The kids may do worse or they may botch a program, but then, failure is one of the best ways to learn. And youth groups always seem to be able to accept the failures of their peers. High-school students are much less critical of other high-school students than they are of adults. Peer ministry is credible exactly because it is not professional.

We recommend two very valuable resources to help you in the area of peer ministry:

1. Brian Reynolds. *A Chance To Serve*. Winona, Minn.: St. Mary's Press, 1983.

2. Barbara B. Varenhorst. *Real Friends*. San Francisco: Harper and Row, 1983.

TEAM-CENTERED MINISTRY
For lack of guidance a nation falls, but many advisers make victory sure (Prov. 11:14).

Effective youth ministry means there is no such thing as a one-person show. It is always better to have a team of leaders relating to kids than just one person. (In a small church or rural community, of course, it is better to have one person than no persons.)

We have all heard of the youth program that fell apart after the youth worker left. Why did it fail? Because the program was based on the personality and gifts of one person, but not based on stability. One of the advantages of team ministry is *stability*.

Another advantage is *diversification*. Team ministry is not getting a bunch of cookie-cutter college kids, as diverse as a sackful of Big Macs, to work with your youth group; it is gathering together a group of adults with different ages, different gifts, and different strengths to minister to all the kids in the group.

Teamwork is work. Not only should there be a diversity of adult leadership, there must be a real team attitude. It takes time to develop unity among diverse people. Each of the members of the team needs to agree on the central goals of the program and learn to live with the differences in each other that don't matter. A team ministry requires that the members of the team see the benefits in diversity and cannot function if one or more of the members tries to get everyone to be like them. A team ministry needs to be characterized by these words of Jesus, "By this will all men know that you are my disciples, if you have love for one another" (John 13:35). As an adult staff develops into a team, the love that is generated between them will be a significant witness to the young people in the group.

How to recruit a team. The most difficult task in any church is finding people who are willing to work with youth. Most adults will heartily agree that youth work is important, but they do not believe they have anything to offer. *Recruitment is a never-ending exercise of faith.* There are no easy ways to recruit adults, but we do have a couple of suggestions:

1. Go to your church leadership (board, elders, session, consistory, deacons). Ask them for a list of people in the church they believe would make good youth sponsors. Approach the people on the list by pointing out that they were recommended by the church leadership. Often, when adults realize that the church leadership believes in them, they will be more willing to help.

2. Go to the members of the youth group. Ask your high-school students to come up with a list of people they would like to see as youth workers. Most adults refuse to work with kids because they are afraid the kids won't like them. When they find out that the kids suggested their names, it really encourages them to volunteer.

CONTENT-CENTERED MINISTRY

As we have mentioned, most youth programs have no plan, no sense of direction, no long-term or short-term goals—especially when it comes to content. What do you want the kids to know by the time they leave the group? What topics do the high-school kids need to have grasped before they graduate from high-school? At the heart of the gospel is the belief that the Christian faith is truth. How much of that truth do we want a high-school student to know?

Setting objectives and goals. First of all, gather your team of youth workers together for an evening. Begin with the understanding that you will probably have most of your high-school students for two years. (We realize that most high-school programs are three to four years, but many kids move or drop out before that time.) Two years represents 104 weeks of content. Ask the group to brainstorm this question: "If we only have a high-school student for two years, what do we want them to know about their faith at the end of those two years?" Here's a partial list of topics that we would want our high-school students to know about:

1. The Bible (the Old and New Testaments, where the

Bible came from, the difference between a translation and a paraphrase, what a canon is)

2. *Church* (a biblical doctrine of our church, our church's beliefs, what other religions believe, what the church is)

3. *Doctrine* (what doctrine is; what doctrines our church believes; the different doctrines about baptism, communion, priesthood, conversion, forgiveness)

4. *Marriage* (what the Bible says about marriage, divorce, separation, remarriage, living together outside of marriage)

5. *Parents* (what the Bible says about parents, what it means to honor our parents)

There are many more subjects we could list (sex, ethics, responsibility, relationships, poverty, mission and service, Jesus), but we are sure your list will be different than ours. That doesn't matter, as long as you have a list of the most important content areas and a plan to cover those areas.

The plan. Look at the two years as 104 units of time. Take the categories you have brainstormed and break them down into units. No unit should be longer than six weeks, and some units might last just a week or two. Vary the units, so by the end of two years you will have covered the subject of marriage four times, the subject of the Bible six times, the subject of church doctrine four times, etc. As you can see by the chart, if the high-school students in your group attend your church fairly regularly, they will have been exposed to all the content areas several times.

After you and your committee of youth workers have mapped out the subjects, the length of the units, and the order of subjects, evaluate each of those subjects according to three criteria: content, experience, and relationship.

Content. Each area of content requires new information. It is not enough just to know kids' opinions, so everyone sits around pooling their ignorance. Content programing will probably be more lecture-oriented as you expose kids to the opinions of the church, the church fathers, theologians, modern thinkers, philosophers, and the Bible.

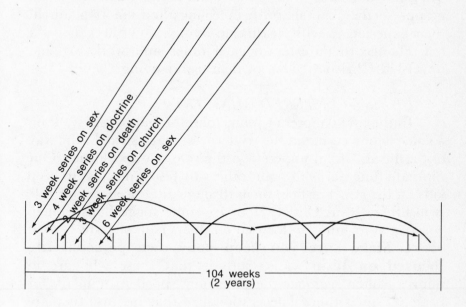

3 week series on sex
4 week series on doctrine
2 week series on death
3 week series on church
6 week series on sex

104 weeks
(2 years)

Experience. Now comes the difficult part. Now you must make sure that all of the information you've given gets into the real world of the students. Suppose, for instance, you were doing a unit on death and dying. The content part of your program would expose the kids to all of the biblical passages about death and dying, the views of theologians and philosophers, and the ideas of church fathers and the church. The experience part of the program would try to give the kids an experience with death and dying, so they could begin to think realistically about it. You might want to have the youth group visit a children's hospital and baby-sit the brothers and sisters of kids with leukemia while they receive their chemotherapy. As the kids see for the first time other kids with terminal illnesses, they begin to really struggle with their views about death.

Relationship. After the hospital experience, you could bring the kids back to the church and divide them into small groups so they can share their feelings and emotions about their experiences with death and dying. Now the kids get a real chance to minister to each other and work together toward a Christian view of death and dying.

CHRIST-CENTERED MINISTRY

In the first chapter of John, John the Baptist says, "I am a voice of one crying in the wilderness, make straight the way of the Lord." John understood the role of every leader. Our ultimate function is to point others to Jesus, not just to keep kids off the street or help them through adolescence. Our role is to lift up Jesus Christ. Here are some suggestions to help you *keep* your ministry focused on the person of Jesus Christ:

1. Make sure you keep your own personal life focused on Jesus. The truth is that those who are in ministry often *substitute* the time they spend in ministry for personal quiet time. They rationalize that because they are spending time in Christ's work, they don't have to spend time with Christ. Not so. It isn't long before the telltale signs of an inadequate relationship with Christ begin to appear. We begin to repeat the same things over and over again. We start experiencing burnout, and we begin to point kids to ourselves or our program instead of Jesus.

We are not saying that you have to spend hours a day in a personal quiet time, but we are saying that you need to spend *some* personal time with God *regularly*.

2. Don't allow kids to put you on a pedestal. When kids find an adult they respect and admire, it is easy for them to romanticize who you are. It is also easy for those of us who are adult leaders to *let* kids put us on a pedestal. You can't keep people from admiring you, and you can't order people to not like or respect you—but you can:

    a. Share the platform with others so that you are not the only one in front of the kids.

    b. Keep limits to the time you spend with kids and let them know that there are certain times you will not be available to them.

    c. Let kids see you in real situations. Invite them over to your house and let them see how you relate to your wife and kids. You cannot accomplish this with a formal dinner, but you can ask a kid over to help you fix your stopped-up toilet.

3. Continue to challenge kids. Kids like being around people who never ask anything from them. Like anyone else, they feel uncomfortable when they are around adults who push them, who keep challenging them to grow. Good youth workers push kids into situations where they need to call on Jesus more.

4. Keep the focus on Jesus. It's easy to fill youth programs with activities and meetings that deal with very relevant subjects (sex, drugs, parents). It is very easy to talk about religious subjects (the Second Coming, the end times), but do we keep coming back to the object of our faith, Jesus Christ? Of course, we are not suggesting that every meeting be about Jesus directly, but somehow there needs to be a conscious effort on the part of your leadership team to keep every meeting and activity in the shadow of the person of Christ.

THE MINISTRY PYRAMID

Beginning to feel overwhelmed by the strategies already suggested? Our purpose, of course, is not to frustrate you, but to give you many different options so that you can tailor-design a program that will minister effectively to your specific group.

It's hard to say just where the pyramid idea began. The idea is so practical and so useful that it has been used by many in youth ministry to get a handle on a strategy for ministry. Here's how it works:

The student population in general. This block in the

pryamid represents all of the students that live within your ministry area. Many of these young people have no idea who you are, but that doesn't matter. What matters is who these young people are and what they are like. To minister effectively to *your* kids, you have to know what *your* kids are like. You may hear about a ministry program that is working great in Southern California, but it would never work in Omaha. If you live in Omaha, you need to understand what the kids in Omaha are like. The point is that there are a lot of kids in your ministry area who have not been ministered to, and ministering to as many of them as possible is one of your goals. But remember, addition is only one of your goals. You are also interested in multiplication.

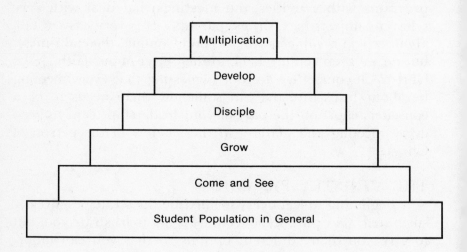

The "Come and See Level." There is only one commitment kids at this level have—and that is *to come.* Every youth group should have some "come-level" activities. That is, part of your program should be geared to those kids who will only come if something is going on that they like. These kids are simply checking your group out. They will attend the ski retreat because they like to ski or they like the girls in the youth group. They are not coming because you are a church or you talk about Jesus. It is easy to understand why you can have eighty kids at a water-ski weekend and ten kids at the Bible study. That is because many kids have only a come-level commitment. Note: It is important to understand that it is *normal* to have a lot of kids at the "come" level and only a few who have a deeper commitment. In our opinion, that is just fine *as long as you always have elements of your program designed for the kids who want a deeper commitment.*

Let's push this a little bit further. When you define an activity as a "come-level" activity, then you understand that you should not fill the program with activities geared for kids with deeper commitments. In other words, you won't plan a Christian rock concert and then have the musician or yourself talk about Jesus for fifty minutes. First of all, you are being dishonest, and secondly, you are turning off the kid who came for the music.

Let's go one step further. A number of youth workers have discovered that most kids attending their Sunday school were forced to come and had basically no commitment. When these youth workers changed the program in Sunday school to be compatible with come-level commitment, attendance and enthusiasm increased. Sunday school changed from a serious Bible study to a light, fast-paced program with a skit, lots of lively singing, and a short talk on a relevant topic.

The grow level. There are some kids in your youth group who are open to going deeper than just the "come" level. These kids are not actively engaging in deep Bible study, but given the opportunity the grow-level person will not be turned off by the prospect of a deeper commitment. These kids won't ask to grow, but if *you* ask them, if you plan activities for them with growth as a goal, these kids will go.

The disciple level. This group of young people is ready to take on responsibility. They are open to structure and discipline in their lives and they are beginning to take initiative for their spiritual growth on their own.

The develop level. Kids at this level are ready for responsibility. They are ready to develop their leadership skills and minister at the peer level.

The multiplication level. These kids are ready to share their lives with others.

A good viable youth ministry program will have something in their program for each of these levels. Such a program will not only give lip-service to a well-balanced youth ministry, but it will provide the activity and the money to minister to kids at every level. Some programs aim at only one of the levels, resulting in limited attendance as well as limited spiritual growth.

THE FUNNEL AND THE PYRAMID

If you visualize your ministry as a funnel, with activities at each level of the funnel that coincide with the pyramid (see diagram), you will understand how to formulate your strategy. At the top of the funnel, where it is easy to enter the program and easy to get out, are the come-level activities. As you get deeper in the funnel, more commitment is required.

But a few things should be noted:

1. *As commitment increases, attendance decreases.*

2. Remember that because today's high-school student is more active and more inclined to be working, *you cannot expect most kids in your group to attend everything.* The days of high-school students showing their commitment by attending everything are over. Most kids today are forced to pick and choose the parts of your program they can attend. This will

require a change of attitude on your part and much more flexibility in your program.

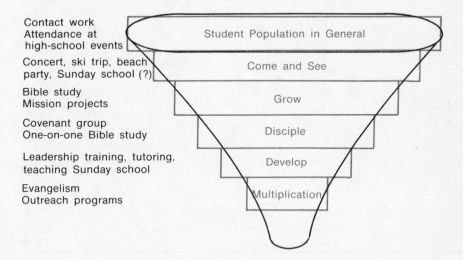

Contact work
Attendance at
high-school events

Concert, ski trip, beach
party, Sunday school (?)

Bible study
Mission projects

Covenant group
One-on-one Bible study

Leadership training, tutoring,
teaching Sunday school

Evangelism
Outreach programs

8   The Problems of Programing

Russ Bradley led an exciting high-school youth group. Every week the program was something new and different—from Polaroid Scavenger Hunts to ski trips and service projects in Haiti. After Russ had been leading the group for a little over a year, he noticed that the attendance began to drop off. Concerned, Russ contacted some of the group dropouts and asked them why they weren't coming anymore. Their answers: The youth group wasn't as exciting as it was a year ago. In the past few weeks, the meetings had become predictable and boring.

What happened to Russ Bradley's group? Nothing. Nothing unusual, that is. Young people today have short attention spans, so they get bored easily. The sooner Russ understands that developmental reality, the more he can adjust his program to meet the needs of the kids. The problem with Russ's group was that the spectacular soon became commonplace; he was lacking a balance between crazy, fun things and solid, continuing, meaty studies. Just because kids have a short attention span doesn't mean you have to encourage it, but it does mean that you must recognize the problem exists and accommodate your program to deal with it. For example, when someone is recovering from a leg injury, the physical therapist accepts the fact that the leg has not been used for a while and comes up with exercises that take the weakness of the leg into account *and* strengthen it at the same time. Do likewise.

There are four characteristics of young people that you must take into account when choosing programing for your high-school youth group: boredom, preoccupation, fear, and superficiality. To fail to design your program around these four problems is to risk failing in your ministry to the adolescents you serve.

BOREDOM

It's a sin to bore a kid.—Jim Rayburn, founder of Young Life.

You don't have to be around high-school young people very long before you've heard the word "boring" at least a thousand times. Church is boring, parents are boring, summer is boring, youth group is boring, the speaker is boring, the party is boring—everything seems boring. The worst thing a high-school student can say about something is that it is boring. These young people have watched so much television, seen so many movies and videos, and had so many exhilarating experiences, they've developed frighteningly high standards for what makes a program worth listening to and a depressingly low tolerance for anything that doesn't immediately captivate their attention. *Today's high-school students are easily bored.* If you want to reach them, you must accept their tendency toward boredom and take steps to counter it.

Kids don't want to be bored. Once we understand that kids *do not want to be bored,* the easier it will be to work on what's causing the boredom. Too often adults working with high-school kids respond to their complaints of boredom by becoming defensive or blaming the young person for not being spiritual enough. Since *no* one likes to be bored, your efforts to relieve boredom will be met with acceptance, not resistance.

Don't counter boredom with excitement. The answer to a boring program is *not* nonstop entertainment. As soon as the entertainment stops, the kids will stop coming because—

you guessed it—they are bored. The answer is to provide a balanced program with differing levels of involvement.

Nine times out of ten, boredom is not a spiritual problem; it is a program problem. Granted there are some high-school young people who simply do not want to listen, but in those cases boredom is only a symptom of a much more serious problem and is the exception, not the rule. Usually kids are bored for a reason, and that reason has something to do with your program.

Boredom can be the result of a lack of understanding. Let's be honest. The Christian faith is not always easy to understand. And sometimes when high-school kids are struggling with a difficult issue, they reach an impasse and give up. When that happens, it isn't long before terminal boredom sets in. Again, our response should not be a lecture or a spiritual admonition; our response should be to spend whatever time it takes to help the high schooler understand.

Boredom can be the result of noninvolvement. No high-school youth program can function very long if the kids are not involved. No matter how good the program is, no matter how interesting those in control may be, if kids aren't involved they soon get bored and drop out. Every kid can get involved in some aspect of your program. The more involvement, the more attentive and interested your kids will be.

Sometimes students are bored because the program or speaker IS boring. Christians do not have to pretend that boring things are not boring. There is legitimate boredom, and when it crops up in your group, it's best to admit it, learn from it, and go on.

It is always better to find a way, without hurting anyone, to end a boring activity. Here are two things to remember. First, if a skit isn't funny and it still has ten minutes to go, there is nothing wrong with stopping the skit before it is done. Obviously, there are times (when someone is speaking, for example) when you can't just cut them off, but you can usually stop something like a skit, movie, or activity. Being bored for ten minutes is better than being bored for twenty minutes.

Secondly, it's better to give kids too little than too much—better for kids to wish the program had lasted longer than for them to wish it had ended sooner. If you're going to err when you are working with kids, err on the lean side.

Boredom can result from too much excitement, from too much stimulation. Strange as it may seem, one of the most common causes of boredom is a program that is too entertaining. That was the problem with Russ Bradley's group (in the introduction to this chapter). You can count on this rule of thumb: What is entertaining today is boring tomorrow. A good program has to do more than entertain; it has to engage people.

Boredom can be the result of forced participation. Some parents force their children to attend youth group; the adolescents sometimes respond by refusing to listen or participate. The solution is not to force their participation but to ignore their inattentiveness (unless it's disruptive) and give them lots of love and empathy.

Boredom can be a symptom of a personal crisis. When a high-school student is preoccupied with a personal problem (girl friend, parents, school), he often appears to be bored. If you are sensitive to the kids in your group, you should be able to recognize when a young person is preoccupied.

Boredom can be caused by a lack of challenge. Activity is not the same thing as challenge. Often in the church, we assume that if we can keep kids busy, if we can keep them active or preoccupied, then we are doing a good job of ministry. But kids can be externally active and internally bored. When high-school students are challenged mentally, spiritually, physically, and emotionally, they are forced to utilize all of their energy to meet the challenge.

Boredom can be a symptom of burnout. On occasion,

a young person raised in the church all his life and involved in the youth group both as a member and a leader suddenly loses interest. This is a serious problem that requires a youth leader who is willing to listen, empathize, and love uncondi- tionally.

Boredom can occur when things are perceived as irrelevant. There are two reasons an adolescent perceives something as irrelevant. Let us suppose that you have a series of meetings about parents. The subject sounds relevant and probably is to most of the kids. Linda Donaldson legitimately feels that she gets along with her parents just fine, so she doesn't need any help. As a result, the subject of parents is *irrelevant* to Linda, so she's bored. If a topic is irrelevant, it is boring because it isn't relevant *at this particular time to this particular kid*.

Let us suppose that a sincere high-school Sunday school teacher decides to give a lesson on biblical archaeology. Most high-school students can see no connection between biblical archaeology and their lives, so they become disinterested and bored because they consider the topic *irrelevant*. If the teacher makes biblical archaeology relevant by showing the connec- tion between it and a current problem in the life of his students, then they will not be bored.

Boredom is always the result of a personal decision. No matter what the reason for the choice, it is still something we choose to do. Sometimes the choice to be bored is justified; sometimes it must be tolerated, but it is not some hypnotic trance cast on us by forces out of our control. We ultimately are responsible for our own boredom. Our task in youth work is to help high-school kids decide not to be bored more often than they decide to be bored.

PREOCCUPATION

Preoccupation may seem similar to boredom, but there is a difference. Boredom is the state of being uninterested; preoccupation is an inability to focus or difficulty in keeping one's attention fixed on something. Preoccupation is the most common reason high-school students cannot concentrate. High-school students can be preoccupied with lots of things: girl friends/boyfriends, family problems, and school-related problems (tests, grades, athletics, and so on).

Preoccupation is a normal part of adolescence. It only causes concern when it seems to be a continuous problem over a prolonged period of time. When you notice that one of your students is preoccupied, talk to the student *privately* to see if you both can identify the problem and begin working on it.

FEAR

There are particular fears that haunt adolescents specifically. Here are some of the most common ones:

Being "uncool." High-school kids do not like to look stupid or uncool, so they are hesitant to do anything that might cause others to laugh at them or make fun of them. By the time many adolescents are in the tenth grade, they consider themselves too sophisticated to play parlor games or participate in games that might cause them to sweat, get messy, or look dumb.

Be sensitive to this fear because it has some legitimacy. Sometimes adults who don't understand high-school kids force them to do things that would be ridiculous for anyone to do. A priest in charge of recreation at a conference tried to get a group of three hundred high-school students to make sounds like a chicken. The kids not only didn't respond but also began to make fun of the priest. He was so insensitive to the crowd that he became hostile and forced them to respond to his requests. Obviously, the priest was out of touch with high-school kids. Don't ask the kids to do things you wouldn't do yourself.

On the other hand, there are times when kids will refuse to participate in a game or program you know they'd enjoy once they got involved. In a case like that, the leader usually has to get involved in the game personally and entice a few key kids to join in. Let the kids know that if the game doesn't work, you'll try something else. Church and youth group are not school but electives—choices that high-school students have. Youth workers have to be careful they do not publicly ridicule or discipline kids because they were unprepared or misbehaving. Kids should be disciplined privately and not embarrassed when they do not have an answer to our questions.

Not being liked. High-school kids are extremely self-conscious. Most adolescents believe that if everyone around them knew what they were *really like*, they wouldn't be liked. You can imagine how those fears are compounded in the church and in youth group where adolescents now have to answer to a God who knows everything. Church kids not only have to worry about whether their friends like them, they also have to wonder whether God likes them. As youth workers, we must spend a great deal of time affirming kids' worth and helping them understand the grace of God by learning to love them unconditionally. Loving high-school kids unconditionally does not mean that what kids do doesn't matter; it means what kids do *does* matter. Whatever they do doesn't change the fact that we love them.

Failure. Forced to make a decision about whether to do the same old thing or try something new that might fail, kids will opt for the same old thing because they don't like to fail. They believe that to fail is to be a loser—a failure. And they believe that failure is the opposite of success rather than a stepping stone to success.

The effective high-school minister recognizes that failure is the fertilizer of growth. Failure is a part of life. It is painful, yes, but it is also the place where learning begins. We not only have to provide high-school kids with opportunities to fail, but we must also offer them an atmosphere of acceptance, so that when they fail, they are surrounded with support, love, and understanding that gives them the motivation to learn from their failure and go on.

SUPERFICIALITY

We live in a spectator society where we would rather let others do the thinking and the work for us. We like to be entertained, to watch, to be spoon-fed.

High-school kids are no different. They would rather come to a youth group and just watch—just be entertained—and not get involved. But one of the primary purposes of high-school ministry is to help high-school students learn how to think. Thinking is the process that enables high-school students to distinguish what *matters*, decide what is an issue and what is a nonissue. Too often, high-school youth programs emphasize the nonissues and don't talk about the real issues. For example, it is easy to get high-school students to talk about rock music or the end times instead of issues like commitment (how do I make decisions that I don't *feel* like making?) and responsibility (how do I take responsibility for my own life?). In high-school ministry we try to help adolescents understand the fabric of their faith (love, forgiveness, grace) rather than just the externals of their faith (smoking, drinking, dancing).

Question making. Sigmund Freud once criticized the church by saying, "The church is in the business of teaching kids to ask only the questions the church has answers for." Too many youth workers view high-school ministry as the place where teenagers get answers to questions, instead of the place where we teach teenagers how to *ask* questions. We want them to ask even the questions we don't have answers for; after all, most young people lose their faith not because they discover that Christianity can't answer all the questions but because they discover a whole new set of questions the church never asked. They feel betrayed and begin to wonder *why* no one told them about the tough questions of life. The Christian faith is true not because it has all the answers but because what we can know is true enough to make us able to live with what we don't know and to make us able to admit we don't know all the answers, even though we are never satisfied with not knowing (we always want to know more). The hope that we have in Christ, the recognition that now "we see through a glass darkly" (1 Cor. 13:12), should never dull our desire to know all we can know *now*.

Our strategy for ministry is twofold. We ask lots of questions, and we help high-school students ask as many questions as possible. In fact, *the way we know high-school kids are growing is not by how many answers they give but rather by how many questions they have.*

Let's say you were doing a three-week study about the Holy Spirit. The first week you ask the students to list all the questions they have about the Holy Spirit, and no one responds. What does that mean? That your students have all the answers? No. It means that they do not yet know enough about the Holy Spirit to have any questions. If you were to take the first week of a three-week study about the Holy Spirit and give a one-hour overview, *then* ask for questions, you would be inundated. The more you know about something, the more *questions* you have.

Creating tension. One of the best ways to generate questions and growth from high-school students is to create tension. Tension is created when students are faced with a dilemma that requires a choice from among many possible choices. The tension comes when there is an overlap of values that makes a simple black-and-white response impossible. The more you can force young people to choose among conflicting values, the more you can cause young people to choose one value over other equally compelling values, and the more you will be preparing them for the real world where few issues are black-and-white.

We are not suggesting that you communicate to high-school students that all values are equal or that truth is relative. We *are* suggesting that you communicate that real truth is absolute and alive. To love someone may mean that you may accept an alcoholic into your home, clean him up, put him to bed to recuperate, and keep him until he is ready to go back to work. That very same love may cause you to refuse to talk to him or let him in your house the next night until he is sober. The application of agape love may require acceptance one time and rejection another time.

This is not situation ethics. Situation ethics says that the situation itself determines what is truth. The Bible says that truth determines what you do in a situation. If you truly love someone, you will help him, but that help may take a number of different forms. Life is complicated, and the more we can prepare high-school students for the complications of real life, the more able they will be to see just how true the gospel is.

9 Ministering to High-school Kids in Crisis*

Jeff, a fifteen year old, has changed drastically in the last four weeks. He is not the same boy you used to know. He never talks anymore; he just sits there looking depressed. You know that his parents were just divorced and that his mother is living with another man. What do you do now?

Seventeen-year-old Mike has been kicked out of his house. His parents don't go to church and have nothing to do with your youth ministry program. Mike's description of what happened has made you concerned about possible physical abuse, but your repeated calls to the parents have been ignored. Now what?

Either of these situations sound familiar? We're not surprised. Today's youth worker sees more and more crises, and there's a good reason. Young people in crisis go to people they trust and have a close relationship with. That is why Howard Clinebell calls those in ministry "natural crisis counselors."[1] It is natural for young people to seek help from their youth worker when they face a crisis.

Unfortunately, those young people don't always find help there. One youth worker, for example, asked a high-school senior not to return to the youth group after his girl friend became pregnant. The couple apologized before the entire youth group and broke the relationship off. They were obviously emotionally needy kids at that point—but the young man, at least, didn't get much help with those needs

---

*The authors are indebted to David Lynn, who researched and organized most of the material in this chapter. His work was then edited and combined with material collected by the authors.

from that church. If the youth worker sincerely wants to help adolescents in crisis, then he must pay the cost of facing the problem, understanding its causes, and walking with the person through the crisis.

If a youth worker cares about the kids he is working with, if he has any kind of a relationship with kids, then it will only be a matter of time before he will be involved in some kind of crisis counseling. All youth workers, then, need some understanding of how to minister to kids in crisis if they are ever going to effectively minister to high-school students.

WHAT IS A CRISIS?

Simply stated, a crisis is a situation that causes a person to feel like he has lost control and, as a result, cannot effectively cope.

Every adolescent develops coping mechanisms that enable him to function normally each day. But when a situation arises for which normal coping mechanisms are inadequate, there is a crisis.

Dave knows that when his dad comes home after work it is best to leave him alone to unwind for thirty minutes or so. Dave has learned to cope with his dad's after-work irritability by staying away from him. But when Dave comes to his father two hours after work and asks for the car and his dad responds with a yelling tirade, Dave's normal means of coping have failed—now there is a crisis. In this case it may be a minor one. Dave can probably regroup, think things through, and realize that something must be happening that he is not aware of. Later Dave discovers that his father has been laid off from work and is deeply upset about the future. It will undoubtedly be a trying time for the family, but Dave, equipped with his new understanding, may well be able to cope again.

There are situations, however, that will exhaust all an adolescent's coping mechanisms, or at least the adolescent will *perceive* that all his coping mechanisms are exhausted.

How an adolescent perceives any given crisis will largely determine how he will cope with the crisis. And how the adolescent perceives the situation is really all that matters. A major emotional crisis occurs when an adolescent who perceives a situation as a threat to his well-being does not have adequate support from parents or friends and does not have adequate problem-solving skills. At this point, outside intervention is necessary if the crisis is to be resolved.

And that's a problem—or is it an opportunity?

The Chinese word for "crisis" has two meanings: danger and opportunity. A crisis is a dangerous time because a person may be unable to cope with the situation in a positive way. It is also an opportunity because in a crisis people are forced to grow, to go beyond what they know, and to push themselves a little bit further. The Greek word for crisis means a decision-making time that could turn out for better or worse. Crisis situations are critical because they require decisions that could have both positive and negative results within moments after the decision is made.

Crises are almost always traumatic for adolescents because they usually experience hurt, pain, fear, and anxiety. Crises often cause adolescents to feel isolated and alone, as though they were the only people who have ever had to endure a situation like theirs. Youth workers can minister to adolescents in crisis by *helping them recognize that crises, although painful, are a normal part of growth.* The youth worker who accomplishes this can be a catalyst toward real emotional and spiritual maturity.

TYPES OF CRISES

Developmental crises are crises brought about by the changes that occur as a result of adolescent growth. Conflict with parents, sexual problems, difficulties with friends, and trouble at school are all crises that are normally the result of adolescent growing pains.

Situational crises are precipitated by a traumatic event.

131

The death of a parent, a car accident, rape, serious illness, suicide of a close friend or relative, parents' divorce, physical or sexual abuse—any of these could easily cause a situational crisis. Situational crises are not as predictable as developmental crises and often, not always, cause more pain and anxiety. Usually they happen with little or no warning, catching the adolescent totally off guard.

Psychopathic crises are the direct result of some kind of personality disorder, schizophrenia, or other psychosis. Qualified professional help should be sought immediately.

ANATOMY OF A CRISIS
There are certain general symptoms apparent during any major crisis. Here are the most common ones:

Excessive tiredness
Nausea
Persistent sickness
Low self-esteem
Feelings of worthlessness or uselessness
Feelings of helplessness or powerlessness
Excessive silliness
Childish behavior
Anxiety
Confusion
Inability to make a decision
Desperation
Apathy
Lethargy
Guilt

Any of these symptoms or combination of them may signal the presence of a serious emotional crisis. On the other hand, they may signal the presence of normal developmental problems that are simply part of the growth process. Still, a concerned youth worker takes these symptoms seriously and does whatever is necessary to identify the source of these symptoms. *If a serious emotional crisis is not resolved in a healthy fashion, the adolescent may develop what psychologists call "learned helplessness."* Learned helplessness is the attitude that says no matter what I do or anyone else does, I will not be able to solve my problems. Once an adolescent develops a feeling of learned helplessness, the crisis is much more difficult to resolve.

CRISIS MYTHS
Myth #1. *Those who are well adjusted do not experience crises.*

Not true. Times of crisis are normal for both adolescents and adults because they are the normal result of living in a fallen world. They are catalysts of growth and maturity. Being well adjusted does not mean you are free from crisis, but that you are free from the illusion that crises are abnormal. High-school students need to know that crisis is normal no matter what our relationship to God.

Myth #2. *A well-adjusted person should be able to handle a crisis.*

Not true. Some crises are too difficult for *anyone* to cope with. Sometimes the accumulation of a number of crises creates an emotional overload that would break even the strongest of persons. When someone cannot handle a crisis, what they *don't* need is a condescending or judgmental attitude that would cause them to feel like the crisis is their fault. They do need to feel supported by people who care and want to help them through the crisis, no matter what the cost.

Myth #3. *God can get rid of any crisis if you have enough faith.*

Dangerous. The Bible never promised that if we just believe in God, we will avoid all crises. The Bible *does* promise that, no matter what we go through, He will be there. High-school students in crisis have enough to worry about without worrying whether they have enough faith. Although it may not sound like much of a help to them when they're sunk in the deepest depression of their young lives or discovering firsthand the meaning of such words as *anguish* and *heartsick*, adolescents need to know that the presence of God is all they need, no matter how bleak the crisis.

Myth #4. *Every crisis is an individual crisis.*

Not necessarily. When a high-school student is having a personal crisis over her parents' divorce, we must recognize that *the entire family is having a crisis*. Often by working with the whole family, we can lessen the impact of the crisis on an individual in the family. A father who has been forced to move out of the home because of a divorce may be using the kids to hurt the mother. Kids can face serious emotional consequences trying to cope with the dilemma of being caught between their mother and father. Speaking with the father and getting him to see what he is doing may remove enough pressure from the children that they can now begin to cope with the divorce itself. Remember, virtually all emotional crises involve one or more people other than the adolescent. These other people are called "significant others." Before any crisis can be resolved adequately, the role of the significant other(s) needs to be understood and clarified.

Myth #5. *Adolescent crises are always caused by negative events.*

Not always. There is a personal dimension to the crises of life. What one person sees as a challenge, another may see as an immovable roadblock. *Remember, it is not the crisis situation that determines the crisis, it is the adolescent's perception of the situation.* Sometimes experiences that most of us would consider to be normal or positive (getting a job, graduation, first date, going steady, making the team) can trigger a crisis for someone else. We have no way of knowing when a particular event in a high-school student's life may add just enough stress or trauma to send a person over the edge. We have no way to predict when this seemingly minor event may be the straw that breaks the camel's back—the last of a series of minor events that, together, precipitate an emotional crisis. Individual crisis is unpredictable.

Myth #6. *Every crisis is unique. What you learn by surviving one crisis will not help you in the next crisis.*

The opposite is true. When an emotional crisis has been effectively handled and resolved, the severity of future crises will be reduced because skills learned in the one crisis *can be used in future crises*.

Myth #7. *The most important goal during any crisis is to get the crisis resolved.*

Not necessarily. The average emotional crisis is usually resolved within a month to two months. Resolution of the crisis is not the issue. The real issue is *how* the crisis was resolved: Was it resolved in a healthy or unhealthy way? A high-school student may resolve the crisis over the breakup of his relationship with a longtime girl friend by jumping into another serious relationship immediately. The resolution of the immediate crisis may result in greater emotional dependence and create the climate for an even greater crisis. When we work with young people in crisis, we must be more concerned with healthy responses to crisis than with quick solutions that may do more harm in the long run.

Myth #8. *Crisis intervention can be done only by professionals.*

Ridiculous. Almost all crises that young people face can be helped by a caring, loving adult leader. There is nothing wrong with referring young people to professional help, when needed, but often what is needed is not sophisticated therapy but someone who is willing to listen. Many crises end as mysteriously as they begin, with no visible reason for the resolution of the crisis other than that someone was walking alongside the person in crisis until it was over.

Myth #9. *Crises are to be avoided.*

Yes and no. Of course, no one actively seeks to create crises in the lives of young people. But when they occur, we need to realize that *crises always provide a significant opportunity for growth*. None of us enjoys crisis, but it is almost always true that during a crisis some of our most significant lessons in life are learned and never forgotten.

THE BIBLICAL VIEW OF CRISIS

Starting with Adam and Eve, the Bible is a continuous story of God's people in crisis: Adam and Eve, Cain and Abel, Moses, David and Goliath, Daniel, Israel, Joseph, Jacob, Noah, and on and on. The Old Testament is a continuous list of crises (see Heb. 11), and a quick look at the New Testament (see Paul's epistles) reveals the same pattern: the people of God in continual crisis. It is obvious from a careful reading of both the Old and New Testaments that crises are:

—a normal consequence of living in a fallen world;
—an opportunity for growth;
—tests of the reality, depth, and strength of our faith;
—strengthening experiences;
—potentially devastating experiences.

The Bible teaches that a crisis can either make us or break us and that one of the functions of the church is to serve as a loving, caring community, united as one body to support, edify, and love each other (Eph. 4:2–6). We can have confidence that God's presence will be with us as we work through our crises (Matt. 28:20). He has promised us the greatest comforter in the midst of a crisis, the Holy Spirit (John 14:16–17).

Most importantly, the Bible makes it clear that the real crisis, the crisis at the cause of all crises, is sin. Sin, manifesting itself in pride and selfishness, has tainted all of creation, leaving us in constant crisis. But Jesus came to resolve the crisis. He took upon Himself our sin, experienced the consequences of our sin, and defeated sin. Now we can face any crisis knowing that Christ is with us and that, even though a temporary crisis may defeat us for the moment, we will never be defeated ultimately. Even in the midst of our seeming defeat, Christ is there using even our failure for good (Rom. 8:36-38).

CRISIS INTERVENTION

THE PURPOSE OF INTERVENTION

Dr. Gary Collins says there are four goals for crisis intervention:[2]

1. To help the person cope effectively with the crisis and return to his usual level of functioning.

2. To decrease the anxiety, apprehension, and other insecurities that may persist after the crisis has passed.

3. To teach crisis-solving techniques, so the person is better prepared to anticipate and deal with future crises.

4. To consider biblical teachings about crisis, so the person learns from the crisis and grows as a result.

INTERVENTION BY THE NONPROFESSIONAL

Crisis intervention done by the youth worker differs greatly from that done by a professional counselor or therapist. The nonprofessional youth worker is not interested in exploring the adolescent's deep-seated psychological conflicts or attempting to develop long-term therapy relationships. *The ultimate goal for any youth worker involved in crisis intervention is the return of the adolescent or family in crisis to a precrisis state.* Here are some principles that will help you to that end:

Youth workers should not play psychotherapist. Even though a youth worker has read a few James Dobson books or attended a Bill Gothard seminar, he does not qualify to play professional counselor. You can do a lot of damage playing with someone's emotional past. Most adolescents in crisis need a nonprofessional, neutral adult who will listen and care more than they need a professional counselor.

Generally, the focus of the nonprofessional counselor should be on the present situation. We are not suggesting that reality therapy or dealing with the present situation is the only effective method of therapy, but focusing on the present is the most helpful approach for the nonprofessional. When Kirk comes to you with a drinking problem, it may be that Kirk's parents are alcoholics. But rather than entangling yourself in the lives of Kirk's parents and trying to go back into Kirk's childhood, it is better for you to help Kirk deal with what *he* needs to do now—quit drinking.

One of the most important functions of a youth worker is the process of referral. Young people in real emotional and psychological trouble will often come to a nonprofessional first because they don't know where else to go or who to trust. As a nonprofessional, you can be the bridge between the person in crisis and professional help, if it's needed.

Remember: The beauty of crisis intervention is that you do not have to be an expert to help an adolescent in crisis. You do not have to be skilled in dealing with the adolescent's past or in interpreting all his feelings and emotions. Remember, your role is to support and help the person in crisis back to a precrisis state.

THE ABC'S OF CRISIS INTERVENTION

Here's a simple, commonsense method of crisis intervention that we believe can be effectively used in almost any crisis you encounter. The method was first proposed by psychiatrist W. A. Jones.[3] It has been used extensively as a model for crisis intervention.

Achieve contact with the person in crisis. Achieving contact with the person in crisis is best done through active listening. By providing a safe, warm, and supportive environment you can begin to establish a constructive relationship with the person. Not only does listening communicate caring and empathy, but it also allows you the opportunity to acquire important information about the person in crisis. While achieving contact, remember the focus of attention must be on the present rather than the past. If you focus on the past, you will quickly find yourself mired in past problems that do nothing but divert your attention from the present problem. The sooner you get the individual to focus on the present situation, the quicker the crisis can be resolved.

Boil down the problem to its essentials. The most difficult part of any crisis counseling is bringing the problem into focus. You and the adolescent must pinpoint exactly what the problem is. Let's look at a typical situation.

Gary Donaldson comes to see his youth worker. His first statement is, "I hate my dad and I want to leave home." Initially, it appears that the son is very angry at his father, but after some probing, the youth worker discovers that Gary doesn't hate his father at all. Gary's problem, as it turns out, is that he is upset about his father's new *job*, which now keeps his dad from seeing Gary as much as he used to. Notice in the following dialogue how the youth worker remains neutral by repeating Gary's statements as questions.

Gary: Boy, am I sick of my dad. I hate him.
Youth Worker: You hate him?
Gary: Yes. He's always gone anymore and he just ignores me.
Youth Worker: What do you mean, "he ignores me"?
Gary: I mean he just doesn't care anymore.
Youth Worker: Anymore?

By repeating Gary's words, the youth worker did not put words or thoughts into Gary's mouth. When an adult talks with an adolescent and makes statements that appear to be opinions, young people feel hesitant to contradict them, so they keep quiet or simply go along with what the adult says. Note in the following dialogue how the youth worker affects Gary's thinking.

Gary: Boy, am I sick of my dad. I hate him.

139

Youth Worker: Does he hassle you all the time?
Gary: Yeah.
Youth Worker: Is he gone a lot?
Gary: Yeah, and I try to talk to him about it, but . . .
Youth Worker: But he doesn't listen.
Gary: Yeah, right.

Instead of the youth worker understanding the adolescent's problem better, he could easily conclude from this second discussion what Gary *thinks the youth worker wants him to feel,* instead of what Gary really feels. In the first dialog, by listening and using neutral statements, the youth worker let the adolescent pinpoint the exact problem, so the youth worker could respond to it.

Cope actively with the problem. One of the most effective ways to help someone in crisis is to help him see just how many options there are. Often a person in crisis feels overwhelmed by the problem and can't see any way out. Work with the person by brainstorming all of the possible solutions to the specific problem. As a result, you do not rescue him or force him to take your advice; you give him whatever tools he needs to deal with the problem on his own. After listing what you think are all the possible solutions, encourage him to take specific action on the crisis problem.

Let's look at a crisis situation and see how the ABC method works.

There is a knock at your door at 9 P.M. It is Scott, a fifteen-year-old high-school student from your youth group. He says he was in the neighborhood and just dropped by, but you sense that something is bothering him. Both of you go out back and start shooting baskets in your lighted patio area while talking about the day. The conversation seems normal until Scott starts talking about his dad. Scott stops the conversation, sits down, then blurts out that he has never accepted his parents' divorce, has never understood why God let it happen, and can't understand why his parents aren't able to get back together again. You listen carefully, and let Scott finish his comments. Then, you ask him why he thinks all of this has surfaced this evening. He says he doesn't know, except his mother did mention to him that morning she was thinking seriously of remarrying. Now you begin to focus on the 'problem. Scott does not want his mother to remarry. He is apprehensive of having a stepfather and doesn't want to hurt his real father. You both begin to explore all the possible solutions to the problem. After a couple of hours of intense discussion, Scott decides to tell his mother how he feels, call his real father and talk to him about the situation, and ask both of them to make a family appointment with a counselor to talk about Scott's feelings.

This, of course, is an ideal scenario, but it does illustrate how effectively the ABC model of crisis intervention can work. Only in extreme cases when an individual is so incapacitated by his crisis that he has lost control (psychosis, severe depression, suicide) should *you* take control.

KNOWING WHEN TO INTERVENE
The youth worker would be wise *not* to intervene in every situation that troubles the adolescents he works with. How do you know when to intervene and when to watch and wait?

Evaluate the emergency potential. The first step in deciding when to intervene in a potential crisis is to determine how serious the crisis is. Has there been serious physical or emotional damage? Is there potential for more physical or emotional damage? Is this a life-threatening situation? What is the worst possible thing that could happen?

Evaluate the self-help potential. Not only do you need to understand the seriousness of the crisis, you must also determine the capability of the person involved in the crisis to help himself. How much support does the person have

141

from family and friends? How good are the coping skills of the individual? How has the person handled crises in the past? Can the person solve the problem without your help?

Here is the best rule of thumb: If the emergency potential is high and the self-help potential is low, you probably need to intervene. If you don't have time to determine the emergency potential or the self-help potential, here's another good rule of thumb: It is better to overreact than not react. Sometimes adolescents will deny they need help, even react with hostility when help is offered—but they may be crying out for help behind that tough exterior. It is always better to offer help than not to offer help. It's true that some kids may cry "wolf," but remember that even false cries are a cry for something real—be it attention, love, or some other unmet need.

FOLLOW-UP AND REFERRAL

Often, the most overlooked aspect of crisis intervention is follow-up. Follow-up is the process of checking out, either by phone or in person, how the person in crisis is doing. There is a flurry of activity and attention at the moment of crisis, but once the crisis is over, the person is often abandoned. Follow-up is the best way to ensure that the crisis does not recur. Keep the following points in mind:

1. The most difficult time that people in crisis face *is not the time right after the crisis is resolved; it is a month or two months later*. Right after a crisis, emotions run high, and the person recovering from the crisis feels a great deal of emotional and psychological support. He *feels* like things are better—like he is special. But slowly, as the support people drop away, as all of the wonderful feelings begin to diminish, he realizes that there are a lot of things that *haven't* changed. He begins to realize how difficult and long the process of meaningful change will be. *This is the time you are most needed*. You need to be there to support and encourage and push the person to stick to the decisions he made a month ago.

2. More often than not, kids who have been in crises show a remarkable turnaround for thirty to sixty days. Many a youth worker has been amazed by how much a troubled child can change. But within two months, sometimes suddenly, the aberrant behavior returns with a vengeance. It is almost as though these young people hold it all back— until they can't hold it any longer, and without warning the crisis returns.

If you work with adolescents very long, the opportunity will arise to have a teenager in crisis come to live with you— and you'll probably jump at the chance. At first you are surprised by how easy he is to work with. He has started doing his homework; he is respectful; he seems to be hanging around the right crowd—and then, one day, he doesn't come home. He calls you three days later from a city five hundred miles away telling you everything is okay, and then you never hear from him again. It happens thousands of times a year, all around the country. The important thing to remember is that crisis kids *can* change—but it takes a lot of time and requires a lot from you.

3. Anger is okay. Rejection is not. There is nothing wrong with getting angry at unacceptable behavior, but it is extremely important that you continue to communicate your acceptance and love of the person. You don't have to love and accept what they do, but you do need to communicate that your heart is always open. Too often we get angry at someone we are helping *not because they failed,* but because they hurt our ego. We thought we were on the way to success, and now we are embarrassed. Embarrassment is not the proper emotion to feel when someone lets you (and himself) down. Anger? Yes. But rejection? No!

4. Kids in crisis are *not* normal. These kids require *more* than large doses of unconditional love. They also require large doses of *conditional* accountability. Many of these young people in crisis have learned how to use buzzwords. They have learned how to manipulate well-meaning and caring

143

people. Following up on a young person in crisis requires that you be willing to pay the price of tough love. You love the person in crisis, you feel for them, but you cannot assume they can handle life on their own. You must provide structure, limits, and accountability, or you will end up being used, and the child will not be helped.

Earlier in this chapter, we emphasized the importance of the youth worker as counselor, even in crises; however, there are times when the young people you counsel need professional help. When the person in crisis needs medical attention, is obviously addicted to drugs or alcohol, or shows signs of serious mental illness, you should refer him to an appropriate professional. Sometimes it isn't easy to tell whether professional help is called for. Here's a good principle to follow: If in doubt, refer. Occasionally you may run into resistance from the adolescent you're counseling when you suggest referral. The best way to avoid resistance is to involve the adolescent in the decision. Let him choose, if possible, and offer to go with him to the first session. Assure the person in crisis that you are not rejecting him or trying to get rid of him.

Prepare a referral file—a list of counselors, doctors, psychologists, and crisis experts you can trust with your referrals. It is best to establish a personal relationship with each of the people you have on file, either by phone or in person, so that you agree on philosophy and have a mutual respect for each other. You may also want to include in your file a list of crisis hot lines for those who need emergency psychiatric care or who need immediate attention because of child abuse, sexual abuse, or rape.

CONFIDENTIALITY

Confidentiality is the basis of any relationship between adolescents and youth workers. If you are going to talk to young people about their problems, they have to know they can trust you to keep what they say confidential. Any youth worker who believes he has the right to share with parents the details of private conversations with their children should not be in youth work. Privacy and confidentiality are part of the code of ethics for youth ministry.

Confidentiality will be threatening to some parents because they'll wonder whose side you are on. It is important for you to communicate to parents that, although you must keep certain things confidential, you are not on the adolescent's side opposing the parents. You *are* on the adolescent's side supporting the parents any way you can. And there will certainly be times when you encourage kids to share with their parents what they have told you in confidence.

Now that we've defended the principle of confidentiality in youth work, it's necessary to consider that a great many difficulties will arise with regard to confidentiality. Should you tell parents that their child is going to run away? What do you say when a mother calls wanting to know what her depressed daughter has been saying? What happens when one of the high-school girls confesses to you that she has just had an abortion?

You may decide it is necessary to violate the principle of confidentiality with an adolescent in crisis, particularly in life-threatening situations or where there has been sexual or physical abuse. The decision to break confidentiality should not be taken lightly. If you decide to violate the principle of confidentiality, make sure that only those individuals necessary to help resolve the crisis be notified. It is also best, if possible, to get the adolescent's permission to allow you to tell those who need to know.

Some adolescents try to manipulate adults into a *confidentiality trap*. They will try and swear you to secrecy before they tell you what is bothering them. The best response is something like this: "I believe I have an obligation anytime I talk with someone to keep our conversations confidential, but I honestly cannot say that, if you were in danger or desperately in need of help, I wouldn't do whatever was necessary to help you." It would be terrible, just at the time the adolescent most needs a friend, for him to lose faith in a caring adult who really wants to help him. Make sure you deal honestly with your young people.

DEALING WITH THE POTENTIAL FOR SUICIDE

SUICIDE MYTHS

At the time this book was written, over five thousand adolescents a year were taking their own lives, and for every one that succeeded there were fifty to one hundred others who attempted suicide. That translates into the sobering figure of about a half million attempts each year. Truly, adolescent suicide is an epidemic. Chances are, if you work with adolescents for any length of time, you will encounter some who are contemplating suicide and, tragically, some who will succeed.

First of all, because most of us are not experienced with suicidal adolescents, let's dispel some common myths:[4]

People who talk about suicide won't do it. The truth is that about 80 percent of those who commit suicide have talked about suicide, *but most of those they talked to did not take them seriously*. Anyone talking about suicide should be taken seriously.

Mentioning suicide may give the person the idea. Many people are afraid if they ask someone whether he has contemplated suicide, they could actually cause him to consider suicide when he had not previously considered it. Not true. If you suspect someone is considering suicide, check it out. Just plain ask them directly. Talking about suicide with someone who is contemplating it actually works as a preventative by encouraging the person to talk about it.

Suicide occurs without warning. Not only do suicidal people give warning, they usually give lots of warning signs. Hindsight is always 20/20, and after someone has committed suicide, friends and family are usually shocked when they realize how many warning signs they missed. The warning signs can be any combination of moodiness, withdrawal, sudden changes in behavior, chronic physical complaints, sudden traumatic event (especially the breakup with a longtime boyfriend or girl friend), violent behavior, or a history of drugs and alcohol. There are usually more than enough warning signs, but those who are closest to the person simply can't believe that a friend of theirs would actually take his own life.

All suicidal people are mentally ill. Too many people believe that suicide only happens to people who are mentally ill, mentally retarded, or very poor. They can't imagine that a *normal* person would want to take his life. The truth is that only about 15 percent of those who take their lives have actually been diagnosed as mentally ill.

Suicidal people are totally committed to dying. Not true. One of the most common characteristics of adolescents who are contemplating suicide is *ambivalence*. They have a strong desire to end their life, and at the same time a strong desire to live. Your best approach is to use their ambivalence and encourage their strong feelings about living.

When depression lifts, the suicide crisis is over. Often the lifting of the depression only means that the adolescent has finally decided to take his life. The depression is replaced with a feeling of euphoria, of relief now that the decision has been made. Incredibly, many suicides occur within three months after the people have appeared to overcome the depression.

Suicidal people do not seek medical help. Strangely, research has shown that three out of four people who have taken their lives have seen a doctor within one to three months beforehand.

WHAT TO DO WHEN AN ADOLESCENT IS SUICIDAL

Don't panic. Remember that adolescents are usually ambivalent. They do have a strong desire to live. The

147

important thing is for you to remain in control of your own emotions so you can be of help.

Believe you can help. The fact that the adolescent has come to you tells you that he is looking to you for help. He trusts you. He *wants* to do what you suggest.

Don't call a person's bluff. A person who is seriously contemplating suicide may be pushed over the edge if you try and get him to prove the seriousness of his intent. Whether you think he's bluffing or not, treat him as if you're sure he means it.

Be suspicious of rapid recoveries. When a suicidal person suddenly says he feels much better now, pay close attention. Feeling better is not a good sign—it is a warning sign.

Do not leave a suicidal person alone. Make sure that a responsible person stays with the person threatening suicide.

Alert parents or guardians. Unless the child has been sexually, physically, or emotionally abused, it is always best to alert the family. Many families are oblivious to the suicidal leanings of their own children.

Share the responsibility. Don't try to be a hero. Refer the adolescent to an appropriate agency or therapist. This is no time to try to be the Lone Ranger; this is the time to gather a posse.

When you sense the need to refer, try to get the adolescent's permission. You could say, "I am very concerned about you at this moment and I believe we should talk to a person I trust very much who can help us with this situation."

Pray with and for the person in crisis. Often when we sense that someone is in crisis, we get so wrapped up in analysis and daily care that we forget to focus on the source of our power and our strength. A crisis is a great opportunity to point people to the ultimate source of hope and healing.

YOU CAN MAKE A DIFFERENCE

We have tried not to make this chapter a syllabus of crisis intervention; rather, we have written in generalities. The function of this chapter is not to make you a minipsychiatrist; rather, it is to encourage you, to let you see that although you may not be a professional crisis counselor, you can still love kids. *You* can make a significant difference in the lives of kids in crisis. And to help you do that, here's a list of suggestions that may help you act on the principles we've discussed above:

1. When someone calls in crisis, try to see him as soon as possible. Try not to wait longer than twenty-four hours.

2. Meet the person either in a public place (a restaurant or shopping mall, for instance) or in your home or office (as long as other adults or witnesses are close by).

3. Offer the person a drink of water. People in crisis are often dehydrated. Do not give them anything with alcohol or caffeine.

4. Don't act shocked or disgusted by what you hear.

5. Allow the adolescent in crisis to ventilate his anger and frustration.

6. Be careful about touching an adolescent in crisis. It's true that a hug may comfort the adolescent, but in the emotional confusion of crisis, he may interpret your touch as a threat or as a sexual response.

7. Adolescents in crisis are vulnerable to manipulation from adults. In fact, they are desperate, and they will cling to any advice you give them. Take that responsibility seriously. Don't use the kid's crisis to make you feel good for the moment.

8. If it is someone other than the adolescent who calls for your help, be prepared for hostility, anger, and outright defiance from the adolescent when he realizes that you've become involved. He's likely to feel that his privacy has been unscrupulously violated. Sometimes the best thing you can do is let him know you're willing to help whenever he's willing to ask for it and then leave. You can't force people to accept help when they do not want it.

9. Do not allow yourself to feel sorry for those in crisis. Feeling sorry gets in the way of your ability to give objective and neutral support.

10. Learn to say no. You cannot help every adolescent in crisis and still maintain a family, a job, and your mental health. Don't feel guilty about it. It's a sound principle of youth ministry that any one person can help only so many kids. Have a list of others you can refer the adolescent in crisis to.

11. Make sure that you are not using the crises of the kids to give *your* life meaning. Some people thrive on others in crisis *because their lives have no intrinsic meaning of their own, and only by intruding in someone else's crisis, do they find any meaning at all.*

12. Remember, *whatever you do is better than doing nothing.* Maybe you will never see miraculous changes in kids; maybe you will very seldom see an adolescent in crisis take any of your advice. It doesn't matter. As long as you do what you can, God will honor the rest. The results you don't see are often the most important.

Christ called us to bear one another's burdens. Crisis intervention is one way the youth worker bears another's burdens. It is not easy, and it doesn't always result in visible, gratifying changes, but if Christ had made His decision to go to the cross based on how many strokes He received for it, He wouldn't have gone.

PART III

TOOLS FOR HIGH-SCHOOL MINISTRY

10 Creative Learning Strategies

All of the ideas in this chapter come from the *Ideas* library, published by Youth Specialties, Inc. (El Cajon, Calif.), or from *Ideas for Social Action,* by Anthony Campolo (Grand Rapids, Mich.: Zondervan Publishing House, 1984).

CHAPTER CONTENTS

BIBLICAL QUIZZES
Christmas I.Q. Test / 156
Easter I.Q. Test / 162
Noah and the Ark I.Q. Test / 164
Prodigal Problems Quiz / 168

BUILDING COMMUNITY
Body Life Game / 172
Lamed Vovnik Convention / 174
Love Groups / 175
Uppers and Downers / 176

CHRISTIANITY
Role Bowl / 178
Theological Fictionary / 179
Word Pictures / 180

CHURCH
The Great Fish Controversy / 180
Ideal Church / 182

Images of the Church / 183
The Life-Saving Station / 184

DEATH
Death Fantasy / 186
Run for Your Life / 187

DISCIPLESHIP
Cost of Discipleship / 188
Dear Abby / 190
Tom Meets God / 191

DIVORCE
Divorce Panel / 193

DRUGS AND ALCOHOL
It's Your Decision / 194

ETHICS, VALUES, MORALITY
Life Auction / 195
Monitoring Your Morals / 197
Problem Hot Line / 198
Values Teasers / 199
The Window / 201

HUNGER, JUSTICE
Letter to Amos / 204
Undinner for World Hunger / 205

MARRIAGE
Dating Data / 206
Perfect Pair / 207
To Marry or Not to Marry / 208
Twenty-five-cent Mate / 211

MISSION AND SERVICE
Adopt a Grandparent / 212
Big Brothers, Big Sisters / 213
Bread-Baking Bash / 213
Convalescent Home Ministry / 214
Creative Canned Food Drives / 217
Gardens and Cleaners / 219
Handicapped All-nighter / 220
H.O.P. Club / 221
Labor Day / 222
Ministry to the Retarded / 223
Prison Ministry / 224
Rake and Run / 227
Senior Surprise / 229
Sponsor a Child / 230
Trash Bash / 230
Tutoring Ministry / 231
Welcoming the Handicapped / 231

NUCLEAR WAR
Armageddon Bomber / 233

PARENTS
Dear Amy Letters / 234
How To Raise Your Parents / 238
A Mad Late Date / 238
Parent Blunders and Teen Goofs / 242
Parent Youth Group / 244

PEER PRESSURE
Friend or Foe / 244
The Great Button Controversy / 245
Paul's Dilemma / 245

SELF-IMAGE
Appreciation Game / 249
Building an Image / 249

Encourage One Another / 251
Prestige Game / 252

SEX/SEXUALITY
The Island Affair / 252
Male or Female / 255
Sex in the Movies / 256

SUICIDE
Facts About Suicide / 257
Suicide Role Play / 259

THEOLOGY
Bethany Church / 259
Invent / 264
Values in the Church / 265

WORSHIP
Body of Christ Worship / 267
Progressive Worship Service / 268
Silent Worship Service / 269
Worship Ideas / 271

BIBLICAL QUIZZES

CHRISTMAS I.Q. TEST

Next Christmas, give the following quiz to your youth to determine how much they really know about the Bible's most popular story. The results will undoubtedly be very embarrassing as well as lead to a better understanding of the events surrounding Christ's birth.

Instructions: Read and answer each question in the order it appears. When choices are given, read them carefully and select the best one. Put a "T" or an "F" in the blank on all True or False questions. Guessing is permitted, cheating is not.

1. As long as Christmas has been celebrated, it has been on December 25th. *(True or False)* ___

2. Joseph was from
   a. Bethlehem
   b. Jerusalem
   c. Nazareth
   d. Egypt
   e. Minnesota
   f. none of the above

3. How did Mary and Joseph travel to Bethlehem?
   a. Camel
   b. Donkey
   c. Walked
   d. Volkswagen
   e. Joseph walked, Mary rode a donkey
   f. Who knows?

4. Mary and Joseph were married when Mary became pregnant. *(True or False)* ___

5. Mary and Joseph were married when Jesus was born. *(True or False)* ___

6. Mary was a virgin when she delivered Jesus. *(True or False)* ___

7. What did the innkeeper tell Mary and Joseph?
   a. "There is no room in the inn."
   b. "I have a stable you can use."
   c. "Come back after the Christmas rush and I should have some vacancies."
   d. Both a and b
   e. None of the above

8. Jesus was delivered in a
   a. stable
   b. manger
   c. cave
   d. barn
   e. unknown

9. A manger is a
   a. stable for domestic animals
   b. wooden hay storage bin
   c. feeding trough
   d. barn

10. Which animals does the Bible say were present at Jesus' birth?
   a. cows, sheep, goats
   b. cows, donkeys, sheep
   c. sheep and goats only
   d. miscellaneous barnyard animals
   e. lions, tigers, elephants
   f. none of the above

11. Who saw the "star in the East"?
   a. shepherds
   b. Mary and Joseph
   c. three kings
   d. both a and c
   e. none of the above

12. How many angels spoke to the shepherd?
   a. one
   b. three
   c. a multitude
   d. none of the above

13. What sign did the angel tell the shepherds to look for?
   a. "This way to baby Jesus"
   b. a star over Bethlehem
   c. a baby that doesn't cry
   d. a house with a Christmas tree
   e. a baby in a stable
   f. none of the above

14. What did the angels sing?
   a. "Joy to the World, the Lord is Come"
   b. "Alleluia"
   c. "Unto us a child is born, unto us a son is given"
   d. "Glory to God in the highest . . ."

e. "Glory to the Newborn King"

f. "My Sweet Lord"

15. What is a heavenly host?

a. the angel at the gate of heaven

b. the angel who invites people to heaven

c. the angel who serves drinks in heaven

d. an angel choir

e. an angel army

f. none of the above

16. There was snow that first Christmas

a. only in Bethlehem

b. all over Israel

c. nowhere in Israel

d. somewhere in Israel

e. Mary and Joseph only dreamed of a white Christmas.

17. The baby Jesus cried

a. when the doctor slapped Him on His behind

b. when the little drummer boy started banging on his drum

c. just like other babies cry

d. He never cried

18. What is frankincense?

a. a precious metal

b. a precious fabric

c. a precious perfume

d. an Eastern monster story

e. none of the above

19. What is myrrh?

a. an easily shaped metal

b. a spice used for burying people

c. a drink

d. aftershave lotion

e. none of the above

20. How many wise men came to see Jesus? (Write in the correct number.) _____

21. What does wise men refer to?
   a. nen of the educated class
   b. Eastern kings
   c. astrologers
   d. people smart enough to follow the star
   e. sages

22. The wise men found Jesus in a
   a. manger
   b. stable
   c. house
   d. Holiday Inn
   e. good mood

23. The wise men stopped in Jerusalem
   a. to inform Herod about Jesus
   b. to find out where Jesus was
   c. to ask about the star that they saw
   d. to get gas
   e. to buy presents for Jesus

24. Where do we find the Christmas story?
   a. Matthew
   b. Mark
   c. Luke
   d. John
   e. all of the above
   f. only a and b
   g. only a and c
   h. only a, b, and c
   i. only x, y, and z
   j. Aesop's Fables

25. When Joseph and Mary found out that Mary was pregnant with Jesus, what happened?
   a. they got married
   b. Joseph wanted to break the engagement
   c. Mary left town for three months
   d. an angel told them to go to Bethlehem
   e. both a and d

f. both b and c

26. Who told Mary and Joseph to go to Bethlehem?
   a. the angel
   b. Mary's mother
   c. Herod
   d. Caesar Augustus
   e. Alexander the Great
   f. no one

27. Joseph took the baby Jesus to Egypt
   a. to show Him the pyramids
   b. to teach Him the wisdom of the Pharaohs
   c. to put Him in a basket in the reeds by the river
   d. to fulfill a dream he had
   e. to be taxed
   f. none of the above

28. I think that this test was
   a. super
   b. great
   c. fantastic
   d. all of the above

ANSWERS

   1. False. Not until the fourth century did it settle on the 25th. Other dates were accepted before then.
   2. a. See Luke 2:3, 4
   3. f. The Bible doesn't say.
   4. False. See Matthew 1:18
   5. False. See Luke 2:5
   6. True. See Matthew 1:25
   7. e. No word about the innkeeper. See Luke 2:7
   8. e. No word about it. See Luke 2:7
   9. c.
   10. f. The Bible doesn't specify.
   11. e. The wise men did (they were not kings). See Matthew 2:2
   12. a. See Luke 2:9

13. f. See Luke 2:12
14. d. See Luke 2:14
15. e. Definition is an "army." See Living Bible also.
16. d. Mt. Hermon is snow covered.
17. c. We have no reason to believe He wouldn't.
18. c. By definition.
19. b. See John 19:39 or a dictionary.
20. No one knows. See Matthew 2:1
21. c. See most any commentary. They were astrologers or "star gazers."
22. c. See Matthew 2:11
23. b. See Matthew 2:1–2
24. g. Mark begins with John the Baptist, John with "the Word."
25. f. See Matthew 1:19; Luke 1:39, 56
26. d. See Luke 2:1, 4
27. d. See Matthew 2:13
28. d, of course.

EASTER I.Q. TEST

Here is a quiz that can be used in conjunction with a Bible study about Easter or used to test a group's knowledge of the Easter story as it is presented in Scripture.

Instructions: Place an "X" on the line if you think the answer is biblically correct.

1. The woman (or women) who went to the tomb was (or were)
___ a. Mary Magdalene and the other Mary
___ b. Mary Magdalene, Mary the mother of James, and Salome
___ c. Mary Magdalene, Mary the mother of James, Joanna, and others
___ d. Mary Magdalene
2. The time of early morning was
___ a. when the sun had risen

__ b. while it was still dark

3. At the tomb was (or were)
__ a. an angel
__ b. a young man
__ c. two men
__ d. two angels

4. The reaction of the woman (or women) was one of
__ a. amazement and astonishment
__ b. fear and trembling
__ c. great joy

5. After leaving the tomb, the woman (or women)
__ a. told the disciples
__ b. said nothing to anyone

6. The reaction of the disciples at first was
__ a. they did not believe the women; it seemed an idle tale
__ b. Peter and John went immediately and quickly to the tomb

7. Jesus first appeared to the disciples
__ a. in Galilee, on a mountain
__ b. in an upper room in Jerusalem

8. Jesus seemingly last appeared to the disciples
__ a. on a mountain in Galilee
__ b. on a mountain in Bethany (or just outside Bethany)
__ c. by the Sea of Tiberias

9. The gift of the Holy Spirit was given to the disciples
__ a. before Jesus ascended—in the Upper Room He breathed on them
__ b. after Jesus ascended—on the Day of Pentecost

10. We have many details about the crucifixion and death of Jesus. Which Gospel writer gives the most details about the actual resurrection of Jesus? Which one best describes what happened when Jesus rose from the dead?
__ a. Matthew

___ b. Mark
___ c. Luke
___ d. John

The answers are found in Matthew 28, Mark 16, Luke 24, John 20–21, and Acts 1. In questions 1 through 9, all of the choices are correct, and in question 10, none are correct since none of the Gospels describe the actual resurrection of Christ, only what happened afterward. After reading the answers, discuss the differences between the four gospel accounts and how they can be reconciled to each other.

NOAH AND THE ARK I.Q. TEST

Here's a fun little quiz that generates new interest in the old familiar story of Noah and the ark. Most people assume that they know most everything about the facts of the story, but this test may prove otherwise.

1. Why did God decide to destroy all living things with the flood?
  a. because Israel was disobedient
  b. because the Romans were corrupt and needed to be punished
  c. because everyone was wicked and evil
  d. because He knew it was the only way to get rid of disco dancing and junk food
2. Why did God pick Noah to survive the flood?
  a. Noah was the only guy around who knew how to build an ark
  b. Noah was the only guy around who loved God and would obey Him
  c. Noah won the trip in a sweepstakes
  d. Noah begged God to save himself and his family
3. What was Noah's profession?
  a. animal expert
  b. boat builder

c. farmer
d. temple priest
4. How did Noah find out about the coming flood?
   a. he read about it in the Bible
   b. he had a dream about it
   c. he was notified by a prophet
   d. God told him
5. How long did Noah have to build the ark and get ready for the flood after he found out about it?
   a. 40 days
   b. 1 year
   c. 3 years
   d. 120 years
6. What were the names of Noah's three sons?
   a. Ham, Shem, and Japheth
   b. Ham, Sam, and Jeff
   c. Ham, Turkey, on Rye
   d. Huey, Dewey, and Louie
7. How old was Noah when his three sons were born?
   a. in his 20s
   b. in his 30s
   c. about 60 years old
   d. about 500 years old
8. How big was the ark?
   a. 50 cubits high, 30 cubits wide, and 300 cubits long
   b. 300 cubits long, 30 cubits high, and 50 cubits wide
   c. 300 cubits wide, 50 cubits long, and 30 cubits high
   d. about the size of the *Queen Mary*
9. How long is a cubit?
   a. about the same as three schmuckos
   b. about 2.5 meters
   c. about the length of one's forearm
   d. about a yard (three feet)

10. How many doors did the ark have?
   a. one
   b. two—one on the side and one on top
   c. just the one on the captain's quarters
   d. who knows?
11. How many floors did the ark have?
   a. one
   b. three
   c. a ranch-style, split-level ark
   d. who knows?
12. How many people did Noah take on the ark with him?
   a. 3
   b. 7
   c. 11
   d. 13
13. True or False: Noah took only two of each species with him on the ark.
   a. true
   b. false
14. How old was Noah when the flood came?
   a. 35
   b. 50
   c. 120
   d. 600
15. Where did the flood waters come from?
   a. a broken pipe
   b. from the sky
   c. from inside the earth
   d. both b and c
16. How long did the flood last?
   a. a little over 1 year
   b. 40 days and 40 nights
   c. about 3 months
   d. who knows?
17. What bird did Noah send out first to see if there was dry land?

a. a pigeon

b. a raven

c. a chicken

d. a sparrow

e. none of the above

18. What did the dove return with the first time Noah sent it out?

a. a pepperoni pizza

b. nothing

c. an olive leaf

d. an olive branch

e. an olive pit

19. What did the dove return with the last time Noah sent it out?

a. olive only

b. a message of peace

c. nothing

d. it did not return

20. Where is the story of Noah in the Bible?

a. the Book of Genesis

b. the Book of Exodus

c. the Book of Noah

d. the Book of Moses

21. After the flood was over, what did Noah do?

a. he continued his righteous life, never sinning again

b. he planted a vineyard

c. he got drunk

d. he opened a boat store

e. both b and c

22. God sent a rainbow as a way of saying to Noah:

a. "There's a pot of gold at the end of every rainbow"

b. "Somewhere over the rainbow"

c. "Every cloud has a silver lining"

d. "You don't have to worry about floods destroying everything anymore, Noah"

   e. "Don't forget what happened, Noah. Next time
      it will be worse!"
23. True or False: Recent scientific expeditions have
      found remains of the ark on Mt. Sinai.
      a. true
      b. false
      c. maybe

ANSWERS
  1. c. (Gen. 6:11–13)
  2. b. (Gen. 6:9, 7:1)
  3. c. (Gen. 9:20)
  4. d. (Gen. 6:17)
  5. d. (Gen. 6:3, 7:6)
  6. a. (Gen. 6:10)
  7. d. (Gen. 5:32)
  8. b. (Gen. 6:15)
  9. c.
  10. a. (Gen. 6:16)
  11. b. (Gen. 6:16)
  12. b. (Gen. 7:7)
  13. b. (Gen. 7:2–3)
  14. d. (Gen. 7:6)
  15. d. (Gen. 7:11)
  16. a. (Gen. 7:11, 8:14)
  17. b. (Gen. 8:6–10)
  18. b. (Gen. 8:8–9)
  19. d. (Gen. 8:12)
  20. a.
  21. e. (Gen. 9:20–21)
  22. d. (Gen. 9:8–16)
  23. b. (It was Mt. Ararat, not Mt. Sinai.)

PRODIGAL PROBLEMS QUIZ
   Next time you're doing a study or talk on the parable of
the Prodigal Son, use this little "pop quiz" to get everyone's
attention.

1. According to the parable of the Prodigal Son found in Mark 15:11–31, how many sons were there?
   a. 1
   b. 2
   c. 3
   d. multitudes
   e. none
2. Which son is considered the "prodigal"?
   a. oldest
   b. youngest
   c. middle
   d. the one with the earring
3. When did the oldest son get his inheritance?
   a. when Pop died
   b. at the same time as the other
   c. when the son stood still
4. What job did the prodigal son take when his wealth ran out?
   a. youth pastor
   b. farming
   c. pig slopper
   d. carnival barker
5. (Fill in the blank.) "But while he was a long way off, his father saw him and was filled with _____ for him . . ."
   a. disgust
   b. totalitarianism
   c. compassion
   d. punishments
6. What items did the father give his returned son?
   a. robe, gold chain, and sandals
   b. ring, sandals, and Walkman
   c. ring, robe, and 'rithmetic
   d. sandals, ring, and robe
7. Where was the older son when the younger son returned home?

169

      a. BMX racing

      b. tending the cattle

      c. in the field

      d. out somewhere

8. The older son knew something was up when he heard
   a. the doorbell
   b. music
   c. music and dancing
   d. a still, small voice

9. What did the older son say his father never gave him so he could celebrate with his friends?
   a. fattened calf
   b. party hats
   c. goat
   d. lamb

10. What didn't the younger son feel worthy to be called any longer?
    a. chicken-lips
    b. Jewish
    c. son
    d. prodigal
    e. Buford

11. Who was unhappy at the homecoming?
    a. the fattened calf
    b. the homecoming queen
    c. older son
    d. both a and c

12. According to verse 19, who did the younger son want to be like?
    a. big brother
    b. Dad
    c. hired servants
    d. Pastor Dave
    e. Buford

13. Where did the older brother refuse to go?

a. Africa
b. in the house
c. to the party
d. Bismarck High
e. Mott, ND

14. According to verse 18, what was the mother's name?
    a. Mildred
    b. Rachel
    c. Hildegaard
    d. heaven
    e. uncertain

15. What did the older son say the younger son spent his money on?
    a. video games
    b. friends
    c. women of the evening
    d. wine, women, and song

ANSWERS

1. e. The story is in Luke 15, not Mark 15.
2. b. Verse 12.
3. b. Verse 12 says he divided his property "between them."
4. c. Verse 15.
5. c. Verse 20.
6. d. Verse 22.
7. c. Verse 25.
8. c. Verse 25.
9. c. Verse 29.
10. c. Verse 19.
11. d. The calf probably wasn't too happy about the deal, either.
12. c.
13. b. Verse 28.
14. d. Verse 18 says, "Father, I have sinned against

heaven and against you. So "Heaven" must have been his mother's name, right? Besides, have you ever known anybody named "Uncertain"?

15. c. Verse 30.

BUILDING COMMUNITY

BODY LIFE GAME

This game is a good way to demonstrate the need for cooperation and unity within the body of Christ as presented in New Testament Scripture. Divide the entire group into five smaller groups that symbolize members or parts of the body. Each group should be named accordingly, for example, Eyes, Hands, Ears, Feet, and Mouth.

The object of the game is for the five groups, all members of the same body, to work together and perform their tasks before LIFE dies. To symbolize LIFE, someone can be locked in a box and a road flare lit nearby. When the flare goes out, LIFE will be considered dead. The only way LIFE can be saved is to complete the tasks that lead to the key and to unlock LIFE before the flare burns out (about 30 minutes).

Each of the five groups should be equal in size and labeled in some way (different color armbands or signs). To complete the tasks, each group may work *only* as a normal body works—that is, Eyes can only see, and Ears can only hear. Therefore, everyone except the Eyes must be blindfolded.

When the game begins, the blindfolds go on, the flare is lit, and the group gets its first task. The instruction for that task is written and presented to the Eyes, who whisper it to the Ears, who likewise whisper it to the Mouths, who then verbalize it to the rest of the body. Whenever the group must go anywhere, the Feet must carry the Eyes (the only ones who can see) and the remaining members of the body must follow in a single-file line, holding on to each other's waists.

The Eyes in that case are allowed to speak, giving directions to the rest of the body.

The tasks may be relatively simple ones. Three or four good ones are enough. A few examples are listed here:

1. Crackers and juice should be fed to the Mouths by the Hands while being guided by the Eyes. The Feet will then carry the Ears to (place) followed by the rest of the body in a single-file line.

2. The Ears will be given a number (by the leader) between one and ten. The Ears must then hold up that many fingers for the Eyes to see, who then tells the Mouths, who shout it to the Hands and Feet. Everyone must then get in smaller groups of that number of people. The Eyes may help everyone get together. (This can be repeated.)

3. Splints and bandages can be provided that the Hands use to splint one arm and one leg of each of the Feet, guided by the Eyes.

The above tasks are only samples. It is best to work out a few tasks that specifically fit your locality. The last task should lead to the envelope containing the key. The Hands must use the key to open the box, again guided by the Eyes and carried there by the Feet.

Aftergame discussion could include the following questions:

1. How did each part of the body function?

2. Did everyone do his part?

3. Why didn't some people get involved?

4. Relate this to Paul's analogy of the body (1 Cor. 12:14–26).

This game, although deceivingly simple, must be thought through carefully by the leader before it's played. One youth group used three different bodies and three different keys representing Faith, Hope, and Love. The possibilities are endless with a little creativity.

LAMED VOVNIK CONVENTION

There is a charming Jewish legend that states the world exists due to the presence of only thirty-six righteous people. The Jewish name for these people is *lamed vov* (pronounced "lahmed vov"), which indicates thirty-six. These people may be of any station in life—poor or mighty, men or women, hermits or public figures. The only thing we know about them is that they are alive and that they do not know that they are lamed vovniks. If they claim to be, then they cannot be.

To conduct a Lamed Vovnik Convention, divide your group into as many small groups as you wish and have each group nominate several individuals whom they think might qualify as a lamed vovnik. They should be righteous, selfless, and the kind of persons on whom the welfare of the world might rest. Each group should take ten to fifteen minutes to decide. Set a maximum number of people that each group may nominate.

At the end of the time limit, have a Lamed Vovnik Convention. Each group announces its choices and explains why they nominated whom they did. Write the list on a blackboard and call for a vote to arrive at the entire group's choices for the thirty-six lamed vovniks.

Many famous people will undoubtedly be nominated, but the beauty of the exercise is that many not well-known people will be favorites. At one Lamed Vovnik Convention, a man named David Rapaport was elected when a persuasive young man nominated him with the words, "Most of you wouldn't know him, but when I need help or advice, he's always there to help me or steer me through times of trouble." Another notable nominee was an anonymous man on an immigrant ship who helped the father of one of the young people who said, "He gave dad some food and a little money and did the same for many others on board. But no one remembers his name. . . ." Perhaps the best lesson is the shift of emphasis from fame to humility. True models emerge, and kids begin to realize what righteousness really is.

LOVE GROUPS

This exercise is a five-session project designed for informal times with your youth group or Sunday school class. The purpose is to let the youth be creative and imaginative about the subject of Christian love through many different activities. The youth leader acts as an organizer, supplying very little direct lecture-type teaching.

The group is divided into activity groups. Each of these activity groups works on something directly related to the subject of Christian love. While the activity groups are working, the leader stops all the groups for one of a variety of give-and-take sessions that might include minilectures (three minutes), discussion, or a short film, all dealing with the subject of love. The fifth session is devoted to the presentation of each group's finished project. For example, the Drama Group would act out their drama, and the Love Banner Group would auction off their banners. Adults or other youth groups can be invited to the fifth session.

Here are ten sample groups:

1. *The Signs of Love Slide Show*. This group will shoot pictures of "signs of love" all around them, have them developed, and create a slide show with narration or music.

2. *Drama*. This group will prepare a play on some facet of Christian love. It can be original or a well-known Bible story.

3. *The Multiple Listing Group*. This group will come up with lists centered on Christian love. For example, a list of "What love is" or "What love is not" or "Ways to demonstrate love."

4. *The Crossword Puzzle Group*. This group will design one or more crossword puzzles based on the subject of Christian love.

5. *The Poetry Group*. This group will write original poetry about Christian love.

6. *The Cartoons Group.* This group will publish a booklet of Christian love cartoons. They can be original or from other publications.

7. *The Bible Scholar Group.* This group will research the concept of Christian love in the Scriptures using commentaries, other books, etc., and write a report on the findings.

8. *The Love Banner Group.* This group must have some artistic and sewing ability because they will produce banners on the subject of Christian love.

9. *The Songwriting Group.* This group will compose Christian love songs and perform them. They can be completely original or new words to familiar tunes.

10. *The Love Object Group.* This group will produce love-related art objects to auction off or give away, such as love necklaces, plaques, calligraphy, paintings, etc.

Each group should be supplied with the necessary items to complete their work and encouraged to work at home as well. A textbook, such as Francis Schaeffer's *The Mark of the Christian,* published by InterVarsity Press, can be used during the class sessions as a common study guide.

UPPERS AND DOWNERS

For an excellent exercise in community building, have the kids in your group fill out a chart similar to the one on the next page.

Give the kids these directions for filling out the chart: Ask them to think of a time when someone said something to them that was really a "downer"—something that made them feel bad. This could be a put-down, an angry comment, anything. Then have them think of a time when someone said an "upper" to them—something that made them feel good. If they can think of several entries for the first two columns, encourage them to write them in.

Next, have the kids do the same thing in the third and fourth columns, only this time they should think of times when *they* said an "upper" or "downer" to someone else.

OTHERS		ME	
Upper	Downer	Upper	Downer

If your group is typical, they'll be able to think of many more "downers" than "uppers." Discuss how easy it is to discourage or to put down others without a second thought—how damaging our tongue can be, and how the damage takes so long to repair.

Follow up with a look at Hebrews 10:23–25, which deals with encouragement, and then discuss practical ways to put it into practice.

You can also help kids recognize whether the things they say to each other are "uppers" or "downers." Some may even take the hint and learn to be more careful about what they say. If you are on a weekend retreat, challenge them to confront each other during the retreat when they hear someone giving someone else a "downer." This can cut down on negativism that often ruins youth group meetings and activities.

CHRISTIANITY

ROLE BOWL

Print up the following situations on cards and put them in a bowl. Let each person in a small group pick one out and think about it. Ask the kids to share their solutions to the situation. The more verbal kids will obviously share first. *But don't force anyone to share!* After each person finishes, allow others in the group to comment.

1. I don't get it. If Christianity is true, how come there are so many religions that call themselves Christian? I mean, what's the difference between Baptists, Presbyterians, etc.?

2. If you ask me, the Christian religion makes you a *doormat*—always loving and turning the other cheek stuff.

3. What if I lived like hell for eighty years and then became a Christian on my deathbed? Would Billy Graham and I go to the same place?

4. I have been reading through the Old Testament for English class. How come God ordered His people to kill everybody—even women and children—when they conquered a land? What kind of a God is that?

5. Your mother and I do not believe in all this Jesus stuff, and we think you spend too much time in church. So we want you to stay away from church for a while.

6. If God is God, then how come you can't see Him or it? Why don't you prove that God exists? Go ahead . . . prove it to me.

7. The Bible has some nice little stories in it, but everyone knows it's full of contradictions, errors, and myths. How can you believe it?

8. I know a bunch of people that go to your church and they are supposed to be Christians, but I also know what they do during the week and at parties that I go to. They are phonies. If Christianity is so great, how come there are so many phonies?

9. My little brother died of leukemia, and I prayed like crazy. Don't tell me there is a God who loves us. How come He didn't help my brother?

10. Look, I know I am overweight and even though it hurts me to say it, I'm ugly. And I started coming to your church because I thought the kids in your youth group would treat me differently than the kids do at school. Wrong! They ignore me and make fun of me like everyone else. How come?

THEOLOGICAL FICTIONARY

If your young people sometimes get stumped trying to figure out the meanings of those big *theological* words, here's a game that will whittle those words down to size. It's played like the game "Dictionary."

Make a list of those big words, like "justification," "atonement," "sanctification," "vicarious" and read them to the group. Taking the words one at a time, have each person come up with a definition for that word. The correct definition is not read by the leader until after everyone has given his definition. If a person is not sure, then he should make up a definition that sounds good.

Scoring is as follows:

1. For getting the correct definition—five points.

2. For each time someone agrees with your phony definition—five points.

As the game progresses, it would be wise to rotate, so each person has a chance to be the first guesser (improving his chances that someone will go along with his definition). You might allow kids to change their answers after all the definitions have been given but before the correct definition has been read. The person with the most points is the winner of the game. You'll be surprised at how ingenious your kids are when creating wild new theological definitions. You can use this game with ordinary words too.

WORD PICTURES

Here's an idea that can help your kids learn to examine Bible characters, do word studies, or dig into theological concepts.

Pass out worksheets with a word picture diagram (see sample on the next page). Have your group write a key word (any word or name you choose) in the center. Then have them look at the key word and the guide words on the outside, and ask them to write in the ovals additional descriptive words, as illustrated. Have them complete it like a word-association exercise—in other words, they should write down the first word that comes to their minds. When they're through, discuss the words they've chosen and what those words reveal about the key word. They'll not only end up with a better understanding of the key word—they'll also have learned a new approach to the study of Scripture.

CHURCH

THE GREAT FISH CONTROVERSY

The following parable is excellent for stimulating discussion about evangelism and the ministry of the church.

> For months, the Fishers' Society had been wracked with dissension. They had built a new meeting hall, which they called their Aquarium, and had even called a world renowned Fisherman's Manual scholar to lecture them on the art of fishing. But still no fish were caught. Several times each week they would gather in their ornate Aquarium Hall, recite portions of the Fisherman's Manual and then listen to their scholar exposite the intricacies and mysteries of the Manual. The meeting would usually end with the scholar dramatically casting his net into the large tank in the center of the hall and the members rushing excitedly to its edges to see if any fish would bite. None ever did, of course, since there were no fish in the tank, which brings up the reason for the controversy. Why? The temperature of the

WORD PICTURE

On this worksheet, you'll produce a Word Picture uniquely your own. You'll be surprised at how creative you really are—and at how much more you know about the key word in the middle of the picture than you thought you knew.

Directions: Write the key word in the center circle. Then look at the guide words along the outside and write a word or phrase in each outer oval that fits the "mood" of that oval. You don't have to write down synonyms all the time, or opposites either. Be creative. Some of the words you write may be positive, some may be negative. That's all right—this is *your* picture of the key word, and however you see fit to draw it is okay. Have fun!

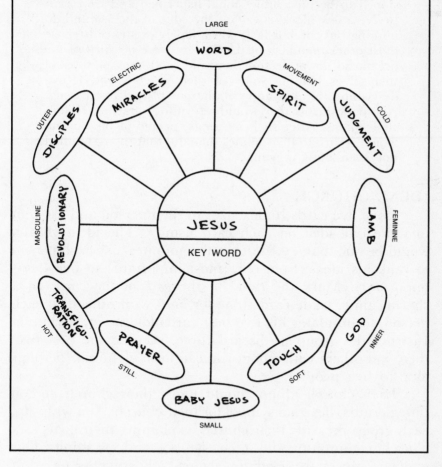

tank was carefully regulated to be just right for ocean perch. Indeed, oceanography experts had been consulted to make the environment of the tank nearly indistinguishable from the ocean. But still no fish. Some blamed it on poor attendance to the Society's meetings. Others were convinced that specialization was the answer: Perhaps several smaller tanks geared especially for different fish age groups. There was even division over which was more important: casting or providing optimum tank conditions. Eventually a solution was reached. A few members of the Society were commissioned to become professional fishermen and were sent to live a few blocks away on the edge of the sea and do nothing but catch fish. It was a lonely existence because most other members of the Society were terrified of the ocean. So the professionals would send back pictures of themselves holding some of their catches and letters describing the joys and tribulations of real live fishing. And periodically they would return to Aquarium Hall to show slides. After such meetings, people of the Society would return to their homes thankful that their Hall had not been built in vain.[2]

IDEAL CHURCH

Issue five cards (index size) to each person and ask him to write one idea on each card using, "The ideal church would be one that . . ." After a few minutes, ask each person to rank his ideas, from one (most important) to five (least important). Mark the rank on the *back* of the card. In a sharing time, trade cards (one for one) with others, so each person accumulates his five best cards for the ideal church. Instruct the group to discard three, keeping the best two, then find others with whom you can form a church (perhaps four to five people).

Each church group should name their church and, if time permits, design a symbol for their church. At a wrap-up, each group presents their church, explaining their goals as a church community and their symbol and meaning. This game is especially good for senior-high students or adult groups because it really motivates them to discuss what is important in the ideal church.

IMAGES OF THE CHURCH

The New Testament uses quite a few metaphors to describe the function of the church in the world. These metaphors are used to help us understand not only who we are as the church but also what our relationship should be to Christ and to each other.

Begin with a study of each of these word pictures of the church and then have the kids rank them from most important to least important or from best to worst. Of course, the idea is not to imply that any of the metaphors are unimportant or more important than others but simply to generate discussion. You might have the kids think of some additional metaphors, borrowing from today's culture to create their own images of the church.

Here is a list of metaphors used in the New Testament:

1. *Bride:* We are the bride; Christ is the bridegroom (see Rom. 7:4, 2 Cor. 11:2, Eph. 5:25, Rev. 19:7).

2. *Branches:* Jesus said that He is the vine, and that we are the branches (see John 15:1–8).

3. *Flock:* Jesus said that we are sheep and that He is the Good Shepherd (see John 10:11–15, also see Matt. 10:16).

4. *Kingdom:* Jesus was called the Mighty King, the King of Kings, and we are brought into His kingdom (see Col. 1:13).

5. *Family:* We are the sons and daughters of God, brothers of Christ, brothers and sisters to each other, joint heirs with Christ, the household of God (see Gal. 4:1–7, Heb. 2:10–11).

6. *A Building:* We are temples of the Holy Spirit, a building not made with hands (see 2 Cor. 5, Eph. 2:19–22).

7. *A Body:* We are all part of the body of Christ, each person being a different part of the body (see 1 Cor. 12, Eph. 4).

8. *Salt:* We are the salt of the earth (see Matt. 5:13).

9. *Light:* We are the light of the world (see Matt. 5:14).

10. *Fishermen:* Jesus calls us to be fishers of men (see Matt. 4:19).

11. *Soldiers:* We are fighting against principalities and powers, wearing the full armor of God (see Eph. 6:10–17, 1 Thess. 5:8).

THE LIFE-SAVING STATION

This is a short parable, which is great for discussion or as a simple thought-provoker on the subject of the church and the world. It may be read aloud or printed and passed out to your group, followed by a discussion using the questions that are provided. The story was written by Theodore Wedel of Washington, D.C.[1]

The Life-Saving Station

On a dangerous sea coast where shipwrecks often occur there was once a crude little life-saving station. The building was just a hut, and there was only one boat but the few devoted members kept a constant watch over the sea and with no thought for themselves, went out day and night tirelessly searching for the lost. Some of those who were saved, and various others in the surrounding area wanted to become associated with the station and give of their time and money and effort for the support of its work. New boats were bought and new crews trained. The little life-saving station grew.

Some of the members of the life-saving station were unhappy that the building was so crude and poorly equipped. They felt that a more comfortable place should be provided as the first refuge of those saved from the sea. They replaced the emergency cots with beds and put better furniture in the enlarged building. Now the life-saving station became a popular gathering place for its members, and they decorated it beautifully and furnished it exquisitely, because they used it as a sort of club. Fewer members were now interested in going to sea on life-saving missions, so they hired lifeboat crews to do this work. The life-saving motif still prevailed in this club's decoration, and there was a liturgical lifeboat in the room where the club initiations were held. About this time a large ship was wrecked off the coast, and the hired crews brought in boatloads of cold, wet, and half-drowned people. They were dirty and sick and some of them had black skin and some had yellow skin. The beautiful new club was in chaos. So the property committee immediately had a shower house built outside the club where victims of shipwreck could be cleaned up before coming inside.

At the next meeting, there was a split in the club membership. Most of the members wanted to stop the club's life-saving activities as being unpleasant and a hindrance to the normal social life of the club. Some members insisted upon life-saving as their primary purpose and pointed out that they were still called a life-saving station. But they were finally voted down and told that if they wanted to save lives of all the various kinds of people who were shipwrecked in those waters, they could begin their own life-saving station down the coast. They did.

As the years went by, the new station experienced the same changes that had occurred in the old. It evolved into a club, and yet another life-saving station was founded. History continued to repeat itself, and if you visit that sea coast today, you will find a number of exclusive clubs along that shore. Shipwrecks are frequent in those waters, but most of the people drown.

QUESTIONS FOR DISCUSSION
1. When was the Life-Saving Station most effective?

2. Where did the Life-Saving Station go wrong?

3. How is the church like a Life-Saving Station? What is the purpose of the church?

4. Is growth always good or desirable?

5. Is growth inevitable if needs are being met?

6. If you don't like the church as it is now, what alternatives do you have?

7. What should the church do with all its money?

8. How can the problems that the Life-Saving Station experienced be avoided in the church? What should the Life-Saving Station have done?

9. Is the church necessary for being a Christian?

10. What are your church's good points? Bad points?

11. If you could write a "moral" for the Life-Saving Station story, what would it be?

DEATH

DEATH FANTASY

Here is a list of questions that have been used effectively to help young people express their feelings about death and dying. By using fantasy or make-believe, young people very often surface their hidden or subconscious feelings about death. These questions can be either a written quiz or a discussion.

1. How do you most frequently see yourself dying?

2. Who died the way you expect to die?

3. What, to you, would be the worst possible way to die? The best possible way?

4. What habits or characteristics of your life may influence the way you die?

5. When do you think you will die? When would you like to die?

6. What is your predominant attitude or feeling about death (defiance, acceptance, fear, longing, curiosity, avoidance)?

7. Imagine you died yesterday . . . what would things be like?

8. What are you doing now to help lengthen your life? Shorten your life?

9. What do you want to accomplish before you die?

Other optional questions:

1. Describe how you reacted to the death of someone

you knew. Did you feel anger, fear, relief, sorrow, pity, frustration?

2. Whose death would bring you the greatest sorrow? The greatest pleasure?

3. Who would care the most if you died? What would they do?

4. Describe your funeral.

5. What would you have inscribed on your tombstone?

RUN FOR YOUR LIFE

Although this activity deals with the subject of death, it is really about life and how we live it. The purpose of this exercise is to help young people evaluate their priorities in light of what is really important. It allows the group to contrast what they are doing now with what they would do if they only had one month to live. Give each person in the group a list similar to the one below.

If I had only one month to live, I would ...

1. Perform some high-risk feat that I have always wanted to do, figuring that if I don't make it, it won't really matter.

2. Stage an incredible robbery for a large amount of money that I would immediately give to the needy and starving of the world.

3. Not tell anyone.

4. Use my dilemma to present the gospel to as many people as I could.

5. Spend all my time in prayer and Bible reading.

6. Make my own funeral arrangements.

7. Offer myself to science or medicine to be used for experiments that might have fatal results.

8. Have as much fun as possible (sex, parties, booze, whatever turns me on).

9. Travel around the world and see as much as possible.

10. Buy lots of stuff on credit that I've always wanted

(expensive cars, fancy clothes, exotic food, etc.) and say to myself, *Sorry, the deceased left no forwarding address.*

11. Spend my last month with my family or close personal friends.

12. Not do anything much different, just go on as always.

13. Isolate myself from everyone, find a remote place, and meditate.

14. Write a book about my life (or last month).

15. Sell all my possessions and give the money to my family, friends, or others who need it.

16. Try to accomplish as many worthwhile projects as possible.

Have the group rank these alternatives (plus any they wish to add) with the first item on their list being the one they would probably do and the last being the one they would probably not do. Ask everyone to share and explain choices, and then discuss the results with the entire group. Another variation is to evaluate the alternatives by putting each one on a continuum. On one end of the continuum would be "Yes, definitely" and on the other end, "Absolutely not." After each alternative is placed on the continuum, compare and discuss with the rest of the group.

Yes, definitely   Absolutely not

DISCIPLESHIP

COST OF DISCIPLESHIP

The following is a list of five New Testament Scriptures significant to the meaning of discipleship. The questions under each passage are excellent discussion starters to help your group focus on the main issue of each passage. This exercise is most effectively done with groups of five to ten people.

Pass out a copy of the following questions and have each young person circle what he considers to be the best answer for each question or write an answer if he feels none of the ones provided are sufficient.

READ LUKE 9:23–25
1. For me, taking up my cross daily means
   a. to do things I hate to do
   b. to face death
   c. to be teased because I am a Christian
   d. to accept anything that God desires of me as part of His plan for my life
   e. none of the above
   f. _____
2. Denying self means denying anything that would prevent complete commitment to Christ. For me this has meant
   a. nothing because I haven't made this type of commitment yet
   b. nothing because I don't understand how to do this
   c. attempting to quit being lazy at work, at home, at school, or at church
   d. not trying so hard by myself and letting Christ take over
   e. giving up my favorite TV show on Thursday to come to this meeting
   f. _____

READ JOHN 17:13–24
1. Being "one" here means
   a. doing things together
   b. never disagreeing—always accepting another's viewpoint

      c. learning to love, share, and work closely with each other

      d. _____

   2. This oneness can be achieved by

      a. denying self—sharing our gut feelings with each other

      b. agreeing with others

      c. getting to know others in the group better

      d. it's too difficult, so I won't try

      e. _____

READ JOHN 13:34–35 AND 1 JOHN 3:23, 24

   1. This type of love means

      a. action—sharing myself with others

      b. attitude—finding the good in other people

      c. love—caring enough to help people with their problems

      d. all of the above

      e. _____

   2. For me, a personal relationship with God means.

      a. asking Christ to forgive me

      b. having visions of God talking to me

      c. accepting Christ as my best friend

      d. won't really happen till heaven

      e. _____

READ 1 CORINTHIANS 15:49 AND 1 JOHN 3:2

Becoming like Christ means

      a. sinning less and less

      b. learning to love as Christ loved

      c. learning to minister better for Christ

      d. growing in knowledge of God and the Bible

      e. _____

DEAR ABBY

    Occasionally young people encounter situations where they would like advice in a Christian atmosphere but are embarrassed about bringing their questions openly before their peers. This activity not only gives the group a chance to help each other (their advice might be better than an adult's), but also gives them a chance to see that others are having problems very similar to their own.

Give each young person a piece of paper and a pencil and instruct them to write, in letter form, some problem that is bothering them—a family problem, a school problem, or a problem that requires Christian advice. The letter should be addressed to "Dear Abby" to give them the feeling of appealing to some uninvolved source and signed with an anonymous signature ("Concerned" or "Wants to Know"). Collect the letters and read them to the group for their advice.

TOM MEETS GOD

Here's a short skit with a message. It requires three players and should be well rehearsed before presentation to the group. After the skit, discuss what happened. Although the skit itself is short, the issues raised are worthwhile.

Tom: *(Knocks and an angel opens the door)* Hi! My name is Tom. I would like to see the person in charge, please.

Angel: Sure, come in.

Tom: Look . . . I know this guy is really important, but do you think He would see someone like me.

Angel: He sees everyone. You can see Him any time you'd like.

Tom: Could I see Him now?

Angel: Go right in.

Tom: Now?

Angel: Yes.

Tom: *(Hesitates and then slowly walks in)* Uh, excuse me, my name is Tom. I wondered if I could see you for a few minutes?

191

God: My name is God, and I've got all the time you need.

Tom: Well, I'm going to high school right now, and I am a little confused about what I should do. . . . A couple of my friends say You can help, but they seem just as confused as I am. To be honest, I haven't really been impressed by Your work. I mean, don't get me wrong, my friends are really good friends, you know, and they really seem to like me, but they haven't got it so good. Bob, one of my friends, has a dad that is an alcoholic, and my other friend's folks are getting a divorce. The crazy thing is my folks are great; I really love them. Everything's going great . . . except . . . except I can't seem to see the purpose of my life. In spite of all the junk that is happening to my friends, they really seem to be convinced that You are important. So that's why I'm here. I just thought You could give me some pointers. I just feel kinda lost.

God: My price is high.

Tom: That's okay because my folks are pretty well off. What is it?

God: All.

Tom: All?

God: Yes, All—everything.

Tom: Sheesh. Don't You have a lay-a-way plan? How about a pay-as-you-go plan? Isn't your profit margin a little high?

God: Actually, My cost was quite high also . . . ask My Son.

Tom: Well, I think I'll have to wait awhile. I appreciate Your taking the time to talk to me and I'm sure You're worth it, but it's just that at my age, it's a little too soon to give up everything. After all, when you're young, that's when the good times happen. Besides, I think I can get what I'm looking for at a much cheaper price.

God: Be careful, Tom. The price may be cheaper, but your cost may be much higher than you think.

Tom: Yeah, sure. Well, nice talking to You, God. Maybe I'll see you around some time.

God: Yes, Tom, and there's no maybe about it.

DIVORCE

DIVORCE PANEL

Here's a program that can help your kids develop a more realistic picture of the effects of divorce than they usually get from TV or the movies. It can teach them how to help a friend whose parents are divorced or divorcing. It's also a supportive experience for kids whose parents are already divorced.

First, ask several kids whose parents are divorced to serve on your "panel of experts." Give them a list of potential questions in advance to help them decide whether they can handle the experience; allow them to decline if they decide it would be too tough on them.

The adult who moderates the panel should be carefully chosen—someone sensitive to the pain most children of divorce experience. Make sure the moderator reads up ahead of time on the effects of divorce on children. Besides the books on the subject available in your local library, a number of articles have appeared in both Christian and secular publications.

Here are some sample questions for the panel:

1. How did you find out about your parents' decision to divorce? Did the way in which you were told help or hinder your acceptance of the divorce?

2. What kinds of feelings did you (or do you) have about the divorce?

3. Did your role in the family change after the divorce? How?

4. What kinds of things did friends do or say in

response to the divorce? What do you *wish* they had done or said?

This can be a powerful and instructive program for both the audience and the panel.

DRUGS AND ALCOHOL

IT'S YOUR DECISION

Use this story as a discussion starter. Tell the story first, then lead a group in discussing the dilemma, using the questions below.[3]

> A friend whose parents left for the weekend has thrown a party. There must be at least fifty people in the living room. You and your friend Chris are having a great time talking to your friends and listening to music. Someone begins smoking marijuana. You want to leave, but Chris says there is no reason to since you are not the ones smoking dope.

What would you do?

Reason:

What should you do?

Reason:

Scriptures for further study: Psalm 1; Proverbs 13:20; 1 Corinthians 8, 10:23–24.

ETHICS, VALUES, MORALITY

LIFE AUCTION

Divide your group into smaller groups and give each group a copy of the paper below. After each group finishes their sheet, bidding begins. When the auction is over, the whole group then discusses and evaluates what happened. The items below can be adapted to fit your particular group.

LIFE AUCTION

You have received $5,000 and can spend the money any way you desire. Budget the money in the column labeled "Amount Budgeted." We will then bid on each item auction-style. Enter the highest amount you bid for each item in the "Amount Bid" column. You don't need to bid on every item. For those items you actually buy in our auction, enter the amount you pay in the "Amount Spent" column. It is your goal to gain the things you most desire.

	Amount Budgeted	Amount Bid	Amount Spent
1. To have a wonderful family life without any hassles			
2. To have all the money I need to be happy			

	Amount Budgeted	Amount Bid	Amount Spent
3. To never be sick			
4. To find the right mate, who is good-looking and fulfills me			
5. To never have pimples			
6. To be able to do whatever I want whenever I want			
7. To have all the power the president of a country has			
8. To be the best-looking person			
9. To have a real hunger to always read the Bible			
10. To be able to understand all things			
11. To eliminate all hunger and disease in the world			
12. To always be close to God			
13. To never feel lonely or put-down			
14. To always be happy and peaceful			
15. To never feel hurt			
16. To own a beautiful home, car, boat, plane, and seven motorcycles, one for each day of the week			
17. To be super smart without ever having to attend school			
18. To be able to excel and be superior in all things			

	Amount Budgeted	Amount Bid	Amount Spent
19. To be filled with God's presence in the most dynamic way			
20. To always know that you are in God's will			
21. To be the greatest athlete in the world			
22. To be admired by everyone else			
23. To become a star on a popular TV show			
24. To always have a lot of close friends who never let you down			
25. To walk close to God			

MONITORING YOUR MORALS

The following are true-false questions to be answered individually by the members of the group, then discussed collectively by the entire group. Explain that the answers given should be honest opinion, not answers that might be considered *correct* by the church or youth director. Be prepared to work through each question thoroughly in the discussion period.

1. Overeating is as wrong as smoking or drinking. _____

2. While your father was walking home from work one night, a robber came from the shadows and demanded all his money. Your father gave his wallet to the robber. He looked in the wallet and asked, "Is this all the money you have?" Your father said, "Yes." The thief ran away satisfied, but your father had lied to the thief. He had a twenty tucked away in his shirt pocket. This was wrong. _____

3. To goof off on your job is the same as to steal money from your boss. _____

197

4. There are degrees of sin with God, and He won't punish us for the little ones. _____

5. Killing a man is justified when a person is called by his government to defend his country. _____

6. As Christians, we are to obey all people who are in a position of authority over us—police officers, parents, teachers, youth directors, etc. _____

7. You are late for church, so instead of driving at the speed limit, you speed. Because you are going to church, this is not wrong. _____

8. Going into your history final, you are just squeezing by with a C. Passing or failing this test could mean the difference between passing or failing the course. There are several questions you don't know, so you look on your neighbor's paper (an A student) and copy from him. When you get your graded paper back, you find you would have flunked without the correct answers from your neighbor's paper. Cheating was justified in this case. _____

9. You are very much in love with your girl friend and plan to get married. On a date, you get carried away, and she gets pregnant. Because you love her as your wife, sex was not wrong. _____

10. There is a guy at school who really gets on your nerves. If there were ever a person you hated, it would be this guy. The feeling you have for him is as wrong as if you had killed him. _____

PROBLEM HOT LINE

Have the group sit in a circle with two chairs back to back in the center of the circle. Choose two people—one to be the hot line worker, the other a caller with a problem—to sit in the center. (It is important that the worker and caller remain back to back.) The worker leaves the room while the group leader assigns a problem to the caller. When the worker returns, the caller pretends to call the worker and explains his problem. The group leader is responsible for cutting off the mock call at the proper time and leading a discussion with the rest of the group about how the problem might be solved. Here are some sample problems:

1. I am not very attractive. People avoid me, and I can tell that most of the people I know make fun of me behind my back. Frankly, I'm ugly. I know it, so does everyone else. What can I do?

2. My parents make me go to church. I like the youth program, but the worship service is a drag. Our minister is irrelevant and boring, and the services don't relate to me at all.

3. My mother is dying of cancer. Every day I am faced with cancer's ugly and depressing toll on my mom. I am forced to accept more and more of her responsibilities at home. But I like to go out with my friends, too. I feel guilty when I go somewhere and have a good time, but if I stay home, I get angry and frustrated. What's the answer?

4. I have always been told that kids who smoke grass and drink really don't enjoy it. I have refrained from doing those things partly because I believed that and partly because I didn't think it was a Christian thing to do—at least until a few weeks ago. I tried pot and drinking, and it was great. I never had so much fun in my life. How can something that feels so good be bad? Were the people who told me how bad these things are lying?

VALUES TEASERS

Here are some values clarification stories that can help your youth group find out what they believe.

THE TALKING FRIEND

A good friend of yours and you are both equally unprepared for a test, and together you cheat and pass. Your friend, however, begins to feel guilty about it and confesses to the teacher. During the confession, your friend implicates you as well, and you both automatically fail the test.

1. Should the friend have confessed?

2. Couldn't the friend just have confessed to God and not the teacher?

3. Should the friend have told the teacher about you?

THE BORROWING BROTHER

You and your brother share the same bedroom. You have made it very clear to your brother that he is to leave your belongings alone. You have a large record collection and a stereo, which you purchased with your own money. You come home from school one day and find many of your best records out getting dust on them and your favorite record sitting on the window sill getting warped by the sun. You blow up at your brother, and he apologizes and offers to buy a new record, but you're still furious. You threaten to tell your parents about it and refuse to accept his apology. You tell him to get out of your room. Finally he has enough and says to you, "I know that you have been seeing Linda even though Mom and Dad told you not to. You have been telling the folks that you get off work at ten but you really get off at nine. And if you keep yelling at me and threatening me, I'm going to tell them what I know."

1. What's wrong with not wanting to let others use valuable possessions that might be wrecked?

2. Which person in this situation is acting worse? Why?

3. Is blackmail wrong?

THE CHANGING PARENTS

One evening a couple of your friends come by, and you decide to attend a movie the next weekend. You ask your parents, and although they have never heard of the movie, they give their permission. The next Friday night your friends come to the house to pick you up, and your folks ask where you are going. You remind them that they gave you permission to go to a movie. Your dad responds, "Well, I did some checking, and I was going to talk to you, but I forgot you were going tonight. From what my friends tell me the movie is no good. It contains a lot of profanity and explicit sex, so I don't want you to see it. Sorry, but you can't go." Your friends look at each other with shock and amazement. They can't believe it. Just as they leave, you see them smile at each other as if they think your folks are real losers. You are embarrassed, humiliated, and angry.

1. Did the parents do the right thing?

2. Do parents have the right to change their minds at the last minute?

3. If you were a parent, how would you have handled the situation?

4. If your parents had done something like that, how would you have responded?

THE WINDOW
Read or tell the following story to the group.

THE WINDOW

There were once two men, Mr. Wilson and Mr. Thompson, both seriously ill in the same room of a large hospital. Quite a small room, just large enough for the pair of them. Two beds, two bedside lockers, a door opening on the hall, and one window looking out on the world.

Mr. Wilson, as part of his treatment, was allowed to sit up in bed for an hour in the afternoon (something to do with draining the fluid from his lungs). His bed was next to the window. But Mr. Thompson had to spend all of his time flat on his back. Both of them had to be kept quiet and still, which was the reason they were in the small room by themselves. They were grateful for the peace and privacy, though. None of the bustle and clatter and prying eyes of the general ward for them. Of course, one of the disadvantages of their condition was that they weren't allowed to do much—no reading, no radio, certainly no television. They had to keep quiet and still, just the two of them.

201

They used to talk for hours and hours—about their wives, their children, their homes, their jobs, their hobbies, their childhood, what they did during the war, where they'd been on vacations, all that sort of thing. Every afternoon, when Mr. Wilson, the man by the window, was propped up for his hour, he would pass the time by describing what he could see outside. And Mr. Thompson began to live for those hours.

The window apparently overlooked a park with a lake where there were ducks and swans, children throwing them bread and sailing model boats, and young lovers walking hand-in-hand beneath the trees. And there were flowers and stretches of grass, games of softball, people resting in the sunshine, and behind the fringe of trees, there was a fine view of the city skyline. Mr. Thompson would listen to all of this, enjoying every minute—how a child nearly fell into the lake, how beautiful the girls were in their summer dresses, then an exciting ball game, or a boy playing with his puppy. He could almost see what was happening outside.

Then one fine afternoon when there was some sort of a parade, he thought to himself: *Why should Wilson, next to the window, have all the pleasure of seeing what was going on? Why shouldn't I get the chance?* He felt ashamed and tried not to think those thoughts, but the more he tried, the worse he wanted a change. He would do anything! In a few days, he had turned sour. *I should be by the window,* he brooded. He couldn't sleep and grew even more seriously ill, which the doctors just couldn't understand.

One night as he stared at the ceiling, Mr. Wilson suddenly woke up, coughing and choking from the fluid congesting in his lungs, his hands groping for the call button that would bring the night nurse running. But Mr. Thompson watched without moving. The coughing racked the darkness. On and on he choked, then stopped. The sound of breathing stopped. Mr. Thompson continued to stare at the ceiling.

In the morning, the day nurse came in with water for their baths and found Mr. Wilson dead. They took his body away quietly with no fuss.

As soon as it seemed decent, Mr. Thompson asked if he could be moved to the bed next to the window. So they moved him, tucked him in, made him quite comfortable, and left him alone to be quiet and still. The minute they'd gone, he propped himself up on one elbow, painfully and laboriously, and strained as he looked out the window. It faced a blank wall!

This beautiful story is not only an excellent illustration for talking with a youth group about a variety of subjects but lends itself easily to good discussion possibilities. The following questions raise some of the issues but are only suggestions, which do not have to be followed in any order or at all. Feel free to develop your own.

1. What was your initial reaction to the story? Were you shocked? surprised? angry?

2. Describe Mr. Wilson. What kind of man does he appear to be? Do you like or dislike him? Why?

3. Describe Mr. Thompson. What kind of person is he? Do you like or dislike him?

4. Why did Mr. Wilson do what he did? What do you think his motives were?

5. Mr. Wilson's "descriptions" of what was outside the window were (a) lies (b) creative imagination (c) unselfish concern for Mr. Thompson (d) cruel and envy-producing (e) _____

6. Did Mr. Wilson do anything wrong?

7. Why did Mr. Thompson's mood change from enjoyment and appreciation to resentment? Was his resentment justified?

8. Did Mr. Thompson murder Mr. Wilson?

9. Who was guilty of the more serious wrong—Mr. Wilson or Mr. Thompson?

10. Who was most responsible for Mr. Wilson's death? Why?

11. Would both men have been better off without Mr. Wilson's describing the view outside the window?

12. If you had been Mr. Thompson, how would you have felt when you finally looked out the window and saw nothing but a blank wall? (a) disappointed (b) angry (c) guilty (d) grieved (e) grateful (f) puzzled (g) shocked

13. Is it a sin to fantasize?

14. Is it a sin to hide the truth or to exaggerate when it doesn't hurt anyone?

15. Where do you draw the line in the areas of fantasy and imagination?

HUNGER, JUSTICE

LETTER TO AMOS

After a study of the Book of Amos, pass out copies of this letter to Amos and discuss the arguments presented. Some suggested questions for discussion follow.

Dear Mr. Amos,

Your intemperate criticisms of the merchants of Bethel show that you have little understanding of the operations of a modern business economy. You appear not to understand that a businessman is entitled to a profit. After all, a cobbler sells shoes to make as much money as he can; a banker lends money to get a return on his loan. These are not charitable enterprises. Without profits, a tradesman cannot stay in business.

Your slanders also reveal a lack of appreciation for the many contributions made to our land by the business community. Visitors to Israel are greatly impressed by the progress made in the past few decades. The beautiful public buildings and private homes are a proud monument. Increasing contacts with foreign lands add to the cultural opportunities open to our citizens. Our military strength makes us the envy of peoples already swallowed up by their enemies.

Despite the great gains during Jeroboam II's reign, there is some poverty. That we admit. But is it fair to blame us for the inability of some people to compete? You say that the peasants were cheated out of their lands. Not so! They sold their property. Or in some cases, it was sold for back taxes. Some peasants put up the land as collateral on a loan, then failed to meet the payments. No one was cheated. The transactions to which you refer were entirely legal. Had you taken the trouble to investigate the facts, your conclusions would have been more accurate.

The real reason for poverty is lack of initiative. People who get ahead in this world work hard, take risks, overcome obstacles. Dedication and determination are the keys to success. Opportunities don't knock; they are created by imagination and industry.

Our success can be an inspiration to the poor. If we can make it, they can too. With the growth of business, Israel grows. More jobs, better pay, and increased opportunity for everyone. This old saying contains more than a germ of truth: What's good for General Chariots is good for the country.

Yours for Israel,

DISCUSSION QUESTIONS

1. Evaluate the merchant's arguments in light of justice. At what points do the businessmen convince or fail to convince you?

2. Suppose this letter were written today—how would you react? Where do the rights of the individual stop? Can justice be administered without striking a balance between individual rights and rights of the community?

3. What about Justice—Just us or Just U.S.?

UNDINNER FOR WORLD HUNGER

This is a good meal idea to help your group become aware of the world hunger problem that could become an annual event. The following entrees (and others) can be displayed on a buffet with signs indicating price values. It should be explained that everyone can order their choice— 13¢ worth of food, representing the daily food budget of many in the world.

After the dinner, discuss the problems of world hunger and your own personal involvement. The price of a regular

205

dinner can be charged as admission, and the difference between it and the Undinner can be given to Bread for the World or World Vision for distribution.

Menu

Water—1¢

Coffee—6¢ a cup

Sugar—2¢

Milk—2¢

Saltines—1¢ each

American cheese—6¢

Radishes—1¢ a serving

Olives—2¢ each

Orange slices—8¢ each

Hard-boiled eggs—6¢ each

Carrots—3¢ a serving

Sweet pickles—2¢ a serving

Raisins—9¢ a serving

Cookies—3¢ each

MARRIAGE

DATING DATA

This activity provides a good opportunity for kids to express their values and opinions about dating in a relaxed and natural way. Place the following assignments around the room, providing blank paper, felt-tip markers, and resource materials at each station. Ask the kids to choose and complete as many assignments as possible in the time allowed. They may work together in small groups or individually. At the end of the time limit, call for reports and discuss the findings.

ASSIGNMENTS

1. Write a plan for two people who like each other to get together.

2. Devise a foolproof method for deciding the difference between love and infatuation.

3. List at least 20 fun things to do on a date. Each must cost less than $10.00 total.

4. List five guidelines for making a date successful.

5. What advice would you give a Christian who has a

crush on a non-Christian? Include the pros and cons of dating a non-Christian.

6. Write a plan for breaking up in the least painful and most healthy way.

7. List the number of people you tell about your dates and write out 10 pros and cons for talking about your dates.

QUESTIONS FOR DISCUSSION
1. Why do some people seem to date "below" themselves (put up with anger, being used, disrespect, etc.)?

2. Why do some youth find romance earlier than others?

3. How can we be more comfortable on dates?

4. Should girls ask guys out?

PERFECT PAIR
To initiate a good discussion about family and to discover the kids' values, try this activity. Divide into small groups and tell the kids to find the world's most perfect couple, that is, the man and woman best suited to create the ideal home and family and most likely to be happy. Then have them describe their perfect couple. Here are some things to consider:

The items listed are only suggestions, and kids can add to the list. After twenty or thirty minutes of working in their groups, have each describe their perfect couple. Write the descriptions on a blackboard or on an overhead projector. Compare each group's description of their couple. Discuss the differences and similarities, ask *why* certain characteristics were selected, talk about prejudices, and then relate all of these to Scripture. How does God describe His perfect family? What matters and what doesn't? Then discuss the interaction that took place in each small group—the disputes, differences of opinion, prejudices, etc. There are hours of healthy discussion in this activity.

1. The couple themselves
   a. background
   b. age
   c. education
   d. religious affiliation
   e. race
   f. political views

2. Their lifestyle
   a. jobs (employment)
   b. hobbies
   c. sex life
   d. leisure time
   e. entertainment
   f. habits
   g. friends and associations

3. Their possessions
   a. money
   b. furniture
   c. house and neighborhood
   d. books, magazines
   e. appliances
   f. recreational needs
   g. auto(s)

4. Philosophy on child rearing
   a. discipline
   b. education
   c. manners
   d. dress
   e. independence

TO MARRY OR NOT TO MARRY

The following questionnaire is very helpful as a discussion starter on the subject of marriage. Distribute the questionnaires and give the group enough time to think through their answers. Then discuss each question and try to come up with a group consensus. Encourage each person to answer the questions honestly, rather than answering them the way the church, or their parents, or tradition would want them to answer.

1. I think everyone ought to get married. (Put an X on the continuum.)

YES   NO
|_____|

2. I think generally the best age for marriage would be (circle the best answer)
   Girls—16 17 18 19 20 21 22 23 24 25 26 27 28 29 30
        Over 30
   Boys—16 17 18 19 20 21 22 23 24 25 26 27 28 29 30
        Over 30

3. When you are married, are you considered an adult, regardless of age?
(Circle one)   YES   NO

4. What do you think of the following statement: "God has made one special person in the world for you to marry"? (Put an X on the continuum.)

Strongly Agree   Strongly Disagree

5. Marriage is (rank these from 1 to 5)
A legal statement
A social custom
God ordained
A religious ceremony
A parent pleaser

6. Most people get married because (rank these from 1 to 5)
They have to
They want to have kids
They love each other
They want tax benefits
Sex

7. Our concept of marriage is most influenced by (pick top three)
Friends
Television
Movies
Other adults
Parents
Church
Books
Celebrities
Tradition

8. What are the top priorities in marriage? (Rank from 1 to 10.)

> Children
> Sex
> Communication
> Mutual trust/confidence in the other person
> Religion/faith
> Mutual interests
> Finances/security
> In-law relationships
> Faithfulness
> Romantic love

9. Divorce is wrong (choose the best answer or answers)
   > Always (no exceptions)
   > Except when adultery is involved
   > Except when both are incompatible
   > Except when you don't love each other anymore

10. Divorce is (choose the best answer or answers)
    > Better than living together when you hate each other
    > A necessary evil
    > A possibility for any one of us
    > A cop-out
    > Never okay when children are involved
    > Sin

11. Living together (not married) is (put an X on the continuum)

WRONG   OKAY
|——|

12. Living together (not married) is (choose best answer or answers)
    > Better than traditional custom of dating
    > The best way to determine if marriage will last

Is not the same as marriage
Is more acceptable than marriage
Is the best alternative to marriage
None of the above

TWENTY-FIVE-CENT MATE

Give each person a copy of the questionnaire below and enough time to fill it out completely. Then discuss each person's answers and why he answered as he did.

Name: _____

You may spend twenty-five cents to buy a mate. Select all the qualities you wish from the list but do not spend over twenty-five cents. Put the amount in the blank at the right. In the center column, spend twenty-five cents on yourself to be the kind of person you wish to be.

Each of this group costs 6 cents
    A good-looking face   ____ ____
    Very popular   ____ ____
    Quite intelligent   ____ ____
    A great Christian   ____ ____
    Very kind   ____ ____

Each of these costs 5 cents
    A well-built figure and body   ____ ____
    A good conversationalist   ____ ____
    Tactful and considerate   ____ ____
    Happy and good sense of humor   ____ ____

Each of this group costs 4 cents
    Large chest or bust   ____ ____
    Likes sports   ____ ____
    Attends church—is religious   ____ ____
    Honest—doesn't lie or cheat   ____ ____

Each of this group costs 3 cents
    Nicely dressed and well groomed   ____ ____
    Likes drama, art, and music   ____ ____

Well-mannered—comes from nice home   ____   ____
Ambitious and hard-working   ____   ____

Each of this group costs 2 cents
The right height   ____   ____
Gets good grades   ____   ____
Likes children   ____   ____
Brave—stands up for rights   ____   ____

Each of this group costs 1 cent
Choice of color in eyes and hair   ____   ____
Owns a car   ____   ____
Wealthy—or moderately wealthy '   ____   ____
Sincere and serious   ____   ____

MISSION AND SERVICE

ADOPT A GRANDPARENT

This service project is great for young people who are mature enough to make a relatively long-term commitment to something. The first step is to take the entire group to visit a convalescent home or the homes of elderly people who are alone. Allow the kids to mingle and talk with these people, so that they get to know them better.

Afterward, introduce them to the idea of adopting one or more of these seniors as a grandparent. Each young person would be assigned (or would choose) one or two elderly people to visit on a regular basis, to remember on special occasions, to take on short trips now and then, and to be a good friend to. The adoption should be planned to continue for a specific amount of time, perhaps a year or maybe even longer.

During the course of the program, the young people could share with each other how things are going and what problems they are encountering. The youth sponsors would monitor the program and offer help and encouragement to the kids who are involved. At the end of the term, or at least

212

once a year, the group could sponsor a special banquet or some other gathering where each young person brings his grandparent. Of course, there would be some people who are unable to attend because they are confined to beds or nursing care, but there would be others who could attend. Most young people will find this to be a very rewarding experience, and the elderly people involved will appreciate it greatly.

BIG BROTHERS, BIG SISTERS

Your high school and college young people may want to become "big brothers" or "big sisters" to children in your church or neighborhood who don't have "real" older brothers and sisters. That could be as simple as getting to know them by name and making a point to welcome them each Sunday at church or to pay special attention to them in some other way. It might include visiting them at home regularly, planning special activities for the two of them, or picking them up for Sunday school. The teens could teach the children a skill or talent—drawing, playing the guitar, fishing, carpentry, or cooking. It's a wonderful way for your youth to be positive role models for younger kids. •

BREAD-BAKING BASH

Have the kids in your youth group gather up all the ingredients they need to bake up lots of bread—both loaves and rolls. Then have a Saturday of bread baking—preparing the dough, getting it into pans, and then letting it rise.

The kids get free time or organized fun and games while things are in the oven. When the bread is finished, serve some lunch—hot soup and freshly baked bread. (You might have everyone bring a can of soup—any kind—and mix it all together.) After lunch, wrap the other loaves (make *lots* more bread than the kids can eat) and visit the homes of some elderly people in the church. Spend a short time visiting with them and leave them with a homemade loaf of bread and a note of appreciation—"Thanks for being a part of our church family." They'll love it, and it helps to build relationships between the young and the old. You could conclude the day with a discussion of what happened while visiting the elderly and maybe a Bible lesson relating to "bread."

CONVALESCENT HOME MINISTRY

There are hundreds of thousands of elderly people who reside in convalescent hospitals (nursing homes) all over the country. Most of them are there because they need regular medical or nursing care. These resident hospitals provide youth groups with a tremendous opportunity for service. There are probably several convalescent homes close to your church or community that would love to have your group involved in some kind of voluntary service.

Every convalescent home has an "activities director" who will gladly give you information and help you plan whatever you choose to do. Begin by contacting the activities director or the administrator of the convalescent home to find out whether the services of your group will be welcomed. It's unlikely that you'll be turned down. Most convalescent homes have a hard time finding people to come in and do good things for their patients, and they especially enjoy having young people come. If you're interested, the activities director will usually be willing to attend a meeting of your youth group to prepare them for visits to the convalescent home.

Even though convalescent homes take care of people who are losing many of their physical abilities (hearing, walking, sight), they are basically normal human beings— just very old. They enjoy being around other people, they respond to a smile, a touch, kind words, music, and laughter—things that your group can provide for these men and women who often feel isolated from the outside world. Here's a list of ideas:

1. *Begin some one-on-one visits,* perhaps as part of an

"Adopt a Grandparent" program (see page 212). These visits can include conversation, reading aloud (sometimes older folks need someone to read their mail to them, or the newspaper, or the Bible, or other books), writing letters for them, or just being a good listener.

2. Take them on short trips. Most residents of convalescent homes are permitted to leave the hospital for field trips—to go to a restaurant, a movie, a high school football game, or to church. You'll need to arrange it ahead of time with the hospital, of course, but it's worth the trouble—the patients love it. Some convalescent homes will plan their own outings for the patients, like going to the zoo or to a shopping center, if they have sufficient volunteer help to push the patients around in their wheelchairs. Your group can be a big help in this way. And when your young people have an extra half-hour—on the way home from school, maybe—sometimes the older folks enjoy having someone push them around the block, or even around the parking lot. Activities that everyone else takes for granted are available to convalescent home residents only when someone takes the time to help—and they are grateful.

3. Call them on the phone. Most of the residents of convalescent homes enjoy talking to someone who is interested in them. When your kids have established a face-to-face relationship with an older person in a convalescent home, calling those older folks regularly can be important to them. And it's best if it works both ways—with the kids calling the residents, and the residents knowing that they are free to call their young friends anytime.

4. Bring programs to the convalescent home. This can include, for instance, special music, plays, and skits. You might even consider using the meeting hall at a local nursing home for your regular youth group meeting, and allowing the patients to participate. Another idea is to provide a regular Bible Study for the convalescent home. Discuss these ideas with the activities director.

5. Provide music for the patients. If you have any young people with musical talent, encourage them to share their music with the elderly at a convalescent home. Especially liked are the old hymns and the old songs, but almost anything is appreciated.

6. Play games with them. Most of the patients can play games like Scrabble, checkers, and dominoes. And there are a number of not-too-active group games older people enjoy, too.

7. Give them gifts. Like most people, the elderly enjoy receiving gifts of love now and then. A baseball cap to protect their heads when they go outside, a pouch they can hang on the side of their wheelchair to keep things in, a small bouquet of flowers, a book or tape—gifts like these are appropriate and appreciated. They also enjoy giving gifts—and they will.

8. Bring pets or small children to the convalescent home. Most of the residents have almost forgotten what it feels like to hold a small puppy or a kitten, or to touch a small child. Something as ordinary as that can be a major source of joy for an elderly person confined to a nursing home.

9. Plant a garden for the patients. If you can find a suitable small plot of ground near the convalescent home, prepare the soil and plant a garden. Let the patients choose what they would like to plant, and let them help plant and take care of it as they are able. Many of them will look forward each day to going out and watering their tomato plant and watching it grow.

There is really no limit to the helpful things you can do in a convalescent home—just think creatively. What is important is that we do respond to this crucial need just next door. If you aren't aware of any convalescent homes in your area, check the yellow pages, your local doctor, or contact the American Health Care Association, 1200 Fifteenth Street, N.W., Washington, D.C., 20005 for a listing of local and state nursing home associations.

CREATIVE CANNED FOOD DRIVES

Collecting canned goods (or other nonperishable food items) for distribution to needy families is always a useful activity for young people. Here are several creative ways to do it and have fun at the same time.

1. Have a "Can-Collecting Contest." Divide the entire group into teams and send them into the neighborhood for a limited time (like one hour) to collect canned goods. The group with the most cans collected inside the time limit wins. It's amazing how many canned goods your kids can collect when the motivation is a contest of some kind. And for some reason, people respond more when they can help someone win a contest.

2. Have a "Scavenger Food Hunt." Give kids a list of nonperishable food items that they need to find and bring back within a given time limit. They can't buy them—all food items must be donated by other people. Assign each item a particular number of points according to its scarcity. The more of a particular item they bring back, the more points they get. In other words, the aim is to bring back not just *one* of each item on the list, but as many of each item as possible.

3. At Halloween, have your group go "trick or treating" for canned goods. They can wear costumes in real Halloween fashion, but at each house, rather than asking for candy, they ask for donations of canned food items to be given to needy families. Each contributing family should be given a small thank you note explaining the purpose of the collection and where the food is going. Most people will respond very well to "good goblins" like these.

4. This one could be called a "Way Out Weigh-In." Divide the kids into teams (car loads) and have them draw for street names or areas of town. They then have one hour to try to collect as many canned goods or other nonperishable foods as they can from residents of their area. The teams report back and weigh in the food they have collected. The team that has

217

the most (by weight) wins a prize of some kind, and all the food is then given to the needy.

5. *Have the group "kidnap" the pastor* or someone else well known in the church (prearranged, of course!) with the ransom being a certain amount of canned goods (e.g., 100 cans) from the congregation to be used for distribution to needy families. Do it on a Saturday. As soon as your kids have their hostage, they begin telephoning people in the congregation, informing them of the kidnapping and the ransom.

The "drop" can be made on Sunday morning. If the ransom isn't paid, the youth should be prepared to handle the responsibilities of the kidnapped person in the morning service. To add to the drama, you could mail out ransom notes made by cutting letters and words out of magazines. The kids will love it.

6. *This one can be given the name "Begging for Benevolence"* or something like that. The concept is simple: Young people go into the homes of people in the church and "beg" for food for the needy. It should be promoted in advance, with everyone being put on notice that on a certain date the youth group will be coming to people's homes to beg for donatable food items. On the appointed day, the kids head out in pairs with empty boxes, stopping at the homes of as many church members as possible, pleading with them to take canned and packaged food items out of their cupboards to fill up the boxes. For effect, the kids can dress up like beggars when they pick up the food.

7. *How about a "Supermarket Stakeout"?* Have teams of kids stake out the front doors of large supermarkets, with big boxes capable of holding a lot of food. As shoppers enter the supermarket, they are given a slip of paper that simply asks them to purchase one extra item (nonperishable) to be given to the needy. They can deposit that item in the box on their way out. It's a good approach—it gives sympathetic people the opportunity to plan ahead in buying more than one item

to give to the needy, and it also gives people who don't want to participate the chance to decline gracefully without appearing to be unfeeling. People can spend as much or as little as they want. It's up to them. You will, of course, want to clear this with the store manager ahead of time; assure him that the young people will not harass the customers or create any other problems outside the store. Most store managers will realize that it will mean positive publicity for the store and will probably generate more business. Some stores will even contribute a few food items. Be sure to pick a day when the weather won't keep people away. If you have a large youth group, simultaneously stake out several stores.

GARDENS AND GLEANERS

Here are some ideas that will really "grow" on you. They each have to do with vegetable gardens. Everybody loves fresh vegetables, but not everyone is able to plant and tend a garden of his own. So, here are some suggestions:

1. Find some unused land and plant a community garden that can provide food for the elderly, the poor, shut-ins, and other needy folks. Call real estate firms, the city, and look for yourself for a good location. Ask if it could be used for gardening by people who need to supplement their food budgets with fresh vegetables and grains. Then go to seed dealers in the area to see if they will donate packages of garden seeds; many dealers throw away seeds that are about to expire. When you have some land and some seeds, get some free advertising in the local paper or shopping guide. Offer the seeds and the land to the poor of the community. Then have members of your youth group work with these people to develop gardens, pull weeds, and water the crops. After the initial set-up, the project will grow (literally). The people who take advantage of the land and the seeds will gain a sense of independence—as well as a lot of fresh vegetables—and the kids who help will also benefit.

2. Start an "Adopt-a-Garden" program at your church. You

may have people in your church or community—the elderly, the chronically ill, and others—who have land but, for one reason or another, are unable to plant or maintain their own gardens. Have your youth group "adopt" the gardens of these people. The group can supply the seeds, the tools, and the muscle power. They can prepare the soil, plant, cultivate, and ultimately harvest the crops of vegetables for the people who own the gardens, and who, of course, are unable to do the work. It makes for some great interaction between the generations when willing and able senior citizens assist the kids with this project.

   3. Invite members of your congregation to set aside a row or two in their own gardens for giving away to the needy. Again, youth can supply the seeds (if necessary) and after the harvest deliver the food to people who need it.

   4. Try gleaning. If your community has public garden plots or is in a farming area, your group might consider the old custom of gleaning. Going through the fields after the harvest and salvaging what is ripe and useable can produce huge amounts of good food for needy people. But remember to ask permission first.

HANDICAPPED ALL-NIGHTER
   To help your group gain a better understanding of the challenges faced by people who are physically handicapped, try an all-nighter. First, have a discussion about handicapped people and their problems. Then give each kid a disability for the rest of the evening. Design the handicaps so that they are of maximum significance to each person: Star athletes, for example, can be confined to wheelchairs, given walkers, or restricted to crutches. Splint their legs or tape them together. Anyone in a wheelchair is not allowed to use the bathroom without two others to help him or her. Your "motor mouth" can be given a stroke, simulated by a right leg splint, the right arm taped to the side, and mouth taped shut. Other active youth can be blindfolded or fitted with

cardboard glasses that have off-center holes so only side vision is possible. Some can be made to see through several layers of sandwich wrap to give clouded vision. Use your imagination.

As soon as everyone has a handicap, the evening proceeds like any other all-nighter, with dumb games, relays, skill activities, and mixers. Try making and eating pizza, with the youth doing all the work so that they must help one another to succeed.

Finally, have a Bible study focusing on several stories about Jesus healing. At midnight, hold a communion service. As each youth is given the bread and wine, each person can be "healed" of his or her handicap.

Follow with a discussion of what happened, what was easiest and most difficult about the experience, and what they learned. The rest of the night can be spent in the usual youth night activities.

H.O.P. CLUB

H.O.P. stands for "Help Older People" and the H.O.P. Club is a program in which teens and adults work together to assist the elderly with work that they are unable to do for themselves. Skilled adults train the youth to do carpentry, plumbing, wiring, upholstery, or whatever needs to be done, and give direction and supervision while on the job. Younger kids can be involved in such tasks as washing windows and walls, raking leaves, shoveling snow, moving furniture, and writing letters. Many other people who want to be involved, but less directly, can provide financial and other forms of assistance. The important thing is that it be well-organized and carried out regularly. Many senior citizens' groups can provide information on where the greatest needs are, and the elderly community can be informed that this service is available at little or no charge to them.

A program such as this not only provides valuable relief for the elderly who normally must pay to have this work done, but also gives kids the opportunity to give of themselves in a meaningful way and to build relationships with a segment of society that they often ignore.

LABOR DAY

Here's the basic idea: The youth group works for people in the community—doing odd jobs of all kinds—for free. First, pick a day, like a Saturday or a day when all the kids are out of school. Then get the word out that on this day, the kids will be available to work for anyone who needs them, without pay.

You could send out a letter to everyone in the neighborhood that reads something like this:

Dear Neighbor:

The members of the church youth fellowship want to show appreciation for our special friends by a work day. Can we help you in some way? Does your lawn need mowing? Do you need help getting groceries? Would you like your windows washed? Would you like us to read to you? Just visit you?

Just mark on the enclosed card how we can be of some help. If we receive a reply from you, we will come on _____. Of course, there is no charge for this. This is a gift of love.

Sincerely yours,

Another way to do this would be to distribute flyers around the community announcing that on a given day the youth group will be passing by in the church bus looking for work to do. If anyone would like some help, they should simply tie a handkerchief onto the doorknob of their front door. Then, the group just cruises up and down streets looking for houses that have handkerchiefs tied to the front doorknob.

You can make this a one-shot activity or you can have Labor Day once a month or more. You can make it open to anybody who needs work done, or you can limit it to elderly people, those who are handicapped, or people from a certain socioeconomic class. It's up to you.

"Sure," some critics are likely to say, "these kids will work hard for other people, but they won't do any work at home." It's a good point. Help the kids to understand that demonstrating the love of Christ needs to begin at home. By doing their chores without having to be reminded over and over, or by cleaning their room before they head out on another service project, they can expect to get a lot more positive support from parents.

MINISTRY TO THE RETARDED

Every city has institutions that care for the "developmentally handicapped" or mentally retarded. In most cases, those institutions are understaffed and operate on a shoe-string budget. They can use all the help they can get. If there is a mental institution or retarded children's home in your area, your young people have a great variety of opportunities to minister to some special human beings who, like themselves, have been created in the image and likeness of God.

It's important to prepare the participants in any service project, but especially so with a ministry to the retarded. Unprepared young people may become frightened or upset at the actions or conditions of those who are retarded. It's a good idea to start with a visit to the institution rather than to try and "do something" right away. Usually a staff person from the institution can help the group with their questions and concerns.

Here are a few things that any group can do with retarded people who are residents of institutions:

1. *Bring music to them.* Many retarded people love music

intensely. A few young people with guitars or other instruments will go over big.

2. Play games with them. Frisbee throwing, ball games, active games of all kinds are great.

3. Bring some arts and crafts projects and work on them together.

4. Talk to them. Develop a friendship with one person. Help that person with letter writing and other simple tasks that may be difficult. Go on walks or short excursions with that person. Most retarded people are allowed to leave the institution with a responsible person.

5. Provide a church service at the institution. Include a lot of singing and Bible stories.

6. Participate in a Special Olympics. This nationally known event is conducted in local communities all over the country, and most institutions need volunteers who will be coaches, helpers, and escorts.

7. Bring a few retarded young people to your youth group meetings. They will contribute a great deal to the quality of your group.

PRISON MINISTRY

Every city has jails, prisons, juvenile halls, reform schools, detention camps, and correctional institutions of all kinds. One of the specific instructions Jesus gave the church was to minister to the needs of prisoners. It would not be an overstatement to say that to neglect this ministry would be an act of disobedience. Today most of our jails and prisons are filled to capacity with human beings who have been written off as "the least of these." The following ideas, suggested by Chuck Workman of Bravo Ministries in San Diego, are just a few of the ways that your youth group or your entire church might become involved in a ministry to prisoners.

1. Church Services. The best way for a church or youth group to become involved is to provide a good church service within an institution. Because the U.S. Constitution guarantees each of us the freedom of worship, institutions are obligated to allow their residents this privilege. This doesn't grant a church the right to come in and use manipulation, intimidation, or the imposition of guilt, fear, and shame to bring the wicked to repentance. An effective institutional church service should instead focus on the needs of the inmates without violating the rules of the institution and common decency. Special music, movies, and guest speakers can all be used along with traditional singing and preaching to bring to the men and women a message of hope and salvation. Far too often the church is looked upon as irrelevant by both staff and inmates. Good planning and a sense of responsibility and caring can help counteract that misperception.

2. Book Drives. Many libraries within institutions are in terrible shape; the selection is poor and the condition of the books is worse. Churches frequently donate Bibles and religious reading material, but these often pile up in storerooms, ignored. A youth group could offer a tremendous service to an institution by providing books for its library. The institution may have a list of books it needs; if not, the youth group could put together its own list. Include classic books by the world's greatest authors, "how-to" books on languages, typing, and bookkeeping, as well as books on law, philosophy, ethics, history, and other subjects. A practical gift like this would make a profound impact on both staff and residents alike and do much to improve the church's image.

3. Special Music. The church has been faithful in providing good *religious* music. But inmates are often starved for music that is simply entertaining. Music is often an inmate's only communication with the outside world, and maybe his only means of emotional escape. A church or youth group could provide some regular entertainment that would not compromise the principles of the church.

4. Big Brother/Big Sister Programs. It is often possible to pair up an inmate (especially younger ones) with a person from the community who would act as a "big brother" or "big sister." In fact, there may be a similar program already established in your area; if not, you can always create your own. Loneliness can be crippling in an institution, and the presence of a "friend" can make a world of difference in an inmate's adjustment. And after he's released, having concerned individuals and a strong church offering some support is a real encouragement to stay clean and survive.

5. *Pen Pals*. For those who can't or don't want to be involved with the inmates in person, letter writing can be a very good ministry. Inmates are avid writers; many write so often that postage becomes a problem. And receiving a letter during mail-call can be the high point of the day. For churches that don't have a correctional institution close by, this is one way to reach behind the walls and touch someone's life. It's also great for young people who may not be allowed in prisons because they are under age.

6. *Guest Speakers*. Institutions aren't usually intellectually stimulating, and churches could perform a real service by providing good speakers once in a while. There are some excellent speakers (not preachers) who would be very well-received in a prison, such as public figures, politicians, sports figures, people from the entertainment industry, educators, former offenders, and attorneys.

7. *Sports*. Most institutions have some type of intramural sports program, but since they tend to play each other over and over, it gets boring after a while. Churches are usually welcome to bring in a group to play against an institutional team in basketball, softball, volleyball, horseshoes, chess, checkers, or almost any game. It's great fun— and it makes the residents feel part of society again.

8. *Special Services*. Churches are usually storehouses of talent, while most institutions are practically bereft of talent. Churches can offer their talent to the institution for the benefit of the inmates. Medical doctors can volunteer their

services, as can attorneys, psychologists, dentists, teachers, and social workers. Tradesmen can offer their skills in carpentry, wiring, and plumbing. Church members can volunteer to cook and sew for those who can't. Virtually any talent can be employed to help those in need.

9. *Special Gifts.* Even when the economy is booming, most institutions don't have much money to work with. Churches could buy the items most needed by an institution—for example, a new sound system, new chairs, curtains, or sports equipment. If there is no particular item the church wants to purchase, they might consider a cash gift to be used at the institution's discretion.

10. *Political Activities.* Correctional institutions are caught in a tough position today. Society wants its offenders locked away for longer periods of time, yet refuses to approve funds for the construction of more or better prisons. The result is that more and more people are forced into institutions where the quality of life (which never was good) is quickly deteriorating. The church can do much to become knowledgeable and active in the field of correctional reform. This one area, more than any other, could build the credibility of the church among the institutional population. Lobbying, letter writing, rallies, speaking, and books could be used to help persuade voters and legislators to alleviate incredibly bad living conditions and ease the suffering of many hurting people.

All of these ideas are worth checking into. Some are more appropriate for youth groups than others. If you need more information about what is possible in your area, contact your local government, talk to officials who work within the institutions—like the prison chaplain (if there is one)—and they will try to help you decide upon a project that would be appropriate for your group.

RAKE AND RUN

Kids love this service project, and it goes over great with the whole neighborhood. On a given day, all the members of the youth group gather for a day of raking leaves. They should all bring their own leaf rakes. Load everybody up on the church bus, or in the back of a truck, and cruise up and down streets looking for houses that need to have leaves raked. One member of the group knocks on the door of the house and asks whether the people would like their leaves raked. If so, all the kids pile out of the bus and rake the lawn. With fifteen or twenty kids, it will only take five minutes to rake the leaves and bag them. Let people know that this is being done for free.

Be sure to join us in our "Rake & Run" Party this Saturday afternoon from 1:00 until 4:00.

Bring a leaf rake (If you have one) Wear old clothes. We'll ride the bus to various deserving homes and rake their leaves and then run to the next one.

We'll eat too!

Lots of fun while we do something worthwhile for others.

Kids should be reminded that they are on other people's property and that they should be careful not to damage anything by carelessness or horsing around. When the job is finished at each house, the kids can leave a card from the youth group that offers best wishes and lets the people know who they are. Most people are very impressed and the kids really feel good about what they have done.

During the winter, this event can be called "Snow and Blow" (shoveling snow off people's sidewalks). During the spring, you could call it "Splash and Split" (washing people's windows), or "Mow and Blow" (mowing people's lawns). In each case, the idea is the same: to give an unexpected act of kindness to others.

SENIOR SURPRISE

This service project will help bridge the generation gap. Find out the birthdates of the senior citizens in your congregation. (Double-check to make sure you don't miss anyone!) Assign these dates to different members of your group who will be responsible for baking a cake on that day. Besides a cake, you will need to furnish the following: paper plates, plastic forks, a knife, napkins, candles, milk (you can't eat cake without milk), ice cream, a small cooler for the ice cream, a card (this could be made by someone in the group), and even a present if there is someone good at making things like pillows or plaques.

On the senior's birthday, go to his or her house without notice and have everyone sing "Happy Birthday." Then, invite yourself in and tell the senior that he or she is guest of honor. Cut, serve, and pass out the food—and don't forget to clean up the mess.

If you really want to surprise the senior citizens in your church, have a senior birthday surprise party for them to celebrate the day of their *baptism*. That means, of course, that at least at this party they're younger than they thought, since we're celebrating the day of their *second* birth. That will please them—and besides, it won't take as many candles!

Either way, this is an excellent way to get to know the elderly people of your church or community. They will feel loved and you'll be "surprised" at how good you feel doing it.

SPONSOR A CHILD

There are many agencies like World Vision and Holt International that try to find financial sponsors for children in orphanages overseas. Usually these agencies will ask for a certain amount of money to provide food, clothing, and shelter for particular children each month. Most of the time, you can select a child to sponsor by name and receive detailed information about the child, including photos and sometimes handwritten thank-you notes from the child.

Why not ask your church group to adopt one of these children and pledge to support the child monthly? Each person in the youth group can give a certain amount (like $1.00 per month), and the child's progress can be monitored by the entire group. Knowing the child's name, the group will really feel involved in that child's life. The group can also pray for the child on a regular basis. Not only is a project like this easy to do, it helps young people to develop a world awareness and a sense of compassion for others.

TRASH BASH

Collecting trash from streets and vacant lots is a community service project that goes over great with everybody. A "Trash Bash" is one good way to organize and promote this with your youth group. Divide your group into teams of five or six each and assign them to different areas of the community. Each person should carry a heavy-duty trash bag and wear gloves. As each bag of trash is collected, it can be tied and placed in large dumpsters provided by a trash collection agency.

One group has turned this into a "marathon" event, with kids working around the clock (taking turns) to establish a record of 200 consecutive hours of trash collecting. Usually something like this attracts the attention of the local news media and the city officials who give the group a lot of encouragement and praise.

TUTORING MINISTRY

There are many children who need tutoring in basic subjects like arithmetic and reading. Without such tutoring, they have extreme difficulty with the subject and begin to feel like failures. In addition, there are children who have minor learning disabilities which can be overcome with some tutoring and some positive reinforcement.

You may have several young people in your youth group who would be well qualified to tutor a child in a given subject. Usually this means getting together with the child each day, or every other day, to work on homework and to offer some patient instruction in the subject. Maybe your group would see this as a ministry and offer themselves as tutors for free. The parents of some of the tutored children may want to pay something for the service. Either way, it can be a tremendous opportunity for a young person to contribute to the education and development of a child. It's also a good experience for the members of your groups who are thinking about becoming teachers. It would probably be a good idea to seek some professional help (from teachers or professional tutors) to give your youth some training and guidance in the fundamentals of tutoring.

WELCOMING THE HANDICAPPED

Your youth group can have a significant ministry to young people who are physically handicapped. In all likelihood, there are hundreds of teenagers and young adults in your area who are confined to wheelchairs, who are vision- or hearing-impaired, or who are seriously handicapped in some other way. Few of them will be involved in a regular church youth program because most youth groups are unable to make them feel welcome.

Why not encourage your group to follow the example of

231

Jesus and make friends with some handicapped young people? You might begin by bringing in some professionals (doctors, nurses, and social workers) who can help educate the group as to the special needs and problems of the handicapped. Let the kids ask questions and work through any hang-ups that they might have concerning handicapped people.

Then invite some handicapped young people to come to your youth group meetings. Provide transportation if necessary. When they feel at home with the group, and if it is appropriate, ask them to talk about their particular handicap and to share some of their feelings with the group. Allow the other members of the group the opportunity to get to know them. Try to plan your meetings in such a way that everyone, whether handicapped or not, can be included.

You may want to work with local hospitals or other agencies (like schools that provide special education for the handicapped). They can help you contact handicapped young people who might want to become a part of a Christian youth group. Once they are there, conduct your meetings normally—but inclusive of everyone. In most cases you can even continue to play the games and do the active things you always do, as long as you provide your handicapped kids with a way to feel a part. One youth group made a handicapped boy who was confined to a wheelchair their "official youth group photographer." When the rest of the kids were playing games and running around, the handicapped boy was busy taking pictures with an instant camera. After the games were over, the kids would gather around him to look at all the pictures.

Any youth group can be a place where the physically handicapped are welcomed. If you and your youth group are willing to make a few adjustments, the opportunities for ministry are enormous. Of course, it works both ways: Your handicapped young people will have a real ministry to the group as a whole. Their presence will make a positive difference.

NUCLEAR WAR

ARMAGEDDON BOMBER

If played seriously, this can be a great discussion starter. Armageddon Bomber is a simulation game that can be done with several groups in different rooms. Each group should include four people—pilot, bombardier, radio controller, and copilot. Give the following information to each group:

The year is 1999. You are the flight team of an advanced, ultramodern U.S. bomber and you are flying maneuvers over the Atlantic. You suddenly receive a highly classified, coded message from a computer. (The message below should be given to each flight team in coded form. Make up your own code and give each group the key.)

EMERGENCY ALERT: CODE RED
U.S. HAS RECEIVED NUCLEAR ATTACK BY U.S.S.R. CASUALTIES AND DESTRUCTION NOT KNOWN AT THIS TIME. U.S. UNABLE TO RETALI-ATE . . . TOTAL DESTRUCTION IS IMMINENT. YOU ARE CARRYING ADVANCED NUCLEAR WARHEAD. ONLY HOPE. YOUR LOCATION PINPOINTED HALFWAY BETWEEN U.S. AND U.S.S.R. YOUR FUEL AT 50 PERCENT. MAINTAIN RADIO SILENCE AND PROCEED WITH OPERATION RANGER RED. DE-LIVER WARHEAD.

Each group has twenty minutes to decode the message and make a decision among themselves. The decision to fulfill the mission must be unanimous. If you decide not to fulfill the mission, you have several options:

1. You will change course and attempt to land in Greenland and hope the contamination has not reached you.

2. You will attempt to crash the plane in the target area rather than stay alive.

3. You will surrender to the enemy.

4. You will commit suicide and not drop the bomb.

5. You will simply keep flying and hope that you can get a clear picture of the situation and make up your mind at the last possible minute.

6. You will fly back to the U.S. and assess the damage and hope that you can refuel somewhere.

DISCUSSION

After a discussion of the groups' decisions and the reasons for them, here are two further discussion questions:

1. Do the teachings of Jesus apply to this situation? If so, which ones?

2. How much of your decision was influenced by your Christian convictions?

PARENTS

DEAR AMY LETTERS

The following letters are great for starting group discussion on a number of sensitive topics. To use them, print them on sheets of paper (one per sheet) with room at the bottom for an answer to be written. They can be used with kids or with parents. The letters here can be used as they are, or you can adapt them or write some of your own. They can be answered individually or in small groups. The object is to find the best possible solution to each problem.

LETTERS FOR KIDS

Dear Amy,

My parents are always wanting me to go places with them, but I would rather be with my friends. I've had it with this "togetherness bit." How can I convince them that I don't enjoy family outings and don't want to do that scene anymore?

"Olda Nuff"

234

Dear Amy,

My mother insists that I go to church every Sunday, but my dad never goes, so why should I? Now that I'm older I think I should be allowed to make up my own mind about God, church, and all that stuff.

"Tired of Sunday School"

Dear Amy,

Our Bible school teacher says every family should study the Bible and pray together, but our family never seems to have the time for that. Isn't going to church together good enough?

"Busy Betsy"

Dear Amy,

My parents don't like my friends. Whenever I want to go places with my friends, Mom and Dad ask me all kinds of questions. I don't think they trust me either! How can I persuade them to let me go out with whom I want to?

"Ina Cage"

Dear Amy,

I would like to talk to my parents about some of my problems but when I do, I usually just get a lecture. How can I make them see that sometimes I just need to talk and do not want their advice?

"Lecture Hater"

Dear Amy,

My parents are always talking to me about being a minister or a missionary. I am very interested in mathematics and would like to study engineering. How can I talk to them about this without hurting their feelings? I think I can be a good Christian in whatever vocation I choose.

"Undecided"

235

LETTERS FOR MOTHERS

Dear Amy,

My husband and I became Christians as adults, but we want our children to let Christ be their guide during their teen years. Our daughter says we're trying to "cram religion down her throat." How can we help her to understand that she needs Christ now?

"Worried Parents"

Dear Amy,

I try to spend time with my son and talk to him, but when I ask questions about his school, friends, etc., he just clams up. How can I get him to talk over his daily activities as well as his problems?

"Clam's Mother"

Dear Amy,

My husband and I try to have open communication with our daughter. However, it seems that more and more lately she comes to me with her problems but refuses to talk with her father. He resents this and thinks I'm encouraging her in this direction. Please help.

"Caught in the Middle"

Dear Amy,

My husband and I come from very different backgrounds, so our ideas about child rearing are very different. We seem to be always at odds about rules for the children, punishments, etc. How can we change this? Our children are confused, so are we.

"Nita Solution"

Dear Amy,

I try to establish good communication with my family by listening to them, asking questions, and encouraging my children to talk about school, etc., and my husband to talk about his work. But nobody listens to me. I want to talk about my activities too, but no one seems interested. Please advise me.

"Wanda Talk Too"

LETTERS FOR FATHERS
Dear Amy,

I am bewildered by the way things in the world have changed! When I was a kid, life was simple, and parents' word was the LAW. Kids today seem to be living fast and furious. My children think my standards are old-fashioned and impossible in today's society. How can we get together on standards for our family to live by?

"Old-Fashioned Dad"

Dear Amy,

I'd like to spend more time with my kids but I have a demanding job that requires a lot of overtime. I also try to participate in community affairs and do as much as possible for the church. There simply aren't enough hours in the day for me, yet I realize that my children are growing up fast. What do you suggest?

"Full-Schedule Dad"

Dear Amy,

My wife and I cannot agree on how to deal with our son. I think she is too soft on him and too sympathetic. He's never going to learn to "take it" out in the world if we're too easy on him at home. How can I convince her of this?

"Ex-Marine Dad"

Dear Amy,

My daughter and I used to be very close. We talked a lot and did a lot of things together. But now she's in high school and she seems to have changed completely. She seldom talks to me anymore and spends more and more time away from home. What can I do?

"Losing the Apple of My Eye"

237

HOW TO RAISE YOUR PARENTS

In the box on the next page are some good questions for a discussion about parents. For best results, print them up and pass them out to each person. Give the kids time to answer all the questions individually, then discuss them one at a time with the entire group.

A MAD LATE DATE

The following short play is useful for starting discussion on the obvious areas of friction developed in the play as well as in family and parent-teen relationships.

Characters needed:

Father
Mother
Daughter (Christy)
Son (Donald)

The setting is the breakfast table. Everyone except Christy is seated. Father is reading the paper, Mother is pouring coffee, and Donald is toying with his cereal. Christy hasn't come in yet.

Mother: Quit playing with your food, Donald. You'll be late for school.

Father: I'll have some more coffee, dear.

Donald: Speaking of being late, what about Christy last night? Man, if I came in that late, I'd be flogged till daylight.

Father: You let us worry about your sister. Anyway, you have to be able to get a date first.

Donald: Funny, funny!

Mother: You know, I am worried about Christy. This is the third time this has happened, and— (*Christy enters and interrupts.*)

238

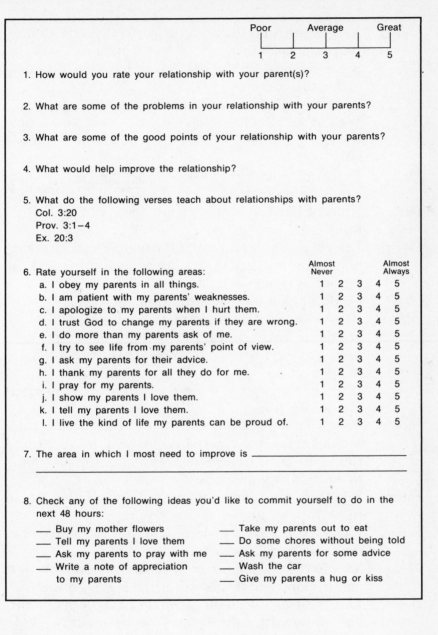

	Poor	Average	Great
	1	2	3	4	5

1. How would you rate your relationship with your parent(s)?

2. What are some of the problems in your relationship with your parents?

3. What are some of the good points of your relationship with your parents?

4. What would help improve the relationship?

5. What do the following verses teach about relationships with parents?
   Col. 3:20
   Prov. 3:1–4
   Ex. 20:3

6. Rate yourself in the following areas:

	Almost Never				Almost Always
a. I obey my parents in all things.	1	2	3	4	5
b. I am patient with my parents' weaknesses.	1	2	3	4	5
c. I apologize to my parents when I hurt them.	1	2	3	4	5
d. I trust God to change my parents if they are wrong.	1	2	3	4	5
e. I do more than my parents ask of me.	1	2	3	4	5
f. I try to see life from my parents' point of view.	1	2	3	4	5
g. I ask my parents for their advice.	1	2	3	4	5
h. I thank my parents for all they do for me.	1	2	3	4	5
i. I pray for my parents.	1	2	3	4	5
j. I show my parents I love them.	1	2	3	4	5
k. I tell my parents I love them.	1	2	3	4	5
l. I live the kind of life my parents can be proud of.	1	2	3	4	5

7. The area in which I most need to improve is _____
_____

8. Check any of the following ideas you'd like to commit yourself to do in the next 48 hours:

   ___ Buy my mother flowers   ___ Take my parents out to eat
   ___ Tell my parents I love them   ___ Do some chores without being told
   ___ Ask my parents to pray with me ___ Ask my parents for some advice
   ___ Write a note of appreciation   ___ Wash the car
       to my parents   ___ Give my parents a hug or kiss

Christy: And every time there was a perfectly good excuse. Just like last night.

Donald: Some reasons! Out of gas, flat tires. What's it going to be this time?

Christy: It's none of your business, smart aleck.

Father: Well it is *my* business, Christy. You know how worried your mother and I become when you are late.

Mother: Yes, you could have at least called and let us know you had problems.

Donald: Kind of hard to find a phone booth out at Folsom Lake.

Christy: Knock it off, bird brain. I couldn't call. Coming home from the game we stopped at Eppie's and the service was just terrible.

Mother: Couldn't you have called from there?

Christy: No, Mom. We left in plenty of time—11:00. But we hit some traffic downtown because of the big fire. Just no way we could know that was going to happen.

Donald: Ha! That greaser you were with probably planned the whole thing.

Father: That's enough, Don. Christy, you know the rules around here. We've asked you to be in by 12:00, and this is the third time you've been late. I'm just going to have to ground you for one week.

Christy: But Dad, you don't understand. We couldn't help it!

Father: I know you have a good reason, but rules are rules. And this isn't the first time.

Christy: So what if it's the fifteenth time? I couldn't help it and I don't think it's fair that I get grounded.

Donald: Fair? If it had been me, I would have been chained and muzzled to the bedpost for a month!

Christy: Yeah, you should be chained and muzzled with that mouth of yours.

Mother: Regardless, Christy, we have rules, and both of you must obey them. I think your father is right. Anyway, I don't know if I like your dating that . . . that . . . oh, what is his name?

Donald: You mean Greasy Gary?

Christy: Shut up dummy! Now I know why I'm grounded, you never have liked anybody I've dated. If it wasn't him, you'd find something else—

Father: *(interrupts)* Now just a minute. The matter of liking who you're dating has nothing to do with it. I might say, however, you could be a little more choosey.

Christy: Choosey! Who would you want me to date? One of those creeps at the church?

Mother: Creeps? Where did you pick up that language?

Donald: From Greasy Gary. I think that's his middle name.

Christy: Okay, smart mouth . . .

Father: Both of you calm down. If this is going to be your attitude, Christy, you can forget about going anywhere for the following week as well. Your mother and I could use a little help around here.

Christy: What, you can't be serious! What about Donald? All he does is sit around and flap his mouth, making corny jokes.

Mother: Now Christy, that's enough. There's no need to bring your brother into this. I think it is time we be just a little more considerate of each other.

Christy: Why don't you start with me? I come in a lousy forty-five minutes late, and you act like it was three hours. Then you start harping on who I date. All you're concerned about is your silly rules.

Father: You don't need to raise your voice to your mother. Rules are something to be concerned about, but more important is your behavior to those rules. Either you shape up or else.

Donald: Or shape out . . . that shouldn't be hard for you.

Christy: *(in tears)* I've had enough! I'm leaving! Nobody understands me. You just don't care.

Mother: We do care, Christy. You are the one who doesn't understand. Why, when I was your age . . .

Christy: Now comes the second lecture! Well, times are different, and you are *not my* age!

Father: I think I've heard enough. Both of you get off to school, and Christy, I want you home at 4:00 sharp.

PARENT BLUNDERS AND TEEN GOOFS

Give each kid a mimeographed sheet that contains two columns of "Yes" and "No" answers, ten to each column. Then read the following questions to them and have them circle their responses after each question is read. The kids should be as honest as they possibly can and need not put their names on their answer sheets.

In column one, they answer questions relating to their parents' attitudes toward them, and in column two, questions about their attitudes toward their parents. The number of "Yes" and "No" answers in each column can be totaled after the quiz and used as a basis for discussion. Normally, whenever the parents score a high number of "No" answers, so does the kid, and vice-versa. For example, if a kid says his parents do not act like they trust him, he will undoubtedly answer "No" to the questions about trying to earn and keep his parents' trust. The answers should show that both parents and teens have a fifty-fifty share of the responsibility for their problems.

PARENT BLUNDERS

1. Do your parents listen to you when you have a family discussion?

2. Do your parents act like they trust you?

3. Do your parents treat your friends nicely and make them feel welcome?

4. Do your parents admit their mistakes when they have been wrong?

5. Do your parents openly express and show their affection for you?

6. Do your parents avoid comparing you to brothers and sisters or other youth?

7. Do your parents keep the promises they make to you?

8. Do your parents show their appreciation and give you credit when you do something good?

9. Do your parents set a good example for you in their personal honesty?

10. Do your parents use the kind of language in front of you that they tell you to use?

TEEN GOOFS

1. Do you listen to your parents when they want to share an idea or advice with you?

2. When your parents say "No" to your plans, do you accept that answer without complaining?

3. Do you try to understand the pressures and problems that sometimes make parents grumpy and hard to live with?

4. Do you say "Thank you" for everything that your parents do for you?

5. Do you try to plan something nice that you can do for your parents occasionally?

6. Do you say "I'm sorry" when you know you have said or done something you shouldn't?

7. Do you try to earn and keep your parents' trust by doing what they expect of you?

8. Do you play fair with them and discuss things honestly, without covering up for yourself?

9. Do you ask your parents' advice about decisions that you have to make?

10. Do you try to avoid problems and arguments by doing what you're supposed to before you have to be told?

PARENT YOUTH GROUP

For one evening, day, or weekend, do with the parents of the kids in your group what you would normally do with the kids. Play the kids' favorite games, sing the songs they like best, conduct a discussion, do a skit, or anything else that you would do with the youth group on a typical day. Then ask the parents to answer these questions:

1. What are the good and poor things you notice about the group?

2. What would you like to see happen in the future?

3. How can we better help your son or daughter?

4. How can we better serve your family?

It is a good idea to meet periodically with parents, and this is a good way to let them know exactly what is going on with the kids and the youth group.

PEER PRESSURE

FRIEND OR FOE

This game is designed to illustrate how we are often influenced in our lives and how difficult it is to determine who is giving us good advice and who is giving us bad advice. Have a person wait outside the door while the room is being set up. Place a variety of obstacles, such as pop bottles, around on the floor, so you will have to avoid them to walk across the room. Blindfold the person waiting outside and bring him in. The object of the game is for the blindfolded person to walk from one side of the room to the other without knocking over any of the obstacles.

The blindfolded person must get directions to cross the room from others in the room, but he does not know who is friend and who is foe. It is up to the person who is trying to cross the room to determine who is giving good advice and who is giving bad advice. Whether the person can cross the room without knocking over any obstacles depends upon whom he decides to listen to. He may decide to listen to no one at all and try to make it on his own.

After that person crosses the room, someone else can try if he thinks he can do better. (Rearrange the room each time.) Afterward, ask the group questions like these:

1. (To the blindfolded persons) How did you decide whom to listen to?

2. (To the blindfolded persons) How did you feel when you followed a direction, and it turned out to be bad advice?

3. (To the friends and foes) What tactics did you use to keep the person on or off the right course?

4. (To the group) How is this situation like the world around us? In what ways does the world try to influence us? How can we learn to stay on course?

If the group is a large one, it would be best to have only six (or so) be the friends and foes, while the others watch the action. This game provides fun as well as good learning.

THE GREAT BUTTON CONTROVERSY

As an object lesson on conformity, put one or two dozen buttons in a box and pass them around the group. Have each student count the buttons and remember how many were in the box. By prior arrangement, the next-to-the-last person removes one button from the box secretly, so the last person's count is off by one. When you ask the kids how many they counted, everyone will agree except for that one person (hopefully). In all probability, the different person will change his count to conform to the others, even though he is sure he is right. Follow up with a discussion about group pressure and denial of personal convictions to be accepted by the group.

PAUL'S DILEMMA

The following is a contrived situation involving a teenage boy named Paul. He faces a problem for which he receives *advice* from friends and relatives with various points of view. This situation can be either read to the group by the leader or acted out in role play. After presenting the situation to the group, including all the advice that Paul receives, discuss the questions provided at the end.

THE SITUATION

Paul is a junior in high school. He is relatively well accepted by his friends. He makes average grades and is a member of several school organizations: choir, the basketball team, and student council. He has been friends with one group of five guys through most of his junior-high and high-school years. His parents are respectable members of the community: His father is a lawyer, and his mother the secretary of a popular civic organization. The whole family is active in a local church where his father and mother hold leadership positions.

Paul's problem is this: He has been close with this group of five guys for a long time, and their values have always been quite similar. But lately, the guys have been experimenting with drugs and alcohol. Although Paul has participated, he is beginning to feel more and more uncomfortable. He has discussed the problem with his buddies, and they do not feel uncomfortable. If Paul decides to stop going along with the group, it may cost him his relationship with the guys. He approaches a number of acquaintances, seeking advice.

Youth Group Sponsor: He is concerned that Paul may get pulled into the habits of his buddies. His advice is to break the relationship. He points out that Jesus never allowed relationships to get in the way of His convictions. He refers to others, such as Martin Luther, who did what they knew was right, regardless of the circumstances.

Paul's Uncle: His favorite uncle, who is also a lawyer, listens nervously as Paul confides that he really doesn't see what is so wrong with all of these things but he doesn't feel right. Paul's uncle immediately cites statistics to show the dangers of marijuana and alcohol. He attempts to investigate rationally all of the "phony" justifications for using grass and alcohol and makes a case for abstinence—the only really logical and safe conclusion.

Sunday School Teacher: He points out that you are either "with" Christ or "against" Him, committed or not committed. What is at stake is behaving like a Christian should and renouncing every "appearance of evil" or capitulating and being "worldly" and sold out to sin.

Youth Director: He relates to Paul a true story of a close friend who was bothered by the direction his friends were going but didn't have enough courage to stand for his conviction. The result was that he became heavily involved in drugs, disgraced his family and friends, and eventually committed suicide. He suggests that Paul has great potential to influence hundreds of young people and could destroy his chances of potential greatness. In fact, the youth director confides, he was just going to ask Paul to take a leadership position in the group.

A Neighbor (who is also a policeman): He confronts Paul with the fact that he saw a report on some of Paul's friends who were on the brink of getting into trouble with drugs, etc. The neighbor is concerned that Paul understand the legal implications of his friends' behavior and counsels him to stay away lest he and his friends get busted. Then he explains that he personally does not see what's wrong with a kid experimenting with marijuana, but we must all obey the laws; otherwise there would be total chaos. Laws are for our protection, and we must follow them.

The Pastor: He points out that the church has always spoken out against "non-Christian behavior" and that ever since the church was founded such things were not acceptable for church members. The purity of the church, whether it's a local body of believers or "the church universal," has always been a focal point for "our doctrine."

His Girl Friend: She says she doesn't care what anyone else says, he must do what's right. If he made the wrong choice, he would never be able to live with himself. She reminds him that if his parents knew he was experimenting with marijuana and alcohol, "his mother would be crushed" and "his father would be humiliated." "Besides," she says, "what about me and our relationship? You know what I think of your group of friends and what they are doing, and if I mean very much to you, you'll think carefully about what you're doing."

Paul's Older Brother: He thinks Paul is too narrow and making an issue out of nothing. He feels Paul is experiencing false guilt produced by the unenlightened views of their parents. He points out that he regularly smokes pot and drinks and still maintains a high grade-point average and also holds down a good job. He counsels Paul not to get involved in heavy drugs or excessive drinking but warns him not to sacrifice his good friendships for a "nonissue."

QUESTIONS FOR DISCUSSION

1. Evaluate each of the arguments given to Paul. What are the strengths, if any, and what are the weaknesses, if any?

2. Which person do you most agree with? Why? Least agree with? Why?

3. What answer would you have given Paul? What would you do in Paul's situation?

4. Is there a "right answer" to Paul's dilemma?

5. What were Paul's alternatives?

6. If Paul had weighed all the alternatives and made what you considered to be a wrong choice, what would you say to Paul if you were

a. a close friend
b. a girl friend
c. a parent
d. a brother/sister

e. a youth director
f. a minister
g. a school counselor

SELF-IMAGE

APPRECIATION GAME

This is a small-group experience to be followed by a discussion. Form groups of five to seven people. The groups each sit in a circle with a chair in the center. One person in the group sits in the center chair with the rest of the group around him. As long as he sits in the center chair, he must remain completely silent. Each person in the circle then tells the person in the center three or four things he appreciates about him. The kids are instructed to (1) be honest—as deep or as superficial as you like, (2) speak directly to the person in the center, (3) be specific and detailed. This continues until everyone has sat in the center chair and been verbally appreciated. Following this experience, have the group discuss the following questions:

1. Was it easy to receive these compliments? To give them? Why?

2. Did you feel uncomfortable? When?

3. Did you want to avoid communicating directly with the other person?

4. Did you want to avoid, dismiss, or reject these messages of liking?

5. Did some people in your group find it difficult to follow directions about silence? About saying things of appreciation without cutting down the other person? About respecting the rights of others to speak?

BUILDING AN IMAGE

Here's a learning experience for your youth group that involves role playing and observation. It focuses on character traits and peer approval.

Divide into small groups of eight to ten kids. Each group is to function independently. Hand out the following list of character traits to each person, instructing them to go quickly through the list and assign a number value to each trait on a scale of 1 (low) to 10 (high):

1 = an absolutely worthless or negative character trait
5 = neither good nor bad
10 = essential to being someone you respect and like

CHARACTER TRAITS

___ Critical, fault-finding
___ Inquisitive
___ Gullible
___ Spineless
___ Analytical
___ Picky, fussy, over-concerned about details
___ Daydreaming
___ Selfish
___ Competitive
___ Vain, conceited
___ Scheming, conniving, devious
___ Caring
___ Confident
___ Cooperative
___ Compromising
___ Courteous
___ Flattering
___ Decisive
___ Inflexible, one-track mind
___ Sensitive, touchy, easily offended

___ Aggressive
___ Energetic
___ Melodramatic
___ Verbose, wordy, talkative
___ Indecisive
___ Impatient
___ Patient
___ Big Shot
___ Accusing, blaming
___ Frank, outspoken, blunt
___ Insensitive, unloving
___ Grateful
___ Friendly, cordial
___ Apathetic, indifferent
___ Stubborn, inflexible, intolerant
___ Self-critical, self-abasing
___ Pushy
___ Respectful
___ Mocking
___ Cool
___ Funny, joking
___ Serious

Next, put a batch of role plays in a hat. They can be of any type: crisis resolution, humorous situation, everyday experience, or whatever. Also put everyone's name on paper slips in a different hat. Select one name. That individual is to pick a role play. Then select more names out of the hat to fit whatever other roles are needed for the play.

All the people involved in the role play are to look over their list of character traits and select three that they will use during the role play.

Now perform the role play. The leader should allow about three minutes per situation. As the kids act their roles, the rest of the group members must attempt to discern (privately) which traits each of the role-players is dramatizing.

After time is called, the group confers to decide which traits were being acted out, and awards each member the cumulative points for their 3 traits. The points come from each group member's list.

On the next round, a name is again chosen from the hat, and another role play is performed. This time the kids try to pick the character traits which will win them the most points. The object is not so much to accumulate the most points as it is to figure out what personality types are most acceptable to their peers, and to act that way.

You'll know you're nearing the end of the game when every kid acts just like every other kid. Sound familiar?

Follow up with a discussion. Here are some good questions:

1. Which are the most desirable character or personality traits? Why?

2. Why are these traits so important to your friends?

3. Which coincide with biblical values? Which contradict biblical values?

4. What happens to the kids who try to go against the flow of their peers' opinions?

ENCOURAGE ONE ANOTHER

Give everyone a piece of paper and have someone else pin it on his back. Ask the group to circulate and write one thing they like about each person on his piece of paper. After five to fifteen minutes, depending upon the size of the group, allow time for everyone to read his own piece of paper. Follow with a devotional about the need to encourage each other, using passages such as 1 Thessalonians 5:14 and Hebrews 10:24.

PRESTIGE GAME

This is a simulation game that works well as a springboard to a discussion on self-worth. It is best played with a group who knows each other well. To begin, ask each person to make a list of items that enable someone to gain prestige. If you have high schoolers, ask them to list items that gain prestige in school—good grades, nice car, good looks, being a student body officer, being a football player, being a homecoming queen, and so on. Have people share their lists and the leader select six to ten of the most popular items to use in the next step.

Now give everyone $200 in play money and have them make up a Values Guide—a list of the selected items with assigned dollar value betweem $10 and $50 to each one (the more prestigious items merit the higher dollar value).

The next step is to have the group mill around and distribute the money according to their Values Guides. Each person gives his money to others based on his own Values Guide and each person receives money from others based on the Values Guide of the other people. For example: "Joe lettered in football, and I assigned 'being a football player' a $20 value, so he gets $20 from me."

After the distribution, each person totals up how much money he has. Revealing the amount that each person has is optional. After the game, people can share how they felt during the game and what it means to have prestige in the world's eyes as opposed to God's eyes. They will see that many times we measure our world's worth by the amount of prestige that the world gives us, forgetting about how God sees us.

SEX/SEXUALITY

THE ISLAND AFFAIR

The two circles represent two islands surrounded by shark-infested waters. As a result of a shipwreck, only five survivors manage to reach the safety of the islands. Albert is separated from his fiancée, Carla. Carla is stranded on the other island with her mother, Della. Bruno, a young man of about the same age as Albert ends up on Albert's island. The fifth survivor is an older man, Edgar. He is a loner and on the same island with Carla and Della.

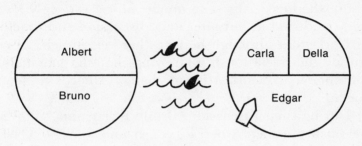

Albert and Carla are deeply in love. After two months of being separated yet seeing each other across the water, they desperately long to be together, but each passing day makes rescue look more hopeless. Carla becomes despondent. One day while walking around the island, Carla discovers a crude boat hollowed out of an old tree. It looks seaworthy. Then Edgar appears. He has just finished making the boat. Carla explains her longing to reach the other island to be with Albert and pleads with Edgar to let her have the boat. Edgar refuses, saying the boat was made for his escape and not hers. After Carla's incessant pleading, Edgar proposes that if Carla will make love to him, he will take her to the other island in his boat. Carla asks for time to consider and runs to find Della. She explains to her mother that rescue looks hopeless and that if they are to be stranded on an island, she should at least be with the one she loves. Della listens with understanding and after much thought says, "I know you sincerely love Albert and I understand your desire to be with him, but I am afraid the cost is a bit high. It is up to you to do what you want, but my advice would be to wait a bit longer. I'm sure a better solution will come, and you will be glad you waited." Carla considers her mother's advice for a number of days. Finally, she decides to accept Edgar's offer. Carla makes love to Edgar. Edgar keeps his part of the bargain and rows Carla to Albert's island. Albert and Carla embrace and are very happy, but during the day's conversation, Carla confesses that she made love to Edgar only because she loved Albert so much. Albert is deeply hurt. He tries to understand but after long discussion and thought, he tells Carla that although he loves her very much, he cannot continue their relationship knowing that she has made love to another man. Carla tries to change Albert's mind but to no avail.

During their discussion, Bruno is listening from behind some bushes. When Albert leaves, Bruno comes to Carla and explains that he thinks what she did was admirable. He understands that her experience with Edgar was the result of desperation and was an act of love for Albert. Bruno tells Carla that he would readily accept someone who would pay such a high price for their love and he would be willing to care for Carla in spite of what Albert did. Carla accepts.

Rank the following characters from best to worst:

Carla, Albert, Edgar, Della, Bruno

Reasoning:

Scriptures for further study: Matthew 22:35–40.

MALE OR FEMALE?

For a discussion starter on the complicated subject of male/female roles and societal norms, distribute copies of the list below to your group. Ask them to decide which of the tasks or roles on the list are *male* and which are *female* (they must choose one or the other). After each person has completed his list, have the group break into smaller groups and try to come up with a consensus in those groups. The smaller groups can then report their conclusions to the larger group. Chances are pretty good that there will be a lot of disagreement and heated discussion. Feel free to add your own items to the following list:

1. Cooking supper
2. Grocery shopping
3. Paying bills
4. Maintaining the car
5. Washing windows
6. Painting the house (outside)
7. Painting the house (inside)
8. Caring for children
9. "Making a living" (work)
10. Playing soccer
11. Mastering a musical instrument
12. Initiating a date
13. Paying for a date
14. Proposing marriage
15. Deciding which church to attend
16. Choosing a house or apartment
17. Talking openly about feelings
18. Getting drunk with the gang on weekends
19. Getting high with the gang on weekends
20. Being a good listener
21. Building furniture
22. Hanging pictures
23. Doing laundry
24. Driving a car on trips
25. Disciplining children
26. Saying grace at meals
27. Decorating home/room
28. Attending a concert
29. Watching TV
30. Going to a play

31. Going camping

32. Attending a sporting event

33. Doing dishes

34. Taking out the garbage

35. Crying

36. Choosing a form of birth control

37. Mowing lawn

38. Tending garden

39. Staying home from work with sick child

40. Cleaning house

You may want to expand this discussion into a Bible study by finding Bible characters that exhibit these role distinctions or by studying the teaching of Jesus and the apostle Paul concerning male/female roles in society.

SEX IN THE MOVIES

Teenagers need to take seriously the effects sexually explicit material in movies can have on their lives. To generate discussion, ask some of the kids to tell their favorite movie or scene from a movie, and why. Then tackle the following questions in small group discussion:

1. Do you think it's okay for actors and actresses to act in the nude or in sexually explicit scenes since they are "only acting"? Why or why not?

2. Why do you think movies today contain so much sexually explicit material? What is its purpose?

3. Do you believe that the movies present an accurate portrayal of sexual behavior or male/female relationships?

4. Do you think Christians should attend or view sexually explicit films? Why or why not? Would the age or maturity of the viewer be a factor in this regard?

5. What kinds of effects might viewing sexually explicit scenes have on you? On your relationship to others? On your relationship to God?

After the small groups come back together, have someone read aloud one or more of the following Scripture passages. Ask what light, if any, they shed on the subject under discussion.

Matt. 5:27–30

Eph. 5:1–12
1 Thess. 4:1–8
Gen. 2:22–25; 3:1–12

In the large-group discussion that follows, point out or review some of the possible effects of viewing sexually explicit material. These might include: immediate sexual arousal and lust at inappropriate times; guilt or shame; and a questioning of God's standards for sexual behavior. Encourage the kids to consider these and other possible effects when they're making decisions about film viewing.

SUICIDE

FACTS ABOUT SUICIDE

To introduce a discussion about teenage suicide, give your group a true/false quiz like the one that follows. Have each person write "T" or "F" on a numbered sheet of paper (1–7) after you read each statement aloud. When you read aloud the right answers afterward, ask for a show of hands of those who responded correctly. (Note: Statistics change with the passing of time, so you might want to check the accuracy of those given here, or add other true-false statements as you have information.)

1. *People who repeatedly talk about killing themselves probably will never actually do it.*

FALSE—Most people who commit suicide give clear warnings through their words or actions.

2. *Anyone who tries to kill himself is basically crazy.*

FALSE—Most teens who try to kill themselves are very unhappy or depressed, but only 15 to 30 percent are mentally ill.

3. *If a person is suicidal, he or she will always be suicidal throughout life.*

FALSE—If the causes of the person's unhappiness can be dealt with, he or she can probably lead a normal and full life.

4. *It is best to talk openly with someone who is suicidal about suicide rather than avoiding the subject.*

TRUE—This lets the person know you really care about him or her. Talking with people about suicide doesn't "give them ideas."

5. *More American teens commit suicide today than they did twenty years ago.*

TRUE—In the last two decades, the suicide rate among American adolescents has skyrocketed to a 300 percent increase.

6. *Most teenage suicides occur away from home.*

FALSE—An average of 70 percent of adolescent suicides take place at home, between the hours of 3:00 P.M. and midnight.

7. *Nothing can stop a suicidal person once the decision has been made.*

FALSE—Most people contemplating suicide feel a deep conflict between their desire to die and a desire to live. Intervention can change their minds.

Here are some ideas for following up the quiz:

1. Ask whether anyone in the group has ever known anyone who was thinking about suicide. (They don't have to mention names.) What did they say or do to help the person? What was the person feeling? What were they themselves feeling?

2. Ask for suggestions about why someone would consider killing himself. Is the cause more likely to be external circumstances or an internal problem?

3. If a friend talks about suicide, what do your youth think they should do? Find an adult to talk to about it?

With the current rate of adolescent suicide attempts so high, this is a critical topic for your kids to consider. You may even discover later that young people who have themselves thought about taking their own lives will come to talk about it with you once you've brought up the subject.

Before you conduct a program like this, be sure to

acquaint yourself with the topic by reading available resources or discussing the subject with knowledgeable counselors. If you yourself are not experienced in the area of
adolescent counseling, be sure you know of someone to whom
you could refer young people who may be contemplating
suicide.

SUICIDE ROLE PLAY

The following role play is excellent as a way to make
young people aware of the feelings of people contemplating
suicide and to help them develop counseling skills as well.

Select a group of kids from your youth group and divide
them in half. One half of the group is to research individually
and develop a suicidal character and be able to answer any
question about him. Each person in this suicidal group
should have a different motivation for wanting to take his
own life, if possible. The second half of the group is to
research various counseling techniques that could be used in
dealing with a person considering suicide.

Before the meeting, set up two toy telephones and ask
the two groups to choose one person to role-play. During the
meeting, a suicidal person calls the Help Line, where a
counselor is ready to answer. The two carry on a dialogue
until either the problem is resolved or no progress is being
made. Then have the group discuss and evaluate techniques
used in counseling, whether or not such a conversation could
have ever taken place, and what approaches they might have
taken.

THEOLOGY

BETHANY CHURCH

This is a simulation that deals with church structure,
the mission of the church, unity in the church, and a host of
other issues as well. It would be most effective in a retreat
setting so plenty of time could be allowed if necessary. It will
work well with any age group from junior high up.

Explain to the group that they are all members of a fictional church called Bethany Church. Bethany Church is located in the heart of downtown Gitchigumi, which has a population of 72,000. The church has a membership of 580 adult members. Although the membership has recently been declining, the church is not in any kind of serious trouble. It is served by a senior minister, an assistant minister, and a full-time secretary. The church budget is $80,000 per year and was raised last year with some difficulty. In the past, approximately $9,000 has been given yearly to the mission of the church.

Recently a wealthy resident of the community passed away and left $250,000 in cash to the church. The church is now faced with the decision of how to use that money. The person who left the money did not specify how it was to be used but did specify that everyone in the church unanimously agree on how the money would be used within a certain time limit. Otherwise the money will be turned over to another charitable organization, namely, the Society for the Preservation of Begonias.

With that in mind, the group is divided into a number of interest groups. Each interest group is provided with a role identity, an assigned number of votes, and a set of goals for them. The effectiveness of each group will depend, to a large degree, on the ability of their members to role-play the assigned viewpoints and identity of the group.

After the groups have been assigned, a number of proposals are presented. Each group must decide which of these, proposals, if adopted, would provide the kind of addition to the life of Bethany Church that would be desirable by its own standards. Then, they may devise a strategy for using their group's power or influence to secure other groups' assistance in getting their favorite proposal adopted. They may also try to block, by any means in line with the identity of their group, the adoption of proposals that they feel would adversely affect Bethany Church. If none of the proposals are acceptable to the group, they may suggest alternatives.

THE PROPOSALS

Number One: In light of the large number of people still not going to church in Gitchigumi and in light of the constant tendency of others in the church to fall away, it is proposed that the money be invested to yield $15,000 annually in interest for a week-long evangelism crusade. This fund would allow for obtaining a first-rate preacher, special music, ample advertising including TV, and part-time summer help to follow up new conversions.

Number Two: In the light of severe economic and social distress of many of the aged members of the congregation, it is proposed that the $250,000 be set up in a fund to construct low-cost housing and other facilities for those needy elderly.

Number Three: The $250,000 should be used to finance a modest addition to the current Christian education building that would be helpful to the church in several ways: (1) relieve overcrowding of current Sunday school classes by constructing six new classrooms; (2) provide adequate office facilities for the assistant minister; (3) provide combination gymnasium-activity room to help build a more active youth program; and (4) provide a prayer chapel for small groups within the church and for individual meditation. Since the property is already owned, it is possible to do this for $250,000.

Number Four: Gitchigumi desperately needs more day care for children of working mothers. The church schoolrooms sit unused all week long, while for $100,000 they could be converted and equipped to provide one day-care facility for fifteen to thirty children. The other $150,000 could be invested, and the interest used to finance one full-time professional staff person who, with the help of church volunteers, could run the program. This would fulfill fewer

261

needs of our own church members but would provide help for those outside the church membership.

Number Five: Bethany Church is understaffed. Given the current budget, it would not be possible to hire another minister in the near future. Yet there is needed a person who could go full-time calling on our shut-ins and those in the hospitals and do counseling with those having various difficulties. This would free our other ministers to do their jobs more vigorously and would lead to the eventual building up of the congregation. With the $250,000 in a savings account drawing interest of $15,000 a year, another minister could be hired.

Number Six: The organ in the sanctuary desperately needs to be replaced. The pipes are cracking, and there are notes that do not even play. Since the worship service depends on the organ for music, it is imperative that the organ be replaced. This can be done for only $230,000.

THE INTEREST GROUPS

1. *The Choir (ten votes):* The choir is not the most open group in the church because it is dominated by the members of four or five of the old families in the church. To them, the worship life of the church is central, and at times, music is the center of that worship. Most of the them are over forty-five and very pious, being also the active core of the pastor's adult Bible study group that meets during the Sunday school hour.

2. *Executive Board of Church Women (twenty votes):* These officers speak for the concerns of the women who compose the eight circles of the church. They are perhaps better educated than the congregation as a whole. All of them are married, most of them are homemakers, and they are quite concerned about the church's ministry to young people and children.

3. *The Board (thirty votes):* This is a group of men between the ages of thirty-five and seventy. They are entrusted with the responsibility of raising money and supervising the activities of the church. The majority of them are businessmen. There is also a group of professionals—doctor, lawyer, engineer, and college teacher. Generally the group is rather conservative and traditional.

4. *Young Adult Discussion Group (fifteen votes):* This group of postcollege married couples and singles is the most lively and most progressive group within the church. They meet every Sunday night and study what they choose, emphasizing fellowship, study, and social concern in about equal measure. The pastor speaks of them as the conscience of Bethany because of their willingness to raise unpopular issues and their general contribution to the liveliness of the church.

5. *The Church Staff (twenty votes):* Three people: the senior pastor (fifty-five years old), the assistant pastor (twenty-nine years old), and the church secretary, who has worked here longer than both ministers (fifteen years). They have particular interests and loyalties but also feel, to some extent, a responsibility to look out for the general welfare of the church.

6. *The Youth Fellowship (ten votes):* This group, made up largely of sons and daughters of church members plus a few of their nonmember friends, meets weekly for fun and discussion. They have recently been developing interest in how the church can be more responsive to community needs, though a few members are pressing for a more personally-oriented, evangelical emphasis.

7. *Neighborhood and Street People (five votes):* Though not actually members of Bethany Church, these people are interested in the use and purpose of the church. Some of them resent the church's tax exempt status and feel that it owes the community more specific community services.

INSTRUCTIONS TO THE GROUP
1. Divide into the assigned groups.

2. Read the description of the group you are representing.

3. Decide how you will role-play that group.

4. Decide which proposals you are in favor of and which you object to.

5. Talk with members of other groups at the designated time to convince them of your argument.

6. Hand in a written ballot with your votes assigned. You may vote either for a proposal or against a proposal. For example, if you have fifteen votes, you can cast three votes for the Evangelism Crusade, six votes against the organ, and six votes for the building addition.

7. The votes will be tabulated, and if a certain proposal has a majority of the votes, it will win. If not, another round will be played.

8. If at the end of four rounds, no one proposal can be agreed upon, Bethany Church will lose the $250,000 gift, and it will be given to the Society for the Preservation of Begonias.

Following the simulation, discuss the experience with the entire group, sharing feelings and generally debriefing. This can be tied in with other learning strategies, Bible study, or opportunities for personal growth and commitment. To make the simulation more realistic for your group, use the name and description of your own church here and adapt the entire simulation, including the proposals and the interest groups, to fit your church.

INVENT

Divide your youth group into smaller groups of eight to ten. Describe the situation below and give each group twenty minutes to finish their task. At the end of the allotted time, have the group all meet together and compare their responses.

Situation: You find yourself in a new civilization in which everything is the same as our world is now, but there is no

Bible, no God, no religion, no church, no religious history. You have been selected by your government to create a god who will have the proper attributes to cause people to worship. This god should represent everything that you think will be attractive and yet as the same time, explain things like natural disasters (flood, earthquake, etc.), sickness, suffering, and evil.

Questions to help you as you invent a god: What is its name, if any? Where does it live? Is it visible? Will your god make any demands on people? Any rewards or punishments? How do you worship it? What does it look like? Is there more than one? Does it have any bad attributes? Just let your imaginations run wild and attempt to invent the *perfect* god who will attract the most people.

The discussion should then compare the invented god with the God of the Bible. The following questions could be included in the discussion:

1. Why is God so mysterious?

2. Why did God leave so many unanswered questions?

3. Why doesn't God make Himself visible?

4. What are the most difficult things about God to believe?

5. What things would you change about God if you could?

VALUES IN THE CHURCH

The following exercise will help young people (or adults) set priorities concerning certain values that they have and see the inconsistencies that often exist within the church community regarding priorities and values. Print a twelve-square page (see illustration on the next page) and give one to each person. Each square on the page should contain a statement of concern. Have each person cut the twelve squares apart so they have twelve individual concerns on separate slips of paper. Read these instructions:

1. Rank these statements in order of their importance

with the most urgent or necessary item on top and the least urgent on the bottom. Then list the statements on another sheet of paper, putting the *letter* of the most important item next to the number one and so on through number twelve.

A Raising money and spending it	B Developing the music program of the church	C Getting workers to fill all the jobs in the church
D Spiritual Growth of church members enabling them to become mature disciples of Christ	E Winning local people to Christ	F Building and maintaining larger and more attractive church buildings
G Maintaining or building church attendance	H Helping to relieve starvation and suffering in the famine-stricken areas of the world	I Foreign missionary work
J Helping to relieve poverty and/or racial prejudice in the local community	K Keeping the existing weekly programs of the church going	L Developing a sense of fellowship, love, and mutual concern

2. Now rank them again according to the amount of attention they receive in your local church. Put the one receiving the most attention on top, the one receiving the least attention on the bottom. List their letter sequence alongside the first list.

3. Compare the two lists. How are they different from each other and why are they different? Should they be the same? What changes need to be made on which list? Discuss these and other questions you may have with the entire group.

WORSHIP

BODY OF CHRIST WORSHIP

This activity is good for a youth worship service, emphasizing the body of Christ, not only as relationships between believers, but also the relationship between a corporate body of believers and its Head.

Prior to the service, have an artist in your group (or church) make a life-size (between 5'-6') human silhouette out of colored poster board. Select one color for the legs and arms of the body; another for the head, neck, and shoulders; and a third color for the main part of the body. Next, cut the body, not the head, into a puzzle with the exact number of pieces totaling the number of participants. In bold print with a magic marker, write across the head: "JESUS CHRIST."

Now direct each person, including yourself, to pick up one piece of the puzzle and sign his name in ink on the puzzle part. Next, direct everyone with the same color to gather into a group to fit their pieces together before the whole group puts the entire puzzle together. While everyone is fitting their pieces together, someone should tape the head of the body to the wall (or whatever way you choose to mount the puzzle).

After each group has worked out its part of the puzzle, all three groups should get together to put the puzzle into a complete form. First, direct the group with the neck and shoulders to attach its parts under the head, followed by the group with the main body part, followed by the legs and arms.

Continue the worship service by reading Scripture, such as 1 Corinthians 12, by singing appropriate hymns or choruses, such as "We Are One in the Spirit," by participating in Communion, and by sharing prayers. All of these together combine for an effective and meaningful time of worship.

This worship service vividly demonstrates what Paul was talking about in terms of Christians being parts of the body of Christ because it gives teens and adults an opportunity to work together in building a symbol of the body of Christ. Variations of this basic pattern are possible to illustrate other truths, for example, what the body of Christ is like when certain parts are sick, broken, or missing.

PROGRESSIVE WORSHIP SERVICE

Here's an interesting way to involve young people in worship. It can be done in a church, in homes, or on a weekend retreat. There really is no limit to its possibilities. It works just like a progressive dinner.

A worship service has a variety of elements, just like a dinner does. By taking each element of worship separately and in a different location, it provides a good opportunity to teach young people about these elements of worship. Acts 2:42 and Colossians 3:16 provide a good scriptural base. Here's one way to do it:

1. *Fellowship:* Begin with some kind of group interaction or sharing that provides a chance for the kids to get to know one another better. Something that would put the kids in a celebrative, but not rowdy, mood would be appropriate.

2. *Spiritual Songs:* At the next location, have someone lead the group in a variety of well-known hymns and favorite songs of worship.

3. *Prayer:* Move to another location that provides a good atmosphere for prayer. If outside, a garden would be nice, just as Jesus often chose a garden for prayer. Have the kids offer prayer requests, thanksgivings, etc., and have several kids lead in prayer.

4. *Scripture Reading:* At the next location, have several kids read a lesson from the Old Testament, the New Testament, and perhaps the Psalms. Use a modern English version.

5. *Teaching:* The next stop can be where the sermon is preached. If you prefer, you could accomplish the same thing without being *preachy* by substituting a dialogue sermon, a film, or something of that nature.

6. *Breaking of Bread (Communion):* The last stop can be around the Lord's Table with Communion. Conduct this however you choose, but it should be a time of celebration and joy.

There are other ingredients usually in a worship service (like the offering), which you can incorporate into the others or take separately. Design your own Progressive Worship Service, and you can be sure your group will never forget it.

SILENT WORSHIP SERVICE

This creative service can be a totally different approach to the worship experience. It is completely silent, that is, no one speaks, sings, or makes any verbal utterances during any part of the service. The congregation should be aware ahead of time what will happen and how they are to respond. The youth can be in charge of conducting the service and preparing the church for the worship experience.

The following introduction can be printed in the program to be given to each person entering:

Are you afraid of silence? Do you become uneasy when all the talk stops in a group and people only sit and look away or at each other? Yes, silence can be frustrating in this world of noise and mass media, but it also can be a meaningful time. Silence gives us the chance to digest ideas and analyze feelings. It can be a time of struggle or relaxation.

Our silence today does not approximate deafness, but muteness. Even without anyone speaking, listen to all the other sounds you hear. Have you been aware of all of them? The deaf person cannot ever hear

269

those background sounds. Here are our reasons for having a silent service:

1. *There is more to worship than listening to the words of a sermon.*

2. *We should be aware of all sounds.*

3. *Maybe we do not realize the value of speech and singing.*

4. *Maybe we don't realize the value of silence as an equal to sound.*

5. *It's a real chance to talk and listen to God.*

6. *Communication is possible in silence.*

ORDER OF WORSHIP

The Order of Worship may include the following kinds of things:

1. *Meditative prayer while waiting.* (No organ prelude, etc.)

2. *Greeting.* (Two or more youth come out, shake hands, wave to congregation, get the congregation involved in shaking hands, too.)

3. *Call to worship.* (Youth light candles, open Bible, dramatize the coming of the Spirit to the service.)

4. *Hymns.* (Congregation is instructed in the bulletin or program to turn to this hymn, read, and meditate on its message. Allow them plenty of time for this.)

5. *Meditation on current events.* (A slide presentation can be used to show areas of concern for the church in today's world, followed by silent prayer.)

6. *The Lord's Prayer.* (The words may also be creatively shown on a screen with other slides to illustrate and give added meaning to the prayer.)

7. *Scripture reading.* (Provide Bibles. Read silently.)

8. *Sermon.* (The sermon can take many forms. It can be a printed article that everyone can read; a dramatic presentation done by the youth using only motions, not words; or painted signs held up by the youth combined with a slide presentation, etc.)

270

9. *Communion.* (The youth can feed each other and motion to the congregation to do likewise with the elements provided.)

10. *Doxology.* (This can be used at the conclusion to break the silence with everyone singing together acappella.)

WORSHIP IDEAS

Below are three creative worship ideas that incorporate the use of visual symbols to make each experience more meaningful.

1. By using a rope (about eighteen inches long), tie two people together with one loop around the wrists. Let the people share communion by twos. After the communion, separate the two by cutting the rope two or three inches from the knot. The rope forms the shape of the cross and becomes "the tie that binds." Have the two discuss what the cross means to them and let them decide who will keep it.

2. Using the rope idea, tie two people together with a loop around each wrist. After communing, place the wrists and rope on a block of wood. Separate the two with a blow from a hatchet and say, "With one stroke, God wiped out man's sin." Let the people wear the rope bracelets as a reminder that they have been tied to Christ through another person.

3. Symbols are very meaningful to young people. For a service on the beach, let sand represent sin: "It's dirty and more than you can count." Have everyone make a footprint in the sand, then take some of the sand out of the footprint into a container that can be closed: "This is personal sin." As part of the service, pour wine (or grape juice) over the sand in the container until it is full and close it: "Just as the wine covers all the sand, so the blood of Christ covers all my sin." Let the people take their containers home and put them in a prominent place to be constantly reminded of the forgiveness of sin. As a variation, baby food jars as containers may symbolize the faith of an infant; medicine vials, the "cure" for all of us. Use your imagination to create other variations.

11 Family-Oriented Activities

CHAPTER CONTENTS

Adult-Teen Gap Class / 273
Family Clusters / 274
Family Communion / 275
Family Film Night / 275
Family Newsletter / 276
Family Seed Center / 276
Family Volleyball / 277
Parent Panel / 277
Parent Questionnaire / 278
Parent Swapping / 278
Parent's Perspective / 279
Parent-Teen Camp / 280
Parent Youth Nights / 281
Youth-led Family Night / 285

ADULT-TEEN GAP CLASS

Once a year, invite adults and teenagers in the church to participate in an eight-week, Wednesday-night class. Invite any adult in the church, whether or not he has teenagers living at home. And invite any teenager to come, whether or not he is accompanied by a parent. Stress the activity-centered learning approach to maximize the group experience. Use ideas from other Zondervan/Youth Specialties books (see the list next to the title page of this book) and activities from other curriculum aids you've found helpful but avoid the lecture method. Since it's very hard to find a speaker who relates well to both adults and teens, oftentimes it's best to use role plays, encouraging role reversal where adults play the role of young people and vice versa. Each night, focus on just one concept, such as trust, listening, love, etc. Design your class to facilitate communication and develop feelings of trust and communication between the two age groups.

On the last night, throw a party (an ice cream social or hot dog roast). Give some time for members of the class to share what's happened in their lives and their outlook because of the class.

FAMILY CLUSTERS

If you would like to bring change to your usual Daily Vacation Bible School program, introduce the concept of family clusters. Invite the entire congregation (adults and children alike) to the church for a five-consecutive-night program. Divide the total group into small clusters of eight to ten members each and instruct families to stay together. For example, your clusters will probably consist of a couple of four-member families and a couple of singles or perhaps a family of five, a young married couple with no children, and two older adults. And that's exactly what you want—nuclear families aligned with some outsiders forming new family clusters.

To begin the cluster activity, present a Task Card to each cluster. Design the Task Cards to help a cluster learn the subject of the Scripture being studied for the evening. For instance, if your subject is "Trusting the Lord in All Your Ways," you might have a Task Card instructing the clusters to try the Trust Circle. In the Trust Circle, the cluster sits in a tightly knit circle, legs inward. Then one person stands in the middle of the circle and falls. He is caught, of course, by the members of the cluster and is pushed to another part of the circle, falling and being caught. A variation is the "Trust

Walk" experience where one person, with eyes open, leads the rest of the cluster on a walk. Members of the cluster hold hands and walk in single file with their eyes shut. They are forced to trust the leader for their safety and their learning.

You'll probably discover that not only do people learn concepts during the nightly activities, but that family leaders learn how to lead activities. And this ability is then used by fathers and mothers in family experiences during the rest of the year.

FAMILY COMMUNION

This can be a meaningful experience in a family retreat setting. Following a service emphasizing the family and the importance of family devotions, each family has Communion together as a family unit. Give the fathers the elements of communion and the mothers a candle. Each family then finds a place around the camp area to share Scripture and Communion together. After about fifteen minutes, all the families meet for a closing campfire service. The fathers can together light the campfire with their family's candle.

FAMILY FILM NIGHT

Sponsor a film night for families once a month. Borrow from the public library a Disney film or a set of Laurel and Hardy or Abbott and Costello shorts (most public libraries lend them free of charge, but reserve what you want well in advance) and invite families to come. Encourage parents to bring their children along with popcorn, pop, or whatever they want to eat during the film.

If your public library doesn't have what you want, check with various film outlets. You can usually rent Disney films and other family-oriented films for a nominal amount. If you do rent, charge each family a small sum to help subsidize the film.

If your junior-high or senior-high group needs to raise some funds, have them sell homemade goodies at the film night.

FAMILY NEWSLETTER

Instead of using a church bulletin or church paper to announce family-related events, consider sending a monthly newsletter to all family units of the church. (A family unit consists of any type of living unit—nuclear-family unit, single-parent home, grandparent's home, singles, etc.)

To be most effective, write the letter informally in first person. In addition to announcements concerning family activities, include such items as these: resources for family growth and family devotions, a list of television programs to watch or avoid during the month, questions for family discussions, and thoughts on family finances, managing a household, etc. Share ways you've grown through your own family and include information about what the church and community are doing for family units.

FAMILY SEED CENTER

You can aid the families in your church by developing a Family Seed Center. All you need is a bulletin board, a table, and the ability to find resources and events that pertain to the families in your congregation. Put on the bulletin board items that advertise church-sponsored or community-sponsored events that relate to families, a list of television programs families might profit from watching together during the week, and pictures of families in your church for an excellent way to introduce families to one another.

On the table, put any books or written resources about the family. You may want to begin to build a Family Life Library by buying books on a regular basis that relate to family development. On the table, also include copies of your newsletters (if you decide to publish one) and any magazine articles that relate to the home. Each week, add new items to the table and the board so that people will gravitate to the center. Find a good location, such as the foyer of the church or Christian education area of your church. Analyze the traffic flow of your congregation and put the center where the people are.

FAMILY VOLLEYBALL

Here's a good version of volleyball that works well when families are together. Make sure everyone is in a family group. If someone is present who is not with his family, then find a family that he can join for this game.

Basically, the game is regular volleyball, but each family sends one family member at a time into the game to play for their family. If you have a total of twenty families, then there would be ten people on each side of the net, one from each family. Each family has the freedom to rotate their family members in and out of the game as they please (or whatever organization you choose). Lots of yelling and rooting for your family's player is the most important rule of the game. The results of kids yelling for their parents and parents yelling for their kids are fantastic—it really creates a positive affirming experience for everyone.

PARENT PANEL

This is an excellent transgenerational exercise that can give your youth group an opportunity to understand the parents' point of view. Although this particular idea deals with the subject of dating, any subject could be used by following the guidelines given below.

Choose two moms and two dads to be the panelists. (CAUTION: Do not choose panelists who are related to anyone in your youth group. Do not choose a husband and wife on the same panel. And be sure the panelists have been parents of teenagers who have already passed the dating stage.)

About two weeks before the scheduled panel discussion, have your youth group submit, anonymously, their questions about dating. After all the questions have been submitted, go through and eliminate duplicates, reword poorly stated questions, and then prepare a master list of questions. Duplicate the list and give each panelist a copy a week in advance. On the night of the Parent Panel, give the young people copies, so they can follow along and take notes.

The leader moderates the meeting, question by question, before opening the discussion to the entire group.

PARENT QUESTIONNAIRE

If anyone has an opportunity to speak to a parents' group in the church, the following type of questionnaire can be very helpful in ascertaining the voice of the parents concerning the church and its work.

YOUTH AND THE CHURCH SURVEY

Answer each question briefly and honestly—say what you really believe. If you have no teenage children, answer on the basis of what you know about teenagers from your contacts with them. Do not sign your name.

1. What do you see as the role and the relevancy of the church for today's youth?

2. What do your children think of our church?

3. How meaningful and relevant is it to them?

4. My children attend church school, church, and/or youth groups (or don't attend) because . . .

5. My children's friends attend (or don't attend) because . . .

6. Their biggest gripe about church activities is . . .

PARENT SWAPPING

Organize a weekend family trade for your junior-high or high-school group. Have the kids in your group switch families for a weekend to see what it is like to live with someone else's parents. Then on Sunday, discuss feelings and impressions that the teens had about their experiences. Here are some sample questions for discussion:

1. Did you think that the parents treated you just like they treat their own kids?

2. What rules did you have to obey that you do not have at home?

3. Was it hard to get along with other brothers and sisters?

4. Did you act differently than you would have acted had you been at home?

5. What benefits did you get from this experience?

Using similar questions, you might conduct a discussion with parents, too. No matter who participates, be prepared for an interesting and lively discussion.

PARENT'S PERSPECTIVE

Lead the youth group in a discussion using the questions below. Begin by welcoming them to the meeting as if they were their parents. (Without actually being told what is happening, the kids will catch on pretty fast.) Tell them you want to discuss a few issues that concern them and their teenage children. Allow the group to respond as if they were their parents, reminding them now and then who they are. At the conclusion of the discussion, have the kids read Ephesians 6:1–3 and discuss what it means to them as kids.

DISCUSSION QUESTIONS

1. What would you do if someone you loved very much refused to accept or return your love?

2. How do you communicate with someone who answers every question with "Yes," "No," "I don't know," or with a shrug?

3. How do you free someone who has depended on you for life itself, particularly when you fear that he is going to make some bad choices and get hurt?

4. Where do you get all the money it takes every year to support a child?

5. What would be your reaction if your child always valued his friends' opinions and ignored yours?

6. What would you do if your child regularly disobeyed you?

7. How would you feel if your child outwardly rejected the things that are most important to you?

PARENT-TEEN CAMP

The following retreat idea has been used with great success in establishing a family ministry in the youth program. To attend, there must be at least one teenager and one parent from the same family. The camp begins on Friday at 9:00 P.M. and ends on Saturday at 6:00 P.M. This short schedule allows parents to get away and also keeps the cost down.

Suggested Schedule:

Friday:	9:00 P.M.	All together, guest speaker, crowd breakers, and comedy film
	10:00-10:30 P.M.	Snack time
Saturday:	8:00 A.M.	Breakfast
	9:00 A.M.	Parents—guest speaker Kids—youth leader
	10:00 A.M.	Break
	10:30 A.M.	Meet together, guest speaker
	11:30 A.M.	Recreation
	12:15 P.M.	Lunch
	1:30 P.M.	Film
	2:00 P.M.	Discussions in groups
	3:00 P.M.	Free time
	5:00 P.M.	Dinner
	6:00 P.M.	Leave for home

The first night, some crowd breakers and a comedy film will help loosen everyone up, especially the parents. The guest speaker shares a short message and spends the rest of the evening in fellowship. Have fathers room with sons, mothers with daughters.

The next day, two meetings are scheduled. In the first meeting, the parents and kids are talked to in individual groups, then everyone meets together in one group for a rap session with a guest speaker. Recreation can include volley-ball—where parents must hold hands with their kids to play, or basketball—fathers and guys vs. mothers and gals, but fellows can use only one hand. Games from *Play It!* (Grand Rapids, Mich: Zondervan Publishing House, 1986) work well, too—just be certain to include everyone. During the afternoon, show the film "Parents, Pressures, and Kids" by BFA Educational Media, 2211 Michigan Street, Santa Monica, California. After the film, families meet and discuss pressures in their families. After forty-five minutes, the families join together in the large group to share what they feel they have learned. Then, discuss ways families can do things to understand each other better. Kids can share what they like to do with their parents or what they like about their parents and vice versa. For a short but effective retreat, the long-range results can be very rewarding.

PARENT YOUTH NIGHTS

Here's a six-week program for parents and teenagers that works well during the week in place of midweek group meetings by ages. Make sure that you let both the parents and youth know that the series is not biased in anyone's favor and that no attempt will be made to embarrass anyone or make anyone feel guilty.

FIRST WEEK: "PARENTS' PARTY"

Just a plain, old-fashioned party with games, singing, and refreshments planned and directed by the kids. After the party, have the group meet together to discuss the upcoming series of meetings.

SECOND WEEK: "FAMILY BRIDGE"

Here is a great idea that involves both parents and kids in a cooperative activity. The group should be divided into teams of parents and kids (families should be mixed, so the parents are on a different team than their kids).

The task is to construct a single, cardboard bridge between two cliffs separated by a ten-foot river. The banks of

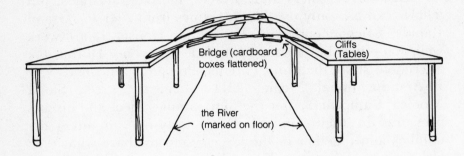

the river should be marked by placing masking tape on the floor beyond the edges of two tables.

Each team of builders constructs their part of the bridge using cardboard boxes (broken flat), string, and masking tape. The teams cannot speak directly to each other nor can they enter the ten-foot-wide river between the cliffs. But each team can appoint a Negotiator (with armband) and a Job Foreman (complete with hard hat) who meet in the middle of the river to exchange strategy every ten minutes, more often if needed, but only for a minute each time. The Job Foreman coordinates his team's efforts to construct their portion of the bridge.

The difficult time comes when both sides have to be joined in the middle. Since none of the builders can work in the river, the task gets rather complicated. The bridge cannot touch the floor nor the ceiling but must be suspended between the two cliffs.

The teams have forty-five minutes to construct the bridge. When construction is over, the bridge is tested by placing a heavy weight in the middle of it, such as a giant Bible. If it stands the test, have a celebration ceremony and follow with a discussion.

THIRD WEEK: "GETTING TO KNOW YOU"
Develop a series of question-and-answer games to see if the parents and young people know as much about themselves as they think they do. As a resource, use the Serendipity Series by Lyman Coleman, which is directed toward families.[1]

FOURTH WEEK: "FAMILY AT PLAY"
What do families do together? Have the families share their traditions, special days, events, camping trips, family nights, and games that they enjoy as a family.

FIFTH WEEK: "FAMILY AT WORSHIP"
Be careful not to offend some families who may not worship much together. Start with lots of suggestions for what families *can* do. Discuss why it is so difficult for families to get together for anything, especially spiritual matters. Then, ask if there are any families doing anything in the area of family devotions, reading, or prayer and have them share.

SIXTH WEEK: "FAMILIES ALIVE"
The purpose of this game is to demonstrate symbolically the importance of cooperation within families because it requires cooperation for each family to complete the game. The game is designed to be played in twenty to thirty minutes but is not a race. Each family completes ten symbolic activities that are performed at ten separate stations (see the listing of stations) and checks off the activities as completed. Restoring Human Dignity must be done first and Living Spring done last. All others can be done at random when the station is vacant.

Each station should be twenty to fifty feet apart and well identified, which will give a sense of accomplishment and also prevent crowding and confusion. Put the final station, Living Spring, in a large, open area that is easily visible. Have clean water in a bucket (the spring) with a second container placed ten feet away from it. Paper cups and a ladle should be easily accessible. Water placed into the second bucket is used to extinguish the flare when all families have completed the ten stations.

To begin the game, a flare is lit representing the time remaining before the world ends. As long as a flare is lit, the game proceeds, so have several flares on hand to relight as others burn out. Once all families have completed all activities, pour the bucket of water over the flare to extinguish it. It is best if the flares are extinguished; however, if the flares are used up before the game is completed, just end the game as if the world's time ran out. Even though the world ended, families can still rejoice in what they have accomplished and join in a discussion of the evening's activities.

Supplies Needed:
String and balloons for everyone, scissors
Crackers (1 box)
Cloth for 5 blindfolds
Empty milk cartons (at least 20)
Scrap paper or newspaper and a trash can (separated by 10 feet)
Band-Aids or tape (scissors)
Large coat and hat
Bible (2 or 3 if you have a large group)
Three flares, matches
Paper cups (one for each family unit)
Two large buckets (or containers), one with clean water (use ladle to fill each family's cup)

Give each family a copy of the following sheet:

1. *Restore Human Dignity* —Tie a balloon (Human Dignity) on each other's waist. Human Dignity must be maintained throughout the game. If a balloon breaks, you must all go back to the Human Dignity Station to obtain another.

2. *Feed the Hungry* —Feed each other crackers.

3. *Lead the Captives* —Blindfold all members but one, so he can lead you to the next station. Remove the blindfolds and return them to the station before doing the next activity.

4. *Rebuild the Nations* —Build a tower by stacking the empty milk cartons. They must remain stacked for fifteen seconds.

5. *Clean up the Environment* —Line up in a straight line. Take a sheet of paper, crumple it up, and pass it down the line to the last person who drops it into the trash can.

6. *Heal the Sick* —Put a Band-Aid on each other. Each person does all the others in the family, so you will have Band-Aids from all the members. Leave them on until the game is over.

7. *Clothe the Naked* —Put on a coat and hat then give it to the next member until all have had a turn.

8. *Welcome Strangers* —Stop another family and greet each of their members, shaking hands and inviting them to visit you again.

9. *Preach the Word* —Select a family member to read aloud Matthew 25:31–46.

10. *Living Spring* —After you have completed all of the above activities, take a cup and fill it full of water from the Living Spring and have each member take a sip of water from it. Refill the cup and pour it into the second water container. Wait nearby once you have finished.

YOUTH-LED FAMILY NIGHT

This event utilizes youth leadership and talent for a family get-together at the church to emphasize family life in the home and in the family of Christ. With the instructions in Exodus 37:1–9 (the Living Bible has modern dimensions), the group is assigned (or assigns themselves) the various tasks required to construct an actual size replica of the ark of the covenant, using plywood, jigsawed cherubim, and ring-type drawer pulls to hold the handles as rings with everything painted gold.

At the family-night event, an informal drama is improvised (better than written and memorized) by the kids themselves to depict a family altar or family worship time. Families enjoy their kids acting out what a Christian home can be like. For balance, Act One could include an exasperating marital experience that could actually stretch the unity of the marriage and home, letting Act Two be the family experience of worship where healing begins. Capsule cures for family problems should be avoided.

Preferably one of the youth (or possibly the pastor) explains the significance of the ark on display. Application is made to the practical way in which God's presence is to be understood in a Christian home and church today.

APPENDIX

RESOURCES
FOR
HIGH-SCHOOL
MINISTRY

A Youth Ministries Bibliography

RESOURCES PUBLISHED SINCE 1977
FOUNDATIONS FOR YOUTH MINISTRY

Author	Book	Publisher
Benson, Dennis and Bill Wolfe	*The Basic Encyclopedia for Youth Ministry*	Group Books
Coles, Robert and Geoffrey Stokes	*Sex and the American Teenager*	Harper & Row
Corbett, Jan	*Creative Youth Leadership*	Judson Press
Dausey, Gary	*The Youth Leader's Source Book*	Zondervan
Green, Ken, ed.	*Insights: Vol I. Building a Successful Youth Ministry*	Here's Life
Hurley, Pat	*Penetrating the Magic Bubble*	Victor Books
Holderness, Ginny	*Youth Ministry: The New Team Approach*	John Knox Press
Jones, Stephen	*Faith Shaping*	Judson Press
Kesler, Jay	*Parents and Teenagers*	Victor Books
Ludwig, Glenn	*Building an Effective Youth Ministry*	Abingdon
Madson, Erik	*Youth Ministry and Wilderness Camping*	Judson Press
Maness, Bill	*Recreation Ministry*	John Knox Press
Richards, Larry	*Youth Ministry: Its Renewal in the Local Church (Revised Edition)*	Zondervan
Richardson, Gary	*Where It's At*	Victor Books
Roadcup, David	*Ministering to Youth*	Standard

Author	Book	Publisher
Stevens, Doug	*Called To Care*	Zondervan
Stone, David	*The Complete Youth Ministries Handbook, Vol I & II*	Abingdon
	Spiritual Growth in Youth Ministry	Group
Warren, Michael	*Youth & the Future of the Church*	Winston Press
Willey, Ray	*Working With Youth Handbook in the 80's*	Victor Books
Wyckoff, Campbell and Don Richter	*Religious Education Ministry With Youth*	Religious Education Press

PROBLEMS AND ISSUES

Author	Book	Publisher
Bayard, Robert and Jean Bayard	*How to Deal With Your Acting Up Teenager: Practical Self-Help for Desperate Parents*	Accord Press
Bimler, Rich, Bill Ameiss; and Jane Graver	*Sex Education Series: The New You, Lord of Life; Lord of Me*	Concordia
Blackburn, Bill	*What You Should Know About Suicide*	Contact Tele-ministries U.S.A.
Burns, Jim	*Handling Your Hormones: The Straight Scoop on Love and Sexuality*	Harvest House
Bush, Florence	*The Best Kept Secret: Sexual Abuse of Children*	McGraw-Hill
Dallas, Truman and Grace Ketterman	*Teenage Rebellion*	Revell
Friesen, Larry	*Decision Making & the Will of God*	Multnomah
Gallagher, Maureen	*Christian Parenting: The Adolescent*	Paulist Press

Author	Book	Publisher
Greenfield, Guy	*The Wounded Parent*	Baker
Hart, Archibald	*Children and Divorce*	Word
Heyer, Robert	*Religious Life of the Adolescent*	Paulist Press
Irwin, Paul	*Care & Counseling of Youth in the Church*	Fortress Press
Lawhead, Steve	*Rock Reconsidered*	InterVarsity Press
Levintron, Steve	*Diagnosis and Treatment of Anorexia Nervosa*	Warner Books
MacLeod, Sheila	*The Art of Starvation*	Schoeken Books
Miller, Mary Susan	*Child Stress*	Doubleday
O'Brien, Bev	*Mom, I'm Pregnant*	Tyndale
Olson, Arvis	*Sexuality: Guidelines for Teenagers*	Baker
Rabkin, Brenda	*Growing Up Dead*	Abingdon
Rekers, George	*Growing Up Straight*	Moody
Rice, E. Phillip	*Morality and Youth*	Westminster
Ridenour, Fritz	*What Teenagers Wish Their Parents Knew About Kids*	Word
Short, Ray	*Sex, Love and Infatuation: How Can I Really Know*	Augsburg
Stafford, Tim	*You Call This a Family?: A Love Story*	Tyndale
White, John	*Parents in Pain*	InterVarsity Press
White, Carl	*Our Dance Has Turned to Death*	Tyndale
Wood, Barry	*Questions Teenagers Ask About Dating and Sex*	Revell
Wright, Norman	*Dating, Waiting & Choosing a Mate*	Harvest House

Author	Book	Publisher
CULTURE		
Becker, Verne, Tim Stafford, and Philip Yancey	*Questions? Answers!*	Tyndale
Campbell, Ross	*How to Really Love Your Teenager*	Victor Books
Collins, Gary	*Give Me a Break*	Revell
Dobson, James	*Preparing for Adolescence*	Victor
Elkind, David	*All Grown Up & No Place to Go*	Addison-Wesley
Hartley, Fred	*Growing Pains*	Revell
	Update	Revell
	Dare To Be Different	Revell
Naisbitt, John	*Megatrends*	Warner Books
Narramore, Bruce	*Adolescence Is Not an Illness*	Revell
Norman, Jane and Myron Harris	*The Private Life of the American Teenager*	Rawson Assoc.
Oraker, James	*Almost Grown*	Harper & Row
Rushford, Patricia	*Have You Hugged Your Teenager Today*	Revell
Smoke, Jim	*Suddenly Single*	Revell
Strommen, Merton	*Five Cries of Youth*	Harper & Row
	Five Cries of Parents	Harper & Row
Wilson, Earl	*You Try Being a Teenager*	Multnomah
Winn, Marie	*Children Without Childhood*	Pantheon
Yancey, Phillip	*Where Is God When It Hurts?*	Campus Life
Yankelovich, Daniel	*New Rules*	Random House

Author	Book	Publisher
LEADERSHIP		
Armerding, Hudson	*Leadership*	Tyndale
Brown, Jerry	*Church Staff Teams That Win*	Broadman
Engstrom, Ted and Ed Dayton	*The Making of a Christian Leader*	Zondervan
	The Art of Management for Christian Leaders	Zondervan
Gerig, Donald	*Leadership in Crisis*	Regal
Griffin, Em	*Getting Together*	InterVarsity Press
Hayford, Jack	*The Church on the Way*	Chosen Books
Nicholas, Ron	*Small Group Leaders Handbook*	InterVarsity Press
Olson, Keith	*Counseling Teenagers*	Group
Paul, Cecil	*Passages of a Pastor*	Zondervan
Powers, Bruce	*Christian Leadership*	Broadman
Richards, Lawrence and Gib Martin	*A Theology of Personal Ministry*	Zondervan
Schaller, Lyle	*The Multiple Staff and the Larger Church*	Abingdon
Varenhorst, Barbara	*Real Friends*	Harper & Row
Watson, David	*Called and Committed*	Harold Shaw
Wilson, Carl	*With Christ in the School of Discipleship*	Zondervan
Wright, Norman	*The Seasons of Marriage*	Regal
DISCIPLESHIP		
Burns, Jim	*Putting God First*	Harvest House
	Making Your Life Count	Harvest House

292

Author	Book	Publisher
	Living Your Life . . . As God Intended	Harvest House
	Giving Yourself to God	Harvest House
	Commitment to Growth	Harvest House
	Leader's Guide	Harvest House
	The 90 Day Experience	Harvest House
Campolo, Anthony	*Ideas for Social Action*	Zondervan
Group Magazine	*Youth Group How-To*	Group Books
	The Best of Try This One	Group Books
	More Try This One	Group Books
	Try This One Too	Group Books
Hadidan, Allen	*Successful Disciplining*	Moody
Hanks, Billie and William Shell	*Discipleship: The Best Writings From the Most Experienced Disciple Makers*	Zondervan
Jackson, Forest W., ed.	*Bible Studies for Special Occasions in Youth Ministry*	Broadman
McAllister, Dawson	*Student Discipleship Manual*	Shepherd Publications (Distributed— Roper Press)
	Discussion Manual for Student Relationships, Vol. 1, 2, 3	Shepherd Publications
	Discussion Manual for Student Discipleship, Vol. 1, 2	Shepherd Publications
	Walk To The Cross	Shepherd Publications
Polleck, Shirley	*Youth Worker's Success Manual*	Abingdon
Reed, Ed and Bobbie Reed	*Creative Bible Learning for Youth Grades 7-12*	Regal
Reichter, Arlo	*The Group Retreat Book*	Group Books
Rice, Wayne	*Great Ideas for Small Youth Groups*	Zondervan
Rodden, Randy	*Student Survival Manual, Vol. 1*	Mott Media

Author	Book	Publisher
St. Clair, Barry	*Discipleship (Reach Out Strategy) Vol. 1, 2*	Reach Out Ministries
St. Clair, Barry and Rod Minor	*Discipleship (Back to Basics) Vol. 1, 2, 3*	Reach Out Ministries
Steward, Ed and Neal McBride	*Bible Learning Activities Grades 7-12*	Gospel Light
Warren, Michael	*Resources for Youth Ministry*	Paulist Press
Yaconelli, Mike and Wayne Rice	*Super Ideas for Youth Groups*	Zondervan
	Far Out Ideas for Youth Groups	Zondervan
	Right On Ideas for Youth Groups	Zondervan
	Way-out Ideas for Youth Groups	Zondervan
	Holiday Ideas for Youth Groups	Zondervan
	Play It!	Zondervan
	Greatest Skits on Earth	Zondervan
	Creative Socials and Special Events	Zondervan
	Tension Getters	Zondervan
	Tension Getters II	Zondervan
	The Ideas Library	Youth Specialties

PERIODICALS

Campus Life
465 Gundersen
Carol Stream, IL 60187

Contemporary Christian Music
P.O. Box 6300
Laguna Hills, CA 92653

Discipleship
P.O. Box 113
Dover, NJ 90801

Group
P.O. Box 481
Loveland, CO 80539

Leadership
P.O. Box 1916
Marion, OH 43305

Ministries
P.O. Box 2374
Orlando, FL 32802

Son Power Idea Sheet
1825 College Avenue
Wheaton, IL 60137

Wittenburg Door
Youth Specialties
1224 Greenfield Drive
El Cajon, CA 92021

Youth Leader
1445 Boonville
Springfield, MO 65801

Youthworker Journal
Youth Specialties
1224 Greenfield Drive
El Cajon, CA 92021

Youthworker Update
Youth Specialties
1224 Greenfield Drive
El Cajon, CA 92021

Books on the Family

BOOKS ON UNDERSTANDING ADOLESCENCE

DiGiacomo, James J. *Understanding Teenagers: A Guide for Parents*. Allen, Tex.: Argus Communications, 1983.

Dobson, James. *Preparing for Adolescence: Straight Talk to Teens and Parents*. Ventura, Calif.: Regal Books, 1978.

Draker, James R. *Almost Grown: A Christian Guide for Parents of Teenagers*. San Francisco: Harper and Row, 1982.

Pipe, Virginia E. *Live and Learn With Your Teenager*. Valley Forge, Penn.: Judson Press, 1985.

BOOKS ON THE FAMILY AND RELATIONSHIPS

Buscaglia, Leo. *Loving Each Other: The Challenge of Human Relationships*. Thorofare, N.J.: Slack, Inc., 1984.

Curan, Dolores. *Traits of a Healthy Family*. Minneapolis: Winston Press, 1983.

Finley, Mitch, and Kathy Finley. *Christian Families in the Real World*. Chicago: Thomas More Press, 1984.

Guernsey, Dennis B. *The Family Covenant: Love and Forgiveness in the Christian Home*. Elgin, Ill.: David C. Cook, 1984.

Hansel, Tim. *What Kids Need Most in a Dad*. Old Tappan, N.J.: Fleming H. Revell, 1984.

Kesler, Jay. *Parents and Teenagers*. Wheaton, Ill.: Scripture Press, 1985.

Kesler, Jay. *Too Big to Spank: Practical Help for Parents of Teenagers*. Ventura, Calif.: Regal Books, 1978.

Ketterman, Grace H. *199 Questions Parents Ask*. Old Tappan, N.J.: Fleming H. Revell, 1986.

Leman, Kevin. *Smart Girls Don't and Guys Don't Either*. Ventura, Calif.: Gospel Light, 1982.

MacArthur, John, Jr. *The Family*. Chicago: Moody Press, 1982.

Rekers, George, ed. *Family Building: Six Qualities of a Strong Family*. Ventura, Calif.: Gospel Light, 1985.

Rushford, Patricia H. *Have You Hugged Your Teenager Today?* Old Tappan, N.J.: Fleming H. Revell, 1983.

Schimmels, Cliff. *When Junior Highs Invade Your Home*. Old Tappan, N.J.: Fleming H. Revell, 1984.

Wells, Joel. *How To Survive With Your Teenager*. Chicago: Thomas More Press, 1982.

Wheeler, Bonnie. *Challenged Parenting: A Practical Handbook for Parents of Children With Handicaps.* Ventura, Calif.: Regal Books, 1982.

White, Joe. *How to Be a Hero to Your Teenager.* Wheaton, Ill.: Tyndale House, 1985.

White, Mary. *Growing Together: Building Your Family's Spiritual Life.* Colorado Springs: Nav Press, 1981.

Wilkerson, Rich. *Hold Me While You Let Me Go.* Eugene, Oreg.: Harvest House, 1983.

Wilson, Earl D. *You Try Being a Teenager: A Challenge to Parents to Stay in Touch.* Portland, Oreg.: Multnomah Press, 1982.

FOR BURNED-OUT CHRISTIAN PARENTS

Gage, Joy P. *When Parents Cry: How to Survive a Child's Rebellion.* Denver: Accent Books, 1980.

Lewis, Margie M. *The Hurting Parent.* Grand Rapids, Mich.: Zondervan Publishing House, 1980.

White, John. *Parents in Pain: A Book of Comfort and Counsel.* Downers Grove, Ill.: InterVarsity Press, 1979.

Notes

AN OVERVIEW
1. Ralph Keyes, *Is There Life After High School?* (New York: Warner Books, 1976).
2. Mihaly Csikszentmihalyi and Reed Larson, *Being Adolescent* (New York: Basic Books, 1984), 11–29.
3. Ibid., 271.
4. Alvin Toffler, *Future Shock* (New York: Random House, 1970).
5. Neil Postman and Charles Weingartner, *Teaching as a Subversive Activity* (New York: Delta, 1969), 11.
6. John Naisbitt, *Megatrends* (New York: Warner Books, 1982), 1.
7. Marie Winn, *Children Without Childhood* (New York: Pantheon Books, 1981), 13.
8. David Breskin, "Dear Mom and Dad," *Rolling Stone* (November 1984).

CHAPTER 1
1. Naisbitt, *Megatrends*, pp. 231–247.
2. Alvin Toffler, *The Third Wave* (New York: Bantam, 1980).
3. Francis Schaeffer, *The Church of the Twentieth Century* (Downers Grove, Ill.: InterVarsity Press, 1970), 88.
4. Jacques Ellul, *The Technological Society* (New York, Vintage Books, 1964), 143.
5. Howard Snyder, *The Problem of Wineskins* (Downers Grove, Ill.: InterVarsity Press, 1975), 114–122.
6. Ibid., 115.
7. Ibid., 116.
8. Jacques Ellul, *To Will and To Do*, trans. C. Edward Hopkin, (Philadelphia: Pilgrim Press, 1969), 185.
9. John 16:8.
10. George Orwell, *1984* (New York: New American Library, 1981), 47.
11. Neil Postman, *Amusing Ourselves to Death* (New York: Viking, 1985), vii-viii.
12. John Francis Kavanaugh, *Following Christ in a Consumer Society* (Maryknoll, New York: Orbis, 1982), 38.
13. Pat Brennan, from a seminar given at the 1985 National Youth Workers Convention in Chicago, Ill. entitled "Youth Culture & Its Effects on Discipling Students."

14. Christopher Lasch, *The Culture of Narcissism* (New York: W. W. Norton and Co., 1979), 5.
15. At first glance, it may appear that adolescents are returning to virginity. But today's young people value *selectivity* more than virginity. Young people are becoming more *selective* of their sexual partners. Not for moral reasons, unfortunately, but for pragmatic reasons—they do not want to risk the possibility of a sexually-transmitted disease.
16. For a detailed study of the divorce of knowledge from the knower, we recommend *To Know As We Are Known* by Parker J. Palmer (San Francisco: Harper and Row, 1983).
17. Herbert Hendin, *The Age of Sensation* (New York: W. W. Norton and Co., 1975), 327.
18. Jacques Ellul, *The Technological Society*, 320.
19. The concept of friendship clusters and the implications of those clusters was first discussed in a book by Donald C. Posterski entitled *Friendship—A Window on Ministry to Youth*, published by Project Teen Canada, 1160 Bellamy Road North, Scarborough, Ontario. This book is the result of a national survey of Canadian youth. Although there are many differences between the American youth culture and the Canadian youth culture, there are also many similarities.
20. Jacques Ellul, *The Presence of the Kingdom* (New York: The Seabury Press, 1967), 105.
21. John Claypool, *Glad Reunion* (Waco, Texas: Word, 1985), 14–15.
22. Robert Capon, *Between Noon and Three* (San Francisco: Harper and Row, 1982), 148.
23. 2 Corinthians 5:14.
24. Erik Erickson, *Childhood and Society*, 2nd ed. (New York: W. W. Norton and Co., 1963), 261–263.
25. Os Guiness, *Knights of Faith: Discovering the Missing Dynamic of Vocation*, pamphlet published by the New York Arts Group.

CHAPTER 2

1. David Elkind, *All Grown Up & No Place To Go* (Reading, Mass.: Addison-Wesley, 1984), 45–67.
2. Ibid, 46–55.
3. Jane Norman and Myron Harris, *The Private Life of the American Teenager* (New York: Rawson Associates, 1981), 169.
4. Csikszentmihalyi and Larson, *Being Adolescent*, 19–26.
5. Ibid., 25.

6. We are by no means specialists in adolescent sexuality. We want to give you an overview to help you understand high-school adolescents a little better, but we do recommend further reading in this area.
7. Elkind, *All Grown Up,* 67.

CHAPTER 3

1. Jerome Kagan, "A Conception of Early Adolescence," in *Twelve to Sixteen: Early Adolescence,* ed. Robert Coles et al. (New York: W. W. Norton, 1972), 103.
2. Elkind, *All Grown Up,* 171.
3. Ibid., 23–43.
4. Winn, *Children Without Childhood,* 191–92.
5. We have provided an extensive list of service projects in section three of this book, all of them taken from Anthony Campolo's *Ideas for Social Action* (Grand Rapids, Mich.: Zondervan Publishing House, 1984), 36–74.
6. Brian Reynolds, *A Chance To Serve,* (Winona, Minn.: St. Mary's Press, 1983), 23–43.
7. Barbara Varenhorst, *Real Friends* (San Francisco: Harper and Row, 1983), 16ff.
8. Reynolds, *A Chance To Serve,* 17.
9. Dan Morgan, *The Washington Post.*
10. Norman and Harris, *Private Life,* 130.

CHAPTER 4

1. Scott Peck, *The Road Less Traveled* (New York: Simon and Schuster, 1978), 194. Author is quoting Alan Jones from his book *Journey Into Christ* (New York: Seabury Press, 1977), 91–92.
2. Garrison Keillor in an interview in the *Wittenberg Door,* No. 82 (December 1984/January 1985), 19.

CHAPTER 5

1. Kenneth Keniston, *All Our Children* (New York: Harcourt Brace Jovanovich, 1977), 18.
2. One Scripture that is often used to produce guilt in parents is Proverbs 22:6: "Train a child in the way he should go, and when he is old he will not turn from it." That verse may not be a guarantee that, if you train your children correctly, they'll turn out wonderfully. It may be another way of saying "My word . . . will not return to me empty" (Isaiah 55:11). In other

words, if you provide a Christian environment for your children, *they will never be able to forget what you taught them,* even though they may turn their back on their faith. The imprint of that truth they were taught will always be there.

3. Butch Ekstrom, "Youth Culture and Teen Spirituality," *Youth Ministry Network Occasional Paper* (Naugatuck, Conn.: Center for Youth Ministry Development, 1985), 22.
4. Tim Stafford, *The Trouble with Parents* (Grand Rapids, Mich.: Zondervan Publishing House, 1978), 11–13.
5. Winn, *Children Without Childhood,* 11–80.

CHAPTER 6
1. Joe Bayly, *A View From a Hearse* (Elgin, Ill: David C. Cook Publishing Co., 1973), 55–56.

CHAPTER 9
1. Howard J. Clinebell, Jr., *Basic Types of Pastoral Counseling* (Nashville: Abingdon Press, 1966), 179.
2. Gary Collins, *Christian Counseling: A Comprehensive Guide* (Waco, Texas: Word Books, 1980), 50.
3. W. A. Jones, "The A-B-C Method of Crisis Management," *Mental Hygiene,* vol. 52 (1968): 87.
4. Based on material in Bill Blackburn's book *What You Should Know About Suicide* (Waco, Tex.: Word Books), 44–47.

CHAPTER 10
1. All of the ideas in this section were taken from the *Ideas* library, volumes 1–39, published by Youth Specialties, Inc., El Cajon, Calif.
2. All of the ideas in the Mission and Service section were selected from *Ideas for Social Action,* by Anthony Campolo (Grand Rapids, Mich.: Zondervan Publishing House, 1984).
3. Taken from the *Ideas* library, volumes 9–12, published by Youth Specialties, Inc., El Cajon, Calif.
4. Taken from the *Ideas* library, volumes 5–8.
5. Reprinted with permission from the *Wittenburg Door* (August 1971), 14.

CHAPTER 11
1. Lyman Coleman et al., *The Serendipity Bible Study Book* (Grand Rapids, Mich.: Zondervan, 1986).